Dollar Harvest

DOLLAR HARVEST

The Story of the Farm Bureau

BY SAMUEL R. BERGER
former aide
to the late
United States Representative
Joseph Y. Resnick

Heath Lexington Books
D. C. Heath and Company
Lexington, Massachusetts

*Dedicated to Joe Resnick,
who had the insight
to see it
and the courage
to pursue it.*

Foreword by Cesar Chavez

THE TRUE STORY of the Farm Bureau should be told and understood. For years, this powerful organization has been pretending to speak for the American farmer, while it has really been promoting the narrow interests of the giant agri-business complex in this country and the largest corporate farms.

Dollar Harvest is a very important book. For those who don't know about the Farm Bureau, it tells a fascinating and shocking story of how an organization, created to benefit a particular interest group in the society, has grown into a huge, self-perpetuating bureaucracy. Instead of serving its members, it has become their master—a self-serving giant with independent interests of its own, interests that are often antagonistic to those of its members. *Dollar Harvest* describes a classic example of an institution, like so many others in our society, which has become encrusted and unresponsive. And in the case of the Farm Bureau, the outrage is compounded because our government, instead of trying to stop this, has actually been promoting it.

For those of us who know the Farm Bureau only too well, *Dollar Harvest* puts together the pieces of a puzzle that was only known to us in its parts. When we learn the staggering dimensions of the Farm Bureau's own agri-business enterprise—nearly $4 billion—its consistent advocacy of positions sympathetic to those interests becomes predictable. When we learn about the links of the organization to the far right in this country, the motivation for its strenuous opposition over the years to such progressive legislation as Medicare, federal aid to education, anti-poverty legislation, and rural public works bills becomes apparent. When we learn about the Farm Bureau's continued tax exemption and its ties to the federal Extension Service, the sources of its strength are more clearly defined.

The Farm Bureau has been one of the most steadfast and consistent opponents of our efforts to unionize the country's farm workers. Arm in arm with other reactionary forces, it has resisted the attempt by farm workers to join together to bargain effectively and lift themselves from the bottom of the economic ladder. It has attempted to defame and discredit our Union and break its strikes. It has led the battle in Washington to cripple unionization with restrictive legislation. It has fought every attempt to improve the conditions of farm workers by opposing legislation to give us such minimum protections as Social Security unemployment insurance and minimum wage and hour legislation.

Dollar Harvest is an important book for those of us working in agriculture because the Farm Bureau has been a powerful, but poorly understood, force. But the book's importance goes beyond agriculture: It dramatically illustrates how we can lose control of our own institutions.

Preface

CONGRESSMAN JOE RESNICK and I originally conceived of this book as a co-authored effort. In the spring of 1969, Resnick had left politics and was back in private business in New York. We decided to reopen the investigation of the Farm Bureau that Resnick had launched when he was in Congress. That investigation, started in 1967, had lasted ten months during which Resnick had strenuously attacked the Farm Bureau for its questionable practices. He had locked horns with his reluctant House colleagues and, when they refused to take action, he held his own public hearings on the Farm Bureau in Chicago, Omaha, Cleveland, and Washington. Our idea in 1969 was to thoroughly reexamine our earlier findings and conclusions, explore aspects of the organization only touched upon previously, and generally undertake a deeper and more comprehensive probe. We set out to answer many of the questions that we had only asked before.

For the next six months, I sifted through the piles of material gathered during and after the Congressional inquiry, and travelled around the country talking with farmers and other rural people, Farm Bureau officials and members, partisans of other farm organizations, rural newspapermen and observers of the Farm Bureau. Then, suddenly, on October 6, 1969, Joe Resnick, at the age of 45, died.

"It would take a book to detail his fights for unpopular or obscure causes in his four years in the House," wrote Washington newsman Lee Hickling at the time, "and another book to describe his industrial career, which would have left Horatio Alger open-mouthed at how reality can outrun imagination." Resnick emerged from a poverty-stricken childhood that forced him to leave school, to build an electronics fortune through his inventive genius and the stubborn aggressiveness of his personality. After he went to Congress in 1964, he was most effective—and perhaps most fulfilled—when he was fighting against musclebound and unresponsive institutions that had set their own self-serving interests above the interests of the people they were supposed to serve. Some of his most characteristic fights were the least publicized: on behalf of the foster parents of a 4½ year old girl who, county welfare officials decreed, they could not adopt because they were too old (48) and had dark hair while the girl was blond; on behalf of a black vagrant who had been arrested, tried, and sentenced without a lawyer in Resnick's home town—all in the course of a few hours one evening; on behalf of a New York State police officer who had been harassed and ultimately discharged by his superiors because he had worked to take politics out of the police department. In the case of the Farm Bureau, as in these other battles, I think Resnick was most angered by the harm being done to people by the very institutions set up to help them.

The investigation, begun in early 1969, was completed some months after Resnick's death, and this book is the result of that investigation. A number of people contributed importantly to the finished product, for which I am deeply appreciative. Specifically: Berkeley Rice for his excellent job of editing; Allen Snyder for his comments on the manuscript; Barbara Young for help far too pervasive to enumerate; Mr. and Mrs. Harold Horvitz for providing me with a peaceful and attractive place in which to work; generally, to Frank Denison, Shirley Downs, John Fergus, Lee Harrison, Bill Lehrfeld, Wes McCune, Dan Roher, and Eli Segal; and especially to my wife Susan for patience, patience, and more patience.

Contents

*Sunlight
is said to be the best
of disinfectants.*

—Louis D. Brandeis

1

Introduction

THE STRUGGLES of our cities have dramatically and justifiably seized the nation's attention. But an equally desperate deterioration has been occurring in our rural areas, a crisis no less serious because it is less visible.

Most Americans have generally avoided face-to-face confrontation with the social ills of the cities. Nevertheless, the morning train from Scarsdale to downtown New York still stops in Harlem; the drive from the Capitol building in Washington, D.C. to the new sports stadium passes through that city's decaying slums; and a trip to the University of Chicago takes a visitor into Chicago's run-down South Side. Some personal contact with the urban problem—however fleeting—is almost unavoidable.

But the average metropolitan American still pictures rural America—the country—in terms of Currier and Ives etchings and Sunday rides to see the autumn foliage. He still retains a trace of the Jeffersonian notion of yeoman farmers satisfying their physical and spiritual needs from the soil. Unfortunately, if that scene ever existed, it no longer does. Rural America is in trouble.

The rural dweller's predicament—the steady, unreplenished flow of human and economic resources to the city and the suburbs—is complicated by several factors. Reduced to a fraction of its one-time population, the rural sector no longer wields the political power it once had to protect itself. It must now draw upon non-rural support to correct serious rural problems. Under these circumstances, it becomes essential for the people who live in the country to convey the urgency of the situation to the people who live in the cities and the suburbs.

But historically, rural dwellers, especially farmers, have been stoic about their plight, attempting to work things out for themselves. And those outbursts of desperation and anger which do occur must somehow overcome the diffuseness of the rural population in order to gather momentum and gain visibility. A rock thrown in frustration by someone living in an urban ghetto makes a shattering noise heard around the nation; but a rock thrown out of the same frustration in a country field resounds with only a deadening thud.

The nation's largest, most powerful, most affluent farm organization—the Farm Bureau—has been in an ideal position to call attention to the rural crisis and to rally national support for enriching the rural-dweller's life. But the Farm Bureau has not been part of the solution to the rural problem. It has been a major part of the problem. At a time when millions of people have been forced to board up their houses and leave rural America, the largest rural organization in the country has been fighting against the social reforms urgently needed to revitalize rural areas. At a time when the American family-farmer is engaged in a quiet struggle for survival, the Farm Bureau has one hand on the shovel that is digging his financial grave.

For more than fifty years, the Farm Bureau has been the self-proclaimed spokesman for the American farmer. With a total membership of nearly 2 million families (over 6 million people) it is far larger than all the other farm organizations combined. It is a national organization, operating in 49 states and Puerto Rico, with organizations in approximately 2800 (of 3000) counties in the United States. In its role as spokesman for the farmer, it has had a profound impact over the years on government policy-making—both agricultural and non-agricultural—at all levels. It is one of the most active lobbies in the nation, and when it testifies before a Congressional committee or a state legislature or a county board of supervisors, it does so as the "voice of agriculture." Generations of legislators have taken it at its word.

But a visitor to the attractive offices of the American Farm Bureau Federation in Chicago's Merchandise Mart; or to its busy Congressional offices in Washington; or to one of its impressive state headquarters like the $5 million home of the state organization in Illinois, is troubled by several striking contrasts. How has the Farm Bureau, supposedly just an organization of farmers, achieved such affluence while the farmers themselves are struggling? Why has the Farm Bureau's membership been steadily increasing over the past ten years while the number of farm households has dropped by more than a million in the same period? Why has the Farm Bureau consistently opposed legislation to upgrade the quality of rural life—medicare, federal aid to education, anti-poverty legislation, housing bills, minimum wage laws—and advocated a farm policy opposed by nearly all the other farm organizations, one that most agricultural economists agree would be disastrous for most farmers?

The answers to these questions emerge from a single fact: the Farm Bureau is far more than simply an organization of farmers, as it so often claims. The nation's biggest farm organization has been quietly but systematically amassing one of the largest business networks in America, while turning its back on the deepening crisis of the farmers whom it supposedly represents. The Farm Bureau has become a $4 billion business empire.

The Farm Bureau was born in a Chamber of Commerce and was nurtured during the 1920s and 30s by the government-sponsored Extension Service. It has never completely broken the umbilical cord. By co-opting the government's vast network of county agents, who sold Farm Bureau memberships and products, it shrewdly gained a unique quasi-governmental status which has been crucial to its financial and political success. The development of this leviathan to its present claim of nearly two million families has been accompanied by a spiraling growth of Farm Bureau businesses. The Farm Bureau business empire now spans the economy: from insurance to oil, from fertilizer to finance companies, from mutual funds to shopping centers. It has even acquired its own travel agency.

A three-year investigation into the affairs of the Farm Bureau reveals a wide discrepancy between official pronouncements about the organization and its actual operation. The Farm Bureau claims it is in business simply to provide "services to its members." But the Farm Bureau business activities now clearly dominate the organization. Much of its business empire is not directly related to farming, apart from the fact that farmers make up the largest part of its market. Over the years, the farmer has increasingly become customer, not constituent, to the Farm Bureau. Some of the Farm Bureau's business interests are even antagonistic to the interests of farmers.

The Farm Bureau has become a giant, self-serving bureaucracy, employing tens of thousands of people around the country. The line between its commercial activities and its organizational activities is distressingly fuzzy. Farm Bureau directors serve as directors and officers of their commercial ventures. The businesses are often conducted in the same office, with the same phones, and by the same personnel as their non-commercial activities.

Despite the fact that the Farm Bureau is now as large as Chrysler, DuPont, or Shell Oil Company, it has retained a tax exemption just like religious, charitable, and educational institutions. Although the Farm Bureau businesses pay taxes themselves, large sums of money generated by the businesses are being transferred to the tax-exempt organization. By means of this device, many Farm Bureau businesses are placed at a competitive advantage over rival enterprises, and the Farm Bureau organizations have access to substantial sums of tax-free income for lobbying and other political activity.

The Farm Bureau claims to be "non-partisan." But despite those claims, and its tax exemption, the Farm Bureau is a potent political force. Local and often state units actively support candidates for office. The president of the largest state organization acknowledges publicly that his organization provided their mailing lists and addressograph machine to reelect a friendly Congressman. Another state organization works to defeat the entire unfriendly wing of the state's Congressional delegation, with astounding success. Many members of the House Committee on Agriculture—which refused to investigate the Farm Bureau—belong to the powerful lobby, an intolerable although currently legal conflict of interest.

Additional sums of the organization's tax-exempt income finances an extensive campaign of right-wing propaganda. The Farm Bureau has become the rural arm of the radical right. Its nearly unlimited financial resources, its respectability as the nation's largest farm organization, and its network of communications to all corners of rural America, make it particularly well suited for such a role. Under the banner of "American citizenship" programs, about a dozen state Farm Bureaus hold elaborate youth conventions each year to introduce young rural Americans to the Farm Bureau's political ideas. Professional anti-communists, hired by the Farm Bureau, speak of the futility of peaceful coexistence, of subversion in our government, and of the alien influences behind the civil rights movement. Some of these speakers are affiliated with the John Birch Society speakers bureau. Nearly all represent the far-right fringe of the political spectrum. No other points of view are presented. Farm Bureaus in many states have become rigidly doctrinaire, espousing a frozen, anti-government, anti-communist, anti-civil rights line. The Farm Bureau has become the right wing in overalls.

The Farm Bureau also claims it is a grass-roots organization, truly representative of farmers. The organization, however, has become more and more autocratic over the years. Policy positions are made at the top of a rigid hierarchy, while attempts at the grass-roots level to change that policy have been ruthlessly stifled. In one dramatic incident, an entire county chapter in Nebraska was expelled because it publicly criticized Farm Bureau policy. Rural ministers and others who have spoken out against the Farm Bureau have been subjected to campaigns that the Farm Bureau refers to as "neutralizing the opposition."

The Farm Bureau claims to be an organization made up of farmers. A large percentage of its members, however, has no relationship to farming. Membership has become little more than a device through which Farm Bureau products and services are sold. Among its members are doctors and lawyers, bankers and barbers, garage owners and grocers.

While there is room in the organization for all those non-farm people, farm workers, who spend their entire life in agriculture, are only entitled to second-class membership, as non-voting "associates." In fact, the Farm Bureau has been one of the most active forces in the nation fighting the efforts of farm workers to ease the harshness of their existence. The Farm Bureau has led a coalition of forces opposing the unionization of farm workers. And although it deals directly in procuring, housing, and transporting migrant laborers, it has been one of the most vigorous and effective opponents of measures to improve their welfare.

Generally, the Farm Bureau claims to be an organization "of farmers, by farmers, and for farmers." But more precisely, it has become principally an agri-business giant. It has its own distinct existence and set of interests quite apart from those of the farmers who theoretically make up the organization. Farm Bureau leaders have placed themselves in an impossible dilemma: serving two masters whose interests are frequently conflicting. They have not performed admirably in resolving that conflict. In a particularly flagrant example, one of the Farm Bureau cooperatives refused to redeem its own stock certificates even upon the death of the holder, leaving the farmers with worthless pieces of paper on which they were required to pay taxes. Such conflicts are not isolated. They reach to the very heart of the Farm Bureau. The organization advocates its policies in the name of the farmer, while largely remaining silent about its own stake in government policy, whether that policy is farm price supports and production controls, the oil depletion allowance, or the anti-poverty program. The bitter irony is that the policies advocated by the Farm Bureau in the name of the American farmer would threaten the survival of all but the largest farms in the nation.

The American people ought to know about the Farm Bureau. They bear the consequences of its impact on the rural condition, on the lives of farmers, on the plight of farmworkers. In fact they are subsidizing this powerful, self-serving and profit-motivated institution that has encouraged the neglect of our urgent social needs.

2

"The Resnick Affair"

THE FARM BUREAU has generally managed to avoid close scrutiny by outsiders—particularly the government—over the years. There is no very effective mechanism in the federal government for examining the affairs of groups who professionally try to influence government action. Lobbyists are required to register with the Secretary of the Senate and the Clerk of the House of Representatives and file certain information about themselves; but although there are penalties for misstatements, there is no enforcement machinery. The Department of Agriculture has never undertaken a thorough study of the role that farm organizations have played in agricultural policy-making, although that role has been significant. Neither the Senate nor House Agriculture Committee has ever seen fit to examine the operations of the groups that daily seek to influence it.

The man who finally made the Farm Bureau an issue on Capitol Hill was Representative Joseph Resnick, a low-ranking member of the House Agriculture Committee. A second-term Democrat from the Catskills resort region of New York state, Resnick had grown up on a farm, before becoming a successful industrialist. Although his Congressional district was not very agricultural, with less than 2 percent farmers, Resnick had become Chairman of the Agriculture Committee's subcommittee on Rural Development. Soon after his reelection in 1966, he began planning a series of hearings on rural poverty to determine the depth of the problem and to dramatize it to the rest of the nation. Toward the end of those hearings, however, he was diverted into investigating the Farm Bureau. The story of that investigation tells a great deal about how that organization operates, as well as how it wields its power in Washington. Unfortunately, it also demonstrates how inadequately Congress protects the public it serves.

The House Committee on Agriculture, despite its responsibility for rural matters, had never held hearings devoted specifically to the problem of rural poverty. Upon becoming chairman of the Subcommittee on Rural Development, Resnick gained the power to initiate such an inquiry. In planning hearings he tried to include a broad range of witnesses—the victims of rural poverty, as well as those with public responsibility to do something about it.

Whenever an announcement is made of impending hearings, the committee or subcommittee holding them customarily receives requests to testify from the various lobbying organizations which consider the subject of the hearings to be part of their domain. Thus when Resnick announced hearings on rural poverty, he soon heard from the Washington office of the American Farm Bureau Federation (AFBF)—parent to the state and county Farm Bureaus.

Anyone who has spent time in Congress, especially on the Agriculture Committee, is of course familiar with the Farm Bureau and the positions it normally takes on both agricultural and non-agricultural issues. Even in Resnick's own non-farming district, there were small county Farm Bureaus that had opposed him in both of his campaigns. But their membership was small, and their opposition had not been significant. From his youth on the farm and his years in Congress, Resnick knew a little about the organization, but not much. Like most of his colleagues on the Committee, he had listened to Farm Bureau representatives testify many times, supposedly on behalf of the American farmer. But he had been completely unaware of the extent of the other interests of the organization pleading its case.

As Resnick explained, "I like to know who I am listening to. This, it seems to me, is more than a personal preference; it is the prerequisite of a system that sanctions the efforts of special interests to influence policymaking. If a representative of General Motors were to testify against a proposed auto safety device, that testimony would be considered and weighed in light of its source. But the Farm Bureau, in its many trips to Capitol Hill to testify on everything from foreign aid to tax bills, never to my knowledge had indicated that there were other interests—business considerations—involved."

On June 21, 1967, soon after the Rural Development Subcommittee hearings opened, John Lynn, then the AFBF's "legislative representative" appeared to present his organization's views.[1] That particular morning, the Subcommittee on Rural Development heard lengthy testimony from representatives of the U.S. Forest Service, and by the time the Farm Bureau's Mr. Lynn sat down to testify, it was nearly time for the House session to begin, and the day's hearings to end. (Because they are restricted to mornings, when the House is not in session House Committee hearings normally last only a few hours a day.)

Despite the little time remaining, Lynn launched into a lengthy dissertation about the fiscal situation in the nation, the need to reduce non-defense expenditures, and the tax burdens on our citizens. Resnick glanced through his copy of Lynn's prepared statement and saw that it was thirteen pages long, and only peripherally related to the subject of the hearings—the effect of federal programs on poverty in rural America. He interrupted Lynn, and asked if he would enter the entire statement in the hearing record and focus on the parts most relevant to the subject of the hearing. Lynn ignored this request, turned back to his testimony, and continued to read. Irked by this arrogance, Resnick stopped him again. They argued for a few minutes, and again Lynn began to read his entire statement.

Once again assuring Lynn that his entire statement would be entered in the record, Resnick explained: "I pointed out in the beginning of these hearings that we are not only interested in the farmer and his problems. As we know, there are many other people living in rural America today to which your fine organization sells insurance, and these people also make up rural America, although they are not involved in the farm economy. These are the things in which we are interested."

Lynn's bristling response startled those left in the Committee room: "If you are insinuating that the Farm Bureau is primarily an insurance company . . . ."

Seeing he had obviously hit a very sensitive subject, Resnick decided to push the point: "I am not insinuating it, I am stating it."

"Well, it is not so," said Lynn. "For the record, it is not so."

"For the record, I am stating it."

"Well, I am stating that it is not true."

When Resnick asked if the Farm Bureau ever issues a statement on how much insurance it writes, Lynn snapped, "Sure, it is a public record." Convinced by now that he had hit upon something interesting, Resnick asked: "As long as this information is all public, will you provide it for the record of these hearings?"

"I will not put it in the record," said Lynn. "The information is available in each state where Farm Bureau has an insurance program."

After this exchange, Lynn retreated to the security of his prepared statement and resumed reading. He and Resnick argued about the Farm Bureau's contention that except for some "pockets of poverty" everything was rosy in rural America. Finally, at about noon, and before Lynn had finished reading his statement, the Subcommittee adjourned to free the Congressmen present for the day's House session.

To appreciate more fully the heated exchange between Resnick and Lynn, one must know something about the diplomacy of Congressional hearings. One of the striking elements of the confrontations that occur during hearings is that even when emotions are running high, the witness under fire invariably remains deferential to his Congressional questioners, out of respect for the institution, if not for the inquisitor. When the witness is not a high-ranking government official, but a lobbyist pursuing his special interests, his ministrations are usually even more exaggerated. Lobbyists pay scrupulous attention to the little courtesies that have become norms. After all, Congressmen are to lobbyists what prospective customers are to car salesmen.

Lynn's abrasive reaction to Resnick's request for information on the Farm Bureau's insurance operation was thus both unexpected and highly unusual. Undoubtedly the Farm Bureau had written Resnick off as a potential supporter; but lobbyists, working with only 535 potential "customers," usually try not to antagonize even those who disagree with them, to avoid making a stronger opponent. In Resnick's case, that is exactly what happened. Later, the Farm Bureau charged that Resnick's entire investigation was the result of a carefully conceived, planned, and organized plot against the Farm Bureau.[2] The fact is that Resnick really did not know much or care much about the Farm Bureau until that morning.

After this incident, Resnick asked one of his staff aides to spend some time checking into the Farm Bureau's business activities. What this aide found—the scope of the Farm Bureau's other activities—began to explain Lynn's reaction. Resnick's sources of information at this point were neither private nor secret. Public statements and documents were indictment enough. Many people already knew portions of what Resnick's investigation turned up, but few had looked at the total picture. Those who most fully understood the Farm Bureau's size and power either did not see anything wrong, or had long since been frustrated by unsuccessful attempts to do something about it.

When a second-term Congressman with little seniority discovers a serious abuse, he has little actual power to do anything about it. He can propose legislation, but hundreds of bills die each session from lack of interest. What power such a Congressman does have is derived from his public platform, his ability to publicize. All that he can really do is arouse public indignation and stimulate enough interest so that the agencies and institutions with specific power to correct the abuses will be compelled to act. This is what Resnick set out to do.

About a week after his initial confrontation with Lynn, Resnick submitted a statement on the Farm Bureau in *The Congressional Record,* outlining some of his staff's findings. The next day he issued a press release, accusing the Farm Bureau of being a "gigantic, interlocking, nationwide combine of insurance companies."[3] The release appeared the same day as the second face-to-face Resnick–Farm Bureau confrontation.

When time had run out on Lynn at the first hearing, Resnick had invited him to return the following week, but "previous commitments" prevented Lynn from returning. In his place came the AFBF's secretary-treasurer Roger Fleming, then as now the number two man in the organization. Fleming has held his office for more than twenty years. In addition to his positions in several of the American Farm Bureau Federation companies, he heads the Bureau's Washington office, and is its political tactician. His official biography states that he graduated from Iowa State with a degree in agricultural economics and worked briefly for the Extension Service before joining the Iowa Farm Bureau. It does not mention that he also attended Harvard Business School.

Although Fleming proved to be far more polished and diplomatic than Lynn, his appearance before the Subcommittee was equally heated.[4] Resnick found that the only way to pin him down was to press him steadily. Fleming insisted that his organization "would be happy to cooperate" with an investigation of farm organizations. "We would be interested in an investigation," he declared, "which analyzed the Farm Bureau and its operation and the other farm organizations." When Resnick pressed him about the occupations of the Farm Bureau's members, Fleming only insisted that "each of the State Farm Bureaus is an autonomous unit. This is a state's rights outfit. . . . They determine the eligibility for membership."

When questioned about the insurance operations of the parent American Farm Bureau Federation itself, Fleming claimed that they consisted of a reinsurance company only. He persisted in that claim even after Resnick read to him from the authoritative source, *Best's Insurance Guides,* that the company had authority to write virtually all lines of insurance, and despite clear evidence that they were in fact writing policies directly.

When Resnick pressed him further on the insurance issue, Fleming launched into a discussion of the history of the Farm Bureau, and refused to give a direct answer. The tension was building and some members of the Subcommittee, sympathetic to the Farm Bureau, asked Resnick to yield. He refused, which as chairman was his prerogative. Finally the hearing was adjourned because the day's House session was about to begin. Since Resnick had many more questions to ask Fleming, and since committees can hold hearings while the House is in session upon the unanimous consent of the House, Resnick requested such permission on the House floor. The single objection of George Goodling (Rep.–Pa.), a member of Resnick's subcommittee, was sufficient to block the request. As Resnick said later, "It troubled me that my colleagues would feel so protective of this lobby group that they would attempt to block the legitimate, if embarrassing questioning of one of its officials. In retrospect, I underestimated their solicitousness to the organization."

As stories of Resnick's early charges—that the Farm Bureau was primarily a business and was not serving its members—began to appear in newspapers around the country, his office was deluged with letters from farmers, rural businessmen, bankers, ministers and housewives. The message was overwhelmingly the same: "You have only scratched the surface. Keep digging." Many recounted at length their own experiences with the organization. Suddenly Resnick had an invaluable new resource—a vast network of in-the-field investigators. One of the most revealing things about the letters was the large number from Farm Bureau members and former members. They explained that they were tied to the organization by insurance or other economic factors, and then went on to urge Resnick's continued scrutiny. "I am positive that three-quarters of the Farm Bureau members who are deriving all their income from farming are behind you," wrote a member from Iowa. An Ohio farmer wrote: "I am a Farm Bureau member for 45 years and I agree with you. If they need investigating, get to it." A member of the board of directors of a county Farm Bureau in Illinois confessed, "I hate to admit it but I'm afraid you are on the right track." Another large group of letters came from Farm Bureau members who had nothing to do with farming—an auto parts dealer, a worker in the Frigidaire plant in Detroit, lawyers, merchants, a union official. They had joined almost invariably when they purchased their insurance.

As these letters arrived, describing questionable Farm Bureau activities, Resnick's staff followed them up, calling government officials, local lawyers, professors at nearby colleges. As new accusations were checked and verified, Resnick released them to the public in press releases and speeches on the floor of the House, charging that the Farm Bureau was abusing its tax exemption, that it was still receiving special benefits from the government-sponsored Extension Service, and that it was carrying many people who were not farmers on its membership rolls. Local papers picked up the new stories, which brought new batches of letters suggesting fresh areas for investigation. Many letters included detailed documentation in support of the charges leveled. Many letters corroborated one another. Resnick's staff soon realized that they had originally seen only the tip of a giant iceberg.

By the end of June, Resnick felt he had enough information to bring the matter to the attention of the Internal Revenue Service. In a detailed, 18-item bill of particulars, he described the abuses which raised questions about the Bureau's right to tax-exempt status. On July 10th, he received the reply he had been waiting for from IRS Commissioner Sheldon Cohen: "I assure you that the Service will carefully investigate the factual allegations in your letter, and will take whatever action may be appropriate."[5] Resnick had won his first victory.

The early optimism proved to be premature. After the confrontations at the hearings, the Farm Bureau had remained silent. Secretary-Treasurer Fleming had disclosed that the organization intended to call on the full House Agriculture Committee—a much friendlier forum—either to disavow Resnick's charges or to undertake an investigation conducted by the entire committee.[6]

The idea of a Congressional committee formally disavowing the statements of one of its members was unprecedented and outrageous. Certainly no one construes the statements of Senator William Fulbright or Representative Wright Patman or Senator James Eastland as those of their committees unless they specifically say so. To make it perfectly clear that he had been speaking only for himself, Resnick had pointed out at his hearings: "I would also like to state for the record that any statements I make, or any requests I make, I make on the basis of an individual Congressman. They do not reflect in any way the feelings of the Subcommittee. As Chairman of this Subcommittee, I am speaking as an individual Congressman."[7]

In spite of that statement, the AFBF sent each member of the House Agriculture Committee one of the most arrogant demands by a professional lobby ever seen by seasoned observers of Congressional politics. The letter cited Resnick's "personal" attack on the Farm Bureau, and demanded:

In the interest of justice and fair play we urge that the full Committee give immediate consideration to the charge made by Subcommittee Chairman Resnick against the Farm Bureau organization (county, state, and national). If the Committee believes that there is basis for these charges, then we respectfully request the full Committee conduct a full scale, in depth, investigation of all farm organizations with special emphasis on organization-related business activities, government contracts in operation, and an analysis of the size and composition of each organization's membership. *On the other hand, if the Committee does not concur in these charges, then we feel that the Committee should clear the record by adopting a resolution in which it disassociates itself from the attacks on Farm Bureau made by Subcommittee Chairman Resnick and by making known to the public at an early date its disposition of this matter* [emphasis added].[8]

Within 48 hours, the Farm Bureau had accomplished its goal, obtaining incredible speed from the same committee that takes years to consider such matters as the food stamp program. Of course the Farm Bureau had several advantages over the food stamp program. Most members of the House Agriculture Committee were Farm Bureau members. Verlon Welch, the top aide of John Zwach (Rep.–Minn.) one of the instigators of the Committee's action, came to work for Zwach in 1966 after five years as legislative director of the Minnesota Farm Bureau.[9]

Responding to the Farm Bureau's call, the five other members of Resnick's own Subcommittee met privately within 24 hours, and adopted a resolution to "disassociate" themselves (the very term requested by the Farm Bureau) from Resnick's charges against "one of our nation's oldest and most respected general farm organizations."[10] They felt all the urgency to vindicate the Farm Bureau that they lacked to feed the rural poor.

Resnick first learned of the action of his fellow Subcommittee members a few hours after they had met. He also learned that a meeting of the full Committee had been called for the following morning. When he arrived on Capitol Hill the next morning, he discovered that the meeting was to be closed to the public and the press. This infuriated him. "If upholding the good name of the Farm Bureau is so crucial to the public interest that it requires an unprecedented Committee action against a dissenting Congressman," Resnick stated, "it should be done in the full light of public scrutiny." Resnick entered the meeting, already in session, and interrupted the Committee Chairman, Robert Poage (Dem.–Tex.). He moved that the meeting be open to the press that had gathered outside the chamber. When this attempt failed, Resnick left, unwilling to submit to a secret inquisition.

By a vote of 27 to 1, the Committee adopted the Farm Bureau resolution:

Resolved, That the Committee on Agriculture of the United States House of Representatives does in no manner endorse, condone, or support the personal attack launched by the Chairman of the Subcommittee on Rural Development upon the American Farm Bureau Federation.[11]

Twelve southern Democrats and fifteen Republicans voted for the resolution. The Committee's two northern Democrats—Frank Brasco of New York, and Tom Foley of Washington, could only summon up sufficient courage to sit on their hands and vote "present." Representative Eligio de la Garza (Dem.–Tex.), the one member to vote against the resolution, later explained his position: "Suppose I want to investigate something or someone. They could do the same thing to me."[12]

Immediately following the action of the Committee, the Farm Bureau proclaimed in a press release: "This judgment by his Congressional colleagues should make it crystal clear that Congressman Resnick's charges against the Farm Bureau Federation are reckless, unwarranted, and unfounded."[13] Despite the fact that the Committee's words were only of "disassociation," the Farm Bureau pronounced itself vindicated. It took the action of a committee that had *refused* to consider the merits of Resnick's charges as a verdict of its innocence, and tried to use that self-proclaimed judgment as a shield against further inquiry.

Later that day, James O'Hara (Dem.–Mich.), then Chairman of the liberal Democratic Study Group, rose on the floor of the House to denounce the Agriculture Committee's vote, calling it "a dangerous precedent when a Subcommittee Chairman cannot question the activities of one of the largest lobbies in Washington."[14] That evening Washington news commentator Joseph McCaffrey spoke of the Committee action:

We now have a Committee which is going to decide what Members of the House should say and what they should not say. The world is being made safe for democracy in a strange and undemocratic way. This will prove to be interesting. It may be developed to such a point where a Member will never say anything until he has had his script cleared by a Congressional Committee. This, of course, will cut down on the adlibs. But then some Members of Congress are pretty bad at adlibbing, so we may be spared much pain.

So big brotherism is now to become operating procedure on Capitol Hill. Members will be told by other Members what they can say, and what they can't say. This is a far cry from what the Founding Fathers had in mind when they met in Philadelphia in 1787 to draft the Constitution. Freedom of speech is precious. For a Member of Congress it should be even more precious.

What is really sad is that the Members of the Committee apparently don't realize the shaft they sunk in the back of freedom. That is what is most disturbing.[15]

The scene of members of a Congressional committee falling all over themselves in their haste to affirm the challenged integrity of one of the largest and most powerful organizations that lobbies before it is a dramatic commentary on the independence of our legislative branch. It raises serious issues of legislative ethics. Should members of Congress join organizations that carry on extensive lobbying before committees on which they serve, even if such memberships are often meaningless political gestures to groups back home? More important, should congressmen be required to disclose all contributions made to their campaigns by organizations with which they have significant legislative contact? Congress will never gain the complete confidence of the American people until all such suspicions are scrupulously eliminated, and until that day its self-righteous criticisms of the irregularities in the other branches of government will smack of hypocrisy.

*   *   *

In retrospect, the Farm Bureau's blatant power-play represented the turning point of Resnick's investigation. It intrigued and angered many, including elements of the press, who had been uninterested until that point. For example, repeated attempts to interest *The New York Times* in writing a story about Resnick's investigation had been unsuccessful; after the Committee's action Resnick had a strong and influential ally in the *Times*. Through the national TV coverage that resulted from the Committee action, millions who had not previously known of Resnick's investigation learned of it, and millions of others who had never heard of the Farm Bureau were introduced to what it was doing. A campaign that would undoubtedly have soon withered away because it could not sustain sufficient public interest had been dramatically boosted. An investigation that lives by the press, dies by the press; it must constantly make news. By hitting the panic button, the Farm Bureau had not only failed to silence Resnick; it had exposed its power and its danger far more dramatically than any critic could have done.

Why had the Farm Bureau so overreacted? Sources inside the organization indicated that Resnick's repeated attacks over the previous few weeks had stirred consternation among Farm Bureaus throughout the country. Farm Bureau leaders were caught between forces demanding bold counter-action and those demanding hard answers to the questions he was raising. Unable to provide the latter, they opted for the former.

Resnick's notoriety provoked a new wave of mail that brought new accusations. It was now clear that there was a need for a full-scale investigation of the entire scope of the Farm Bureau's activities. It would have been preferable if the full Agricultural Committee, with its power of subpoena, had assumed this responsibility. Nevertheless, despite increasing pressure from their constituents (Resnick had urged letter-writers from around the country to write to their own Congressmen expressing their views), it soon became clear that the full Committee would do nothing. Finally Resnick decided to hold hearings on his own, since any Congressman has the right to conduct official ad hoc hearings on any subject of public interest. Because so many potential witnesses were located far from Washington and could not afford the travel costs to the capital, Resnick took his "one-man" hearings to them at his own expense.

His staff arranged a series of open hearings in Chicago, Illinois; Omaha, Nebraska; and finally in Washington. Although Resnick's attention to that point had been focused on the Farm Bureau specifically, he enlarged the scope of the hearings to include all the major general farm organizations: the Grange, the National Farmers Union, and the National Farmers Organization. He wanted to find out whether the Farm Bureau's operations were typical of the other farm organizations, and whether the others felt it necessary to maintain extensive business operations to function effectively.

At each stop, he invited the leaders of each of the state organizations from the surrounding states. In each case, all the organizations appeared except the Farm Bureau. Charles B. Shuman, then president of the Farm Bureau, wrote to Resnick: "Since the Committee has made its position known to the public by disassociating itself from your personal attack on the Farm Bureau, it would have been inappropriate for us to participate in your 'one-man hearings.' " No one seemed to recall that the Farm Bureau's Mr. Fleming had stated at the Subcommittee hearings that his organization "would be interested in an investigation which analyzed the Farm Bureau and its operation and the other farm organizations," and would be "happy to cooperate." The Farm Bureau's basic strategy during this period was to challenge Resnick's motives, rather than answer his charges. Bureau officials accused him of being a publicity-crazed politician, and a fanatic out to smear a reputable organization.[16]

Although Resnick's hearings in Chicago and Omaha had been hastily organized, dozens of farmers appeared at each city to testify, many travelling for hours to do so. Resnick quickly realized that their letters had failed to convey the intensity of their feelings. In Chicago and Omaha the stories were similar: the Farm Bureau is unrepresentative of the farmers' views; internal opposition is stifled; the organization has links to right-wing political activity; there is still a connection with the government Extension

Service; a significant proportion of Farm Bureau members are not farmers. In Chicago, a wiry, weather-beaten farmer of about 70, who had been a member of the Illinois Farm Bureau since it was founded in 1915, walked up to Resnick before testifying: "I would like to shake your hand," he said. "You are the only dude in Washington who had the guts to go into this outfit."

After the Chicago and Omaha hearings, Resnick returned to Washington to prepare for four days of hearings there. Although the Farm Bureau was still boycotting the hearings, the presidents of all the other major farm organizations had agreed to testify, as had government officials, farmers, and rural businessmen from as far away as Nebraska. The president of the National Farmers Organization, the Master of the National Grange, and the legislative director of the National Farmers Union each appeared and freely answered questions about the character of their membership, as well as their financial and political activities. "Farmers should welcome investigation that will give them the answers as to why their problems have not been solved," said NFO president Oren Lee Staley.[17]

The detailed and candid testimony of these representatives indicated that it would be unjustified to lump the other farm organizations in with the Farm Bureau. Their similarities are in fact superficial. The disparity in their financial resources and membership is enormous. By choice or by circumstance, the other farm organizations have not accumulated the mammoth commercial trappings of the Farm Bureau. They have concerned themselves, for the most part, with representing the farmer and trying in various ways to raise his standard of living.

Of the four existing general farm organizations, the oldest is the National Grange. Today, the Grange is largely a rural service organization, with an educational and fraternal character. It readily admits to representing "members of rural communities," rather than just farmers. It has about 700,000 individual members, down from its peak of 850,000, and these are concentrated primarily in the New England and Middle Atlantic states.

The Grange spends about a third of what the Farm Bureau spends on lobbying. Although at one time it was a regular ally of the Farm Bureau, today it is usually aligned with the other farm organizations, across the battle lines from the Farm Bureau on basic issues of farm policy and social reform designed to alleviate rural poverty.

The Farm Bureau's earliest consistent critic was the National Farmers

Union. The National Farmers Union (NFU) represents about 225,000 farm families, down in recent years from about 250,000. Its greatest strength is in the Midwest plain states and the Southwest. Since its inception about 70 years ago, the Farmers Union has been a forceful advocate for the family farmer. Its philosophy and general policies "reflect a general thread of liberalism," explain its officials. The organization has often joined forces with the labor movement to promote social legislation and it generally supported the Kennedy–Johnson domestic policies.

The Farmers Union is connected with a number of cooperatives around the country organized by Farmers Union members. The coops use the organization's name in exchange for a fee. However, these coops are autonomous, elect their own boards of directors, and are managed without assistance from the NFU. Nearly all of the Farmers Union members are farmers.

The newest farm organization on the scene is the National Farmers Organization. Based in the Midwest, the NFO has recently expanded its activities into the South. It is the most militant of the general farm organizations, organized around the principle of collective bargaining for farmers. The major effort of the NFO is to organize farmers into bargaining units that can deal with the concentrated power of the buyers, the processors, and the retailers of farm products. The most widely publicized NFO activities have been its holding actions, where farmers have, for example, dumped their milk production or plowed under their crop, as a tactic to pressure the large buyers into more favorable terms for the farmers. The by-laws of the organization require a potential member to be a farmer, and this has been rigidly upheld. The organization does not disclose its membership figures, contending that this is part of their bargaining strategy. It neither owns nor operates any independent businesses. Although the organization engages in far less lobbying activity than the Farm Bureau, NFU, or Grange, it has generally aligned itself with the latter groups—in opposition to the Farm Bureau.

Armed with this information, gathered at hearings in Chicago, Omaha, and finally Washington, Resnick continued to blast away at the Farm Bureau. Allegations by farmers in Ohio that they had been issued worthless stock by their Farm Bureau coop prompted Resnick to delve into the Farm Bureau cooperative ventures. He found disturbing irregularities in the way in which they were operating. Another round of one-man hearings was held in Cleveland to air the angry complaints of farmers who had been the victims of Farm Bureau cooperative practices.

Meanwhile, pressure was building up within the Farm Bureau to respond to the charges against it. Finally, on September 3, the *New York Times* reported that "The American Farm Bureau Federation, stung by an inquiry into its affairs by Representative Joseph Y. Resnick, . . . has called for an investigation of all farm organizations by the House Agriculture Committee. . . . Mr. Fleming said the request to the Agriculture Committee to investigate its activities had been made in the light of Mr. Resnick's continued attacks on the organization." The wire services carried the same story.[18]

Resnick was delighted. He had become increasingly aware that there was little more he could do alone. Prospects for the corrective legislation he was preparing were dim, especially considering the reluctance of his fellow Congressmen to support the investigation publicly (although privately some of the most powerful members of the House confided in him their support). The abuses had been publicly aired. The IRS had been prodded as much as a junior Congressman can prod, but there had been no response since the initial announcement of an investigation. Hope that that agency would take drastic action was rapidly diminishing. It was now necessary for an official Congressional body—particularly one with power to subpoena witnesses and records—to take over.

Resnick soon learned, however, that the story the *Times* had printed was merely a smokescreen perpetrated by the Farm Bureau, calculated to take the pressure off at least temporarily. Upon checking with the Agriculture Committee, he discovered that no such request for an investigation had in fact been received. As former Governor Al Smith of New York said, "All they knew was what they read in the newspapers." When Resnick blasted the Farm Bureau for this "deliberate deception," the only answer he got referred to the Bureau's original letter to the Agriculture Committee back in July—the one which had demanded "investigation or repudiation."[19]

The Farm Bureau's strategy was not confined to these bizarre verbal contortions. On September 10, syndicated political columnists Evans and Novak reported that, "Although the American Farm Bureau Federation publicly assumes a stance of nonchalance toward the one-man investigation of it by gadfly Representative Joseph Y. Resnick (Dem.–N.Y.) it is working under cover to purge him from public life. Farm Bureau officials here in Washington have privately contacted key New York Republican leaders to ask if a prominent Republican is available to oppose Resnick in 1968, and to offer full resources of the giant farm organization in the campaign."[20]

Fortunately, Resnick had substantial resources of his own, so that this kind of intimidation did not worry him much. It should be recognized, however, that as long as restrictions on the political activities of such tax-exempt organizations are so loosely drawn, and the laws for disclosing the sources of campaign funds remain a farce, most Representatives simply will not stick their necks out to investigate these groups for fear of precisely this kind of reprisal.

In October, following a "four-week inquiry" of its own, the *New York Times* corroborated much of what Resnick had been saying about the Farm Bureau, and disclosed that ". . . the top officials of the . . . organization are displaying uneasiness over the four month attack. . . ."[21]

Despite its public silence, the Farm Bureau's private struggle over the investigation was apparent at its 1967 annual convention in Chicago, on December 12.[22] Secretary–Treasurer Fleming devoted half of his annual report to a direct, if not particularly candid, response to the charges that Resnick had been making during the previous six months. Fleming described "the Resnick Affair" as a "headline-hunting exercise by this multi-millionaire industrialist tycoon from the Catskills of New York State." After describing in great detail the action of the House Agriculture Committee in disassociating itself from Resnick's charges, Fleming, instead of answering the charges, launched into a long discussion of Resnick's motives. After all, if you can impugn the motives, you can ignore the merits. He cited a few "interesting clues," which amounted to a contention that Resnick was the "instigator of a well-organized vendetta."

The Farm Bureau had several fascinating theories about who was behind this well-organized conspiracy. One possibility Fleming raised was the National Farmers Organization. The only proof he offered of the complicity of the NFO was that Resnick had spoken at an NFO rally the previous July in Minnesota. The second possibility put forth was that Resnick's backers were President Johnson and the AFL-CIO. Resnick had indeed spoken to the White House about the investigation, but primarily to keep officials there informed. Likewise it wasn't until September 1967, when Resnick was well into the investigation, that the AFL-CIO executive council endorsed his efforts, and called for a full government probe. The final possibility suggested by Fleming was that Resnick was really acting on behalf of the anti-cooperative forces in the country. In fact, however, Resnick had stated many times that he was not against cooperatives when they are operating consistently with the principles on which they were originally founded.

Apparently, Resnick's investigation had some other interesting repercussions at the Bureau's 1967 convention. For the first time, representatives of the county Farm Bureaus were invited to attend the convention, although in a non-voting capacity. A large, noisy convention looks more democratic than a small, orderly one, and it was obviously felt that the gathering should have at least the appearance of democracy. A new resolution was passed and added to the otherwise more or less unaltered policy statement. The resolution, dealing with "Tax Exempt Groups" read: "Groups otherwise tax exempt should be required to pay property taxes on income-producing property and income taxes on all income derived from commercial activities."[23] Those who saw this as a drastic change of heart—a self-divestiture in the making—were disabused of such naiveté the following year when, with the heat of public scrutiny off, the provision was dropped.

After an unsuccessful bid for the Senate in 1968, Resnick retired from Congress. However, determined to learn more about the Farm Bureau and continue the effort to expose its abuses to the public, he privately financed a new investigation of the organization, more exhaustive and far-reaching than the first. Even after he was no longer a public servant, Resnick continued the job of unravelling the tangled strands of the Farm Bureau story. That, of course, is a tribute to the tenacity and public spirit of one man, but more importantly, it is a serious indictment of Congress itself. Had Resnick been a man of less substantial means, less able to resist the potential retaliation of the special interests he was fighting, or unable to personally finance what should have been the work of government, a powerful organization sorely in need of public exposure would have remained unexamined. The public's right to know hangs by a precarious thread.

3

Membership for Merchandising

THE FARM BUREAU describes itself as an organization of farmers. But despite the fact that critics have been asking for an occupational breakdown of its membership for years, the national organization has refused to produce one. It retreats behind the bastion of state's rights, declaring that membership eligibility is a state affair.[1]

Many of the states break their membership down into voting and non-voting classes. The latter category—called "associate membership"—is theoretically designed for non-farmers. But the classifications are fuzzy, vary widely, and are difficult to obtain. Local- or county-level officials generally have the power to classify an individual as they see fit. For example, The Illinois Farm Bureau (known as the Illinois Agricultural Association) defines voting members as persons "who receive a substantial portion of their income" from the production of agricultural products, including landlords who receive rent from farm ownership. Associate membership is available in Illinois to persons "interested in agriculture," which covers just about anyone.[2]

Clearly sensitive about the percentage of farmers in his organization, Charles Shuman, president of the American Farm Bureau Federation from 1955–1970, has claimed that associate membership is a "privilege . . . extended to a relatively few individuals who are devoting their lives to agriculture, even though they do not own or operate farms."[3] When pressed for an estimate, Shuman recently placed the figure of non-farmer members at 20 percent. Close examination, however, shows that this figure is grossly underestimated. The Kentucky Farm Bureau, for example, acknowledges that more than one-third of its members are associate or non-farm members.[4]

To fully appreciate this matter of Farm Bureau membership, one must look at what has been happening to the farm population over the last several years. While more than three-quarters of a million people were leaving the farms each year during the 1960s, Farm Bureau membership has been steadily climbing. The number of farms in the United States decreased by almost one million from 1961 to 1970, and the farm population shrank by about five million. During that same period, however, the Farm Bureau added nearly a million people (342,000 families) to its rolls. In 1969 alone, while the number of farms dropped by another 70,000, the Farm Bureau increased its membership by about 70,000 families.

Even these diverging figures on farm population and Farm Bureau membership understate the discrepancy. Many of those who are nominally farmers are not farmers at all. According to Willard Cochrane, chief economist for the Department of Agriculture during the Kennedy–Johnson Administrations, nearly one-third of what are statistically listed as "farms" are really part-time, retirement or other non-commercial farms. Many are not really farms at all. "The operators of these farms have, for all practical purposes, left farming," says Cochrane. "They are living in the farmhouses, milking a cow or two, raising a few chickens or pigs, and working in the city. And the retired farmers are retired, not farming, except again for a cow or two and a few chickens or pigs."[5]

In view of these facts and figures on the country's declining farm population, how can one explain the Farm Bureau's dramatic increase in membership? A closer look at the statistics reveals part of the answer. In four of its most active states—Alabama, Florida, Illinois and Indiana—the Farm Bureau has far more family memberships than there are farms. In Illinois, there are nearly twice as many Farm Bureau family members (190,481) as commercial farms. The Indiana Farm Bureau has more than 50 percent more members than the state has farms of all types, including part-time and retirement farms. In several other states, particularly California, Kansas, New Hampshire and Wyoming, there are nearly as many members as there are farms of all kinds.

The most striking disparity is found in Cook County, Illinois, which essentially includes Chicago and some of its suburbs. While the Farm Bureau has more than 7,000 family members in Cook County, the County has only about 1,000 farms. It is difficult therefore to attribute the Farm Bureau's large membership in Cook County to farms unless they are signing up cows as well as people.

One Illinois corn farmer wrote to Congressman Resnick: "The Farm Bureau goes to Washington, D.C. and states they are talking for 2,500 farmers in my county. We have only 1,200 farmers, so just who are they talking for? It sure is not for me and a lot more just like me." Three Indiana farmers reported that "Farm Bureau boasts a . . . county membership of 2,600, whereas we have only 400 farmers."

Farm Bureau leaders respond to this kind of analysis with the argument that some farms support more than a single Farm Bureau membership, namely farms owned by absentee landlords, and farms owned or operated by more than one family. They claim that both the owner and the operator, or in the latter case, both operators, often join separately.

No doubt such multiple memberships exist. What is doubtful, however, is that they exist in sufficient numbers to bring the percentage of farmer members even near 80 percent. Nearly 60 percent of the farms in the country are owned and operated by the same person. Another 17 percent are operated by tenant farmers. Although the owners of these farms may be Farm Bureau members, there are not many tenant farmers in the Farm Bureau for the same reason there are few cobblers in the National Association of Manufacturers.

Among the other third—those farms run by part-owners or managers—there are some multiple Farm Bureau memberships. But it is unlikely that there are substantial numbers. Some of these part-owners have interests in more than a single farm. Some have interests so small that even by the most liberal Farm Bureau view of what a farmer is, they do not qualify. Most important, many joint owners simply balk at the idea of more than one membership for a farm, preferring instead to avail themselves of the Farm Bureau services through a single membership in the name of the farm itself.

If so many Farm Bureau members then are clearly not farmers, just who are they? The answer is simple—anyone. An Illinois hog farmer recently explained the matter to a stranger: "If you get your hair cut in rural Illinois, chances are that a Farm Bureau member will cut it. If you bank in a country bank in Illinois, chances are you will bank with a Farm Bureau member. If you get sick in Illinois, chances are you will go to a Farm Bureau member for medication. And if you are sued in Illinois, chances are that you will consult a Farm Bureau member for legal advice. But if you want to talk to a farmer in Illinois, chances are pretty good that you won't be talking to a Farm Bureau member."

In Illinois, as well as most other states, a large number of Farm Bureau members are factory workers, teachers, lawyers, doctors, merchants and ministers. Why do they join? In view of the Farm Bureau's commercial operations, it is hardly surprising. One enthusiastic Farm Bureau official described the organization as a "supermarket," offering its members insurance, mutual funds, tires, and a host of other products and services. "Pay for this year's DUES with the SAVINGS on your first TWO Safemark [the Farm Bureau's trade name] tires," proclaims a flyer put out by the Wyoming Farm Bureau.[6] It is clear that many people belong to the Farm Bureau for no other reason than to receive these business services. When their address is Chicago, or Detroit, or Birmingham, it is difficult to believe that they are members for any other reason, unless window boxes now qualify as farms.

Comments by Farm Bureau officials show how these commercial ventures influence the makeup of the membership. A former county Farm Bureau secretary from Kansas explained that when his county started a group plan for Blue Cross–Blue Shield insurance through the state Farm Bureau insurance company, he was told to bring in more non-farmers in order to broaden the group. An executive-secretary of long standing with another large county Farm Bureau explained that the competitive situation today requires the Bureau to do business on a volume basis, which has meant expanding the non-farm portion of his county's membership to nearly 40 percent. Former president Shuman admits that some states "have accepted members they shouldn't have because they wanted the money."[7]

For a good example of the Farm Bureau's indiscriminate drive for members, one should look at a current brochure circulated by the Missouri Farm Bureau. Depicting a farmhouse and a suburban residence, the brochure explains that "both rural and urban families" have the common problems of mounting taxes, schools, highways, big government. It then explains what the city man can find in the Farm Bureau: insurance, medical plans, and an organization that works for "individual freedom and our American heritage."[8]

For the city dweller, the difference between Farm Bureau insurance rates and competitive commercial rates can often more than pay for a membership in the Farm Bureau. A study conducted by the Kansas Attorney-General showed that based on 1967 rates, an auto operator over 25 living in Wichita and not engaged in farming pays between $20 and $54 less per year for Farm Bureau insurance than for the same coverage with the four companies to which it was compared. An unmarried Wichita owner and operator under 25 and not in farming can save more than $200 a year with Farm Bureau insurance.[9]

The Farm Bureau business services bind members to the organization indefinitely. Literally thousands of elderly citizens, after retiring from farming, have had to maintain their Farm Bureau membership in order to retain their Farm Bureau life and health insurance. It would be virtually impossible for them to obtain other insurance at their ages. "They are hooked," remarked one Iowa woman explaining the memberships of her mother-in-law and elderly friends.

The Farm Bureau has other special methods of encouraging rural businessmen and professionals to join. One recurrent and bitter theme in conversations about the Farm Bureau with such people is the heavy-handed tactics used by many Farm Bureau membership recruiters in pressuring them to join. "There is a certain type of blackmail, I call it, to get these businessmen to join," explained one Midwesterner. "A farmer member is sent into these business places . . . and asks him to join Farm Bureau, and he also reminds him that he just bought a suit of clothes or just got some teeth fixed or just had a baby. You can guess the rest that goes on."

Some businessmen tell of threatened boycotts if they refuse to join, but few take the risk. An auto body shop owner reported that he must join the Farm Bureau if he wants to get the Farm Bureau auto-insurance repair work. The proprietor of a bowling alley was threatened with the loss of bowling leagues heavily loaded with Farm Bureau members if he refused to join. The following story of one rural bank vice president—a prominent and respected figure in his community—is illuminating and not untypical:

Just last year, a pair of gentlemen who were county officers [in the Farm Bureau] from my banking area called on me in my office and asked me to become a member of the Farm Bureau. I informed them that personally I was not interested, since our bank was already a member. . . . Several years ago the paid professional area Farm Bureau fieldman called on the president of our bank and asked him to see that I become a member. . . . One of their paid professionals told me on the street one day that I lost lots of business because I did not belong. . . . This same well-paid fieldman called on one of my bank customers and called to his attention the fact that he was dealing with a non-member.

Even businessmen in direct competition with Farm Bureau businesses do not escape such lead-piping. One rural insurance salesman who competes with Farm Bureau insurance tried unsuccessfully to discontinue his own Farm Bureau membership. The Farm Bureaus of both counties in his insurance territory sent good customers of his to ask him to renew his membership. "They twisted my arm in this manner, and I felt compelled to sign, and did so." According to this salesman, the county Farm Bureaus in his area applied the same tactics with equal success on the local John Deere farm equipment dealer, a local service station, and a local feed and fertilizer company.

What all this amounts to is exacting tribute from rural businessmen in the regions of the Farm Bureau's greatest strength. And it should be remembered that these economic hostages are counted in the membership figure cited by Farm Bureau lobbyists as they speak in Washington "for the farmers of America."

Another block of the organization's non-farmer members consists of the employees of its business affiliates around the country. Thousands of such employees dutifully subscribe their names to Farm Bureau membership rolls, and remit their dues each year, often after some prodding. Farm Bureau cooperative managers are rewarded with plaques for signing up 100 percent of their employees, and Farm Bureau publications print accounts of their accomplishment.[10]

Besides the non-farmers who "buy in" or who are clubbed in, there is another group of Farm Bureau members with no direct interest in farming, who join for purely social reasons. An Iowa paper, for example, reports that the local Farm Bureau club "has planned a study of Brazil for its fall-winter program. Members will give papers on the history, religion, arts, agriculture and industry of that country. . . . Mrs. Haw's husband works at Firestone, so she has decided to write a report on rubber production in Brazil." The Farm Bureau publication in Ohio not long ago featured a story about one of their county presidents, a retired executive of Procter and Gamble, now a dog breeder, who "is the first to admit he is not a farmer."[11]

Another group of rural businessmen and professionals who, while not pressured to join, feel dependent upon farmers for their livelihood are susceptible to appeals to join the Farm Bureau. Says one lawyer-member: "In this rural community we know that what is good for the farmers is good for the rest of us."

In addition to the large number of non-farmers, the Farm Bureau membership list includes a great number of non-people as well. Businesses, towns, and even counties belong, and pay regular dues. In one county, every school district is a "member" of the Farm Bureau. In Boone County, Iowa, some enterprising Farm Bureau membership chairman has even signed up the county poor house.[12]

These memberships enable the businesses, towns and counties to purchase Farm Bureau insurance, oil, gas, and other services. Sometimes such purchases are made under competitive bidding, sometimes not. But consider the situation here. Not only is the school board or town council or county board paying the full value of the insurance or oil or gas; it is also paying dues to a private organization which is using those dues in part to influence the government itself. Such an arrangement raises serious constitutional questions as to the validity of such expenditures under a doctrine which, simply stated, requires public funds to be spent for public purposes. Although these expenditures are minor for single towns or county boards, they are substantial in the aggregate.

Since Farm Bureau dues are deductible from federal income taxes, many businessmen sign up in the name of their business. Some of the Farm Bureau's two million "member families" are bowling alleys, funeral homes, auto body shops, motels and bars. For example, a 1969 issue of the *Colorado Farm Bureau News* featured a picture of the Thunderbird Motel, displaying out front a Courtesy Coffee sign, a BankAmericard sign, and a Farm Bureau membership sign.[13]

What's wrong with the Farm Bureau having such a large percentage of non-farmer members? First, they haven't been entirely honest about it. Although they are usually careful to express total membership as so many "member families" as opposed to "farm families" (1,943,181 member families at the beginning of 1971), they use the total membership figure in such a way as to leave the impression that it represents only farmers.

A brochure called "This is Farm Bureau," put out by the American Farm Bureau Federation in 1969, describes all aspects of the organization without mentioning that a good portion of the members are not farmers.

In fact it leaves the impression that they all *are* farmers. "Farm Bureau is farm people," it proclaims. "Farm Bureau policies stem from the man on the land." Nowhere is there mention of associate membership, nor any hint that all of those nearly two million members are not farmers.

A lobbying organization values its membership figures as the prime source of its political strength, and when Farm Bureau leaders testify before Congress, they never fail to remind the legislators that they represent nearly two million member-families, "the farmers of America." Many Congressmen have been misled into believing that all Farm Bureau members are farmers. To any Congressman this sounds like an awesome number of farm voters.

Occasionally the misrepresentation is less subtle. At the Democratic Platform Committee hearings in 1964, Idaho Congressman Ralph Harding asked pointedly how many "dirt farmers" the Farm Bureau actually represented. The AFBF's Walter Randolph replied that the organization's total membership represented "farm and ranch families." A brochure currently used by the Florida Farm Bureau proclaims: "Nationally, the American Farm Bureau Federation has become the strong voice of more than 1,800,000 farm families." A brochure put out a few years ago by the Virginia Farm Bureau states: "The American Farm Bureau Federation is the Spokesman for 1,628,000 farm families" (total membership at that time). And an Ohio Farm Bureau pamphlet describes the state body as "a voluntary membership organization of well over 52,000 farm families."[14]

Whether the non-farmer percentage is 20 percent, 30 percent, or 50 percent, it is significant enough to deserve full disclosure to government bodies, and to warrant mention in general descriptions of the organization. When such an organization becomes a powerful influence on national farm policy, the public has a right to know such information. When such an organization receives a tax-exemption as a farm organization, the federal government has a right to know.

4

Insuring the Farm Bureau's Future

THE OFFICIAL of the Farm Bureau who described the organization as a "supermarket" was being modest. In fact, the Farm Bureau is one of the largest business empires in the United States. The Farm Bureau businesses were originally conceived, and are still justified by the organization, as "service to member" projects. But they have long since outgrown that rationale. The Farm Bureau has become a multi-billion-dollar rural colossus, dispensing everything from rented cars to mutual funds.

As the Farm Bureau has added layer after layer of commercial crust, its organizational core has become more and more obscured, until today it is unrealistic to still characterize the Farm Bureau as truly a farm organization. But it still claims to be a farm organization, to Congress and state legislatures, as well as to the Internal Revenue Service and county tax assessors. As the business activities of the Farm Bureau have mushroomed, it has become increasingly difficult for its leadership to resolve the fundamental conflict between the Farm Bureau's role as *salesman* to the farmer and its role as *spokesman* for the farmer.

The cornerstone of Farm Bureau business operations is insurance. The Farm Bureau operates a nationwide network of fifty-five insurance companies with more than $1.5 billion in total assets. In 1968, these companies earned more than $500 million in premiums alone. The Farm Bureau insurance companies have increased their total assets by more than 50 percent since 1960. Farm Bureau life insurance companies have tripled in size over the last decade. They had over $7 billion of life insurance in force in 1968.

Who buys all this Farm Bureau insurance? Murray Lincoln, one of the pioneers of Farm Bureau insurance, has written: "When we first started our insurance company, it never dawned on me that we would ever insure anyone but farmers. But once we started insuring farmers other than Farm Bureau members, we found that we simply could not keep out the barber in the small town, the grocer, the gas-station attendant, the shopkeeper, or any other type of small businessman. Finally, as our company grew, we had to throw out the window the concept of restricting our insurance only to farmers."[1]

To accommodate the natural thrust to "go where the business is," some of the Farm Bureau companies, like the one in Ohio that Lincoln headed, simply changed their corporate articles to permit selling to non-members. Others have discovered more ingenious methods to surmount this obstacle. One of the most common methods is to have the prospective customer join the Farm Bureau when he purchases his insurance. In addition to enabling the company to sell another policy, this has the added advantage of placing another name on the Farm Bureau membership rolls.

As part of his investigation into the activities of the Farm Bureau in 1967, Representative Resnick sent one of his staff secretaries down to a Virginia Farm Bureau Insurance office to try to purchase some insurance. The closest she had ever been to a farm had been to pass over one in an airplane. From her chic appearance, there was considerable reason to doubt that she had just hopped off a tractor. She made no representation of having any connection with farming or agriculture. She merely said a friend had recommended this insurance company for her car insurance.

The insurance salesman asked no questions about her occupation or financial interests, but he did tell her she would have to join the Farm Bureau in order to buy the insurance. She agreed, and upon request made out a $20 check for her dues in the Virginia Farm Bureau. As instructed, she made this *dues* check out to "Farm Bureau Insurance," and was given a temporary certificate of insurance from the Virginia Farm Bureau Mutual Insurance Company. (She also received some literature on other Farm Bureau services, including a tire and battery purchase program for which she was now eligible as a Farm Bureau member.) The ease with which all this was done raises serious questions about the character of Farm Bureau membership, and the financial link between the organization and its businesses.

The outcome of this incident shows that the Farm Bureau itself is well-aware of how delicate the subject is. When Resnick confronted Farm Bureau officials with this story several days later, an interesting chain of events began. Although he did not mention the secretary's name, he did say she was a Washington secretary, and one could easily infer that she was on Resnick's own staff. Since she had gone to the closest Farm Bureau insurance agency, it was not difficult to trace the sale. A week after Resnick's hearing, the young lady received a letter from the Loudon County (Virginia) Farm Bureau stating: "your status does not qualify you for membership." (No questions had ever been asked about her "status" when she purchased the insurance.) Copies of this letter had been sent to the Virginia Farm Bureau headquarters, the Virginia Farm Bureau Mutual Insurance Company, and the American Farm Bureau Federation in Chicago —certainly an unusual procedure for a routine rejection of membership.[2]

Some states have established an alternative method for selling Farm Bureau insurance to non-members. In order to expand the types of coverage offered, and more conveniently service non-farm customers, the mutual insurance companies in these states have purchased or organized separate stock-ownership companies. Eleven such fire and casualty companies are currently part of the Farm Bureau group. These companies generally have no restrictions on who may purchase their insurance. Since life insurance companies, by law, cannot restrict sales to members of a particular group, all the Farm Bureau life insurance companies face no problem in selling to non-members or non-farmers.

Farm Bureau insurance companies aggressively seek non-farm business. Advertisements like that for "City Squire" insurance in Oregon, usually play down the farm element, and do not mention any occupational prerequisites. Sometimes the message is quite blunt. Ads for Farm Bureau insurance in the yellow pages in Illinois declare: "Insurance benefits now available to all persons—members and non-members of Bureau." And a brochure for Farm Bureau Insurance in Virginia advertises its insurance as designed "to meet the needs of FARMERS and RURAL VIRGINIANS."[3]

The results of such aggressive salesmanship to non-farmers is impressive. The Illinois Farm Bureau's Country Life Insurance Company, for example, is the largest one-state life insurance company in the United States, the only one with more than $2 billion of life insurance in force. One out of every six non-Chicago cars in Illinois is insured by Country Casualty Insurance Company.

As the Farm Bureau's insurance operations have expanded through the years, the state organizations have retained tight control over the companies by means of various corporate techniques. The most common technique is the interlocking directorate. The board of directors of a Farm Bureau insurance company is usually identical to the board of directors of the Farm Bureau of the state in which the company operates. As a staff member of one state Farm Bureau explained, "The board of directors of the state organization regularly meets at the state headquarters. When they are finished, they adjourn, go around to the other side of the table, so to speak, and call the meeting of the insurance company to order."

The officers of the state organization often serve as officers of the insurance companies as well. For example, William Kuhfuss (until his election to the presidency of the entire American Farm Bureau Federation in December, 1970) was president of the Illinois Farm Bureau and also president of its Country Insurance companies. Similar relationships can be found in many other state Farm Bureau operations.

Besides this interlocking and overlapping control, the Farm Bureau state organizations have employed other procedures to assure continued control of the insurance companies. These methods vary somewhat, depending partly upon whether the company is a mutual or stock company. According to Murray Lincoln, "In conventional stock insurance companies, policyholders have no voting rights. Only the stockholders vote. In a mutual insurance company the policyholder has the right to vote and the right to nominate and elect directors. Historically, however, mutual policyholders have not exercised the right to nominate and elect directors. Such matters are left to management. Commonly the management of a mutual company will take proxies from policyholders, and in this way insure the election of directors it nominates."[4]

Policyholders in most Farm Bureau mutual companies—despite the "of the farmer, by the farmer, for the farmer" rhetoric—have no more control over company policy than do the policyholders of any large insurance company, mutual or otherwise. For example, when the Farm Bureau Insurance Company of Nebraska was organized into a mutual company several years ago, each policyholder received a letter from the manager of the company explaining the reorganization. Appealing to the policyholders' loyalty to the Farm Bureau, the manager wrote:

As policyholders and owners of this Company we must make certain that the Company is always owned and controlled "lock, stock, and barrel" by the Nebraska Farm Bureau, which means centering the control in the Board of Directors, who are duly elected by the Farm Bureau members.

Few of us policyholders will be able to attend annual meetings in Lincoln and exercise our right to vote. But we must make certain that a quorum is present, either in person or by proxy, and that each policyholder's vote is counted.

We can do this by "permanent proxy," authorizing either the President or Secretary of the Board to cast our votes as the Board directs.[5]

This same letter assures policyholders: "If we intend to attend the meeting in person we can always revoke our proxy for that meeting." However, at the Resnick hearings in Omaha, a Nebraska woman who had sent in a permanent proxy told what happened when she became disenchanted with the Farm Bureau and its insurance company. She testified that despite repeated inquiries to Farm Bureau officials, she was unable to find out when and where the annual meeting was being held.

Farm Bureau control of the stock companies is even more straightforward. In some cases the owner of the stock is the parent mutual company. In other cases the state Farm Bureau itself owns the stock, either directly, or through a holding company established precisely for that purpose. In Illinois, where the state Farm Bureau is known as the Illinois Agricultural Association, the IAA's annual report tells us that "The Illinois Agricultural Holding Co., an affiliated company of the Illinois Agricultural Association, was organized to hold the capital stock of Country Life Insurance Company, and to insure that the control of Country Life Insurance Company would always remain in the Farm Bureau organization."[6] The Board of Directors of the holding company is the same as the Board of the insurance companies, which also happens to be the same as the Board of the state Farm Bureau. Before moving up to take over the national organization, president William Kuhfuss, who (as mentioned above) was president of the insurance companies, was, not surprisingly, president of the holding company. Other states are more circumspect in describing their intentions, but the effect is the same.

In some cases stock in these insurance companies is also owned by certain Farm Bureau members. For example, an exhaustive investigation by Alabama's *Birmingham News* revealed that preferred shares of the Southern Farm Bureau Insurance Companies are owned by Farm Bureau officials and other individuals.[7] Where such ownership of company stock by Farm Bureau officials exists, it raises serious questions about the true goals of an organization which claims to be in business only to serve its members—*all* its members.

In most states the overlap between the Farm Bureau and its businesses goes far beyond their interlocking directorates. Often the businesses share the same office buildings, the same personnel, and the same telephones as the Farm Bureaus. Frequently staff personnel have dual functions—serving organizational needs such as membership recruitment and program development, as well as managing one of the businesses. For example, a probe of the Farm Bureau insurance companies in Kansas by the state Attorney-General revealed that one of the members of the Board of Directors of the Farm Bureau insurance company is also employed by the state Farm Bureau itself. A Farm Bureau newsletter in Vermont recently reported: "The Vermont Farm Bureau Board of Trustees and the Trustees of the Farm Bureau Service Company announce the hiring of Edwin Douglas of Shoreham as staff assistant and tire company manager. . . . In his new job he will to working closely with the county Farm Bureau organizations and the service companies that have agreed to handle the tire program. He will also serve as staff assistant to the president with the Neighborhood clubs, membership work, and committee supervision." What all this means, as the *Birmingham News* concluded, is that "Only corporate lines, and the tax regulations and other laws governing business corporations separate Farm Bureau from its business enterprises."[8]

Farm Bureau officials and insurance executives claim that the relationship between the two is perfectly distinct. They claim that the affiliated companies pay rent for their office space, pay the state organization for their share of operating expenses, and pay a proportional share of the salaries of employees and officers who work for both.[9] But the complicated bundle of benefits flowing between business and organization makes such a simple explanation unrealistic. It is most difficult to deal "at arm's length" with yourself. The organizations provide the affiliated companies with more than office space and secretaries. Some of the other benefits are measurable, and undoubtedly are figured, however roughly, into the formula by which the companies reimburse the organization. But other benefits are less tangible, and less easily measured.

Let us focus for a moment on the workings of the Illinois Farm Bureau organization, the IAA. As a practical matter the IAA is little more than a management arm for a diverse conglomeration of Farm Bureau business enterprises in Illinois, with assets of more than $500 million. The IAA itself occupies only a fraction of the floor space of its impressive new office building in Bloomington. The rest of the building—called the "agri-business pentagon" by Farm Bureau critics—is rented to the "affiliated" companies. The IAA itself is composed of seven divisions, but only one—the organization division—is primarily concerned with the activities usually associated with an organization: membership, programs, committees, and so forth. The other six divisions provide extensive business services to the fifteen affiliated companies. The Legal Division is composed of nine in-house lawyers, including tax and natural resource specialists, who do nearly all of the legal work for the affiliated companies. The Finance Division of the IAA invests nearly one million dollars each week, primarily from insurance premiums of the four IAA-controlled insurance companies.

The Information Division is equipped with one of the most modern communications systems in Illinois. The Bloomington headquarters houses a modern and complete radio broadcasting station with facilities for live broadcast as well as audio and video taping. As one IAA staff man boasted, "most Illinois radio stations would give their 'eye teeth' for that equipment." In addition to using this equipment for IAA newscasts, it is also used to prepare and broadcast advertising for the affiliate companies. The Information Division also has its own full advertising and public relations staff, including commercial artists, admen, photographers and photographic studio, and complete facilities for preparation of advertising— copy, layout, and production. These impressive facilities are used only partially for the organization; they primarily serve the companies.

IAA officials contend that all these services are paid for by the affiliated companies as if obtained from any commercial source. But critics question the reasons for placing these business-related divisions in the organization, rather than operating them as part of the companies. Why, they ask, isn't the Information Division, or at least that major portion of it that does the advertising work for the affiliated companies, organized as the advertising division of the companies? Even more troublesome questions arise over allocating the costs of those promotions which benefit both the companies and the organization. This effort would be difficult enough even if the officials making these decisions did not have their hands in both pies. Such difficulties, as we shall see, led the Insurance Department of Ohio to order the state Farm Bureau to divest itself of its insurance companies, requiring separate identities for each.

Largely due to its financially beneficial relationship to its insurance companies, the IAA consistently shows a healthy budget surplus at the end of the year—almost $400,000 in 1968. Yet the idea of reducing the $25 annual dues, or passing this surplus on to Farm Bureau members in some other way, does not seem to have been seriously considered by the organization's leadership. As a matter of fact, the IAA's dues have increased in recent years.

In addition to the obvious services which the state organizations around the country provide for their affiliated companies, the companies receive a number of other benefits—less tangible, but no less valuable—from the relationship. Farm Bureau lobbyists often support their insurance companies when bills affecting the insurance industry come up in the state legislatures.[10] It is far more effective for a business to be represented by the spokesmen for an organization with a large membership (and proven political strength in the state) than to present its own self-interested position. This raises another financial question. In Kansas, for example, the Farm Bureau insurance companies paid 40 percent of the Farm Bureau's legislative costs for 1967.[11] But is it possible to fairly allocate these legislative costs between companies and organization when they have a joint concern about much legislation?

Legislative proposals do not fall into two neat piles: those that affect the insurance industry, and those that affect Farm Bureau members. Some bills clearly affect the insurance industry, some less clearly. Many affect both the insurance industry *and* the organization membership—for example, tax legislation. How do you distribute the cost of lobbying for those? And what about proposals that affect the companies one way, but the members in quite the opposite way—an insurance rate hike, for example? The insurance companies would support it; the Farm Bureau members who hold policies would oppose it. What would the position of the Farm Bureau lobbyists be, considering that much of their funds come from the insurance companies?

A controversy that erupted in South Carolina a few years ago illustrates this dilemma. After examining the transcript of the rate hearings held by the South Carolina Insurance Department, the state's Chief Insurance Commissioner, Charles Gambrell, charged that the Southern Farm Bureau Casualty Insurance Company had embarked upon a campaign "to induce, if not force" other commercial insurance companies in the state "to lead the way in raising farmers' rates, so that Farm Bureau could follow suit, and avoid the stigma of being first to do so."[12]

South Carolina Farm Bureau president David Sloan immediately criticized Gambrell's charges as "intemperate, unjudicious, and thoroughly biased." The charges, however, received the backing of the State Association of Insurance Agents and the state insurance commission. State Senator James Waddell, chairman of a special insurance study commission, called on the state Farm Bureau to remove itself from the auto insurance field. "If Mr. Sloan would tend to the problems of agriculture," said Waddell, "and forget about selling tires and insurance, maybe the farmers of South Carolina would have better strains of cotton and soybeans."[13]

Along with such "assistance" before state legislatures, the Farm Bureaus provide their insurance companies with an excellent communications network for promotional purposes. The American Farm Bureau Federation's national magazine, *Nation's Agriculture,* has a monthly circulation of nearly two million copies, only slightly less than that of *Newsweek.* The AFBF also publishes a weekly newsletter with a circulation of more than 60,000. Each state has at least one, and sometimes several weekly and/or monthly publications. Most of the more than 2,800 county Farm Bureaus have a regular publication going to members. Most of these are not the cheap variety that could be hastily run off on backroom mimeograph machines. They are often professionally prepared, and have all the gloss and polish of commercial publications.

In all these publications, one of the predominant messages is "Buy Farm Bureau." In some cases the insurance companies may be paying for these ads. But on the county level, where the message is often in the form of news articles about the progress of the companies, or new lines of business, it would be impossible to separate the promotional value from the news value.

The Farm Bureau's commercial ventures also benefit from the organization's extensive radio and television network. The AFBF and many of the state Farm Bureaus produce regular radio broadcasts heard over hundreds of radio stations across the country, as well as on five stations partially owned by Farm Bureau companies.[14] The AFBF prepares and distributes a regular monthly radio program called "Across the Land," composed of Farm Bureau news analysis and interviews. Many states have assembled their own network of radio outlets for their own daily or weekly broadcasts, like the "Alfalfa Network" in California, and the 108 stations in Texas which broadcast the Farm Bureau show daily. Some states, like Illinois and Georgia, even prepare a regular TV show, and distribute it to stations in the state. In many cases the Farm Bureau companies sponsor these broadcasts. Some programs are aired as "public service" broadcasts by the stations, which gives the Farm Bureau businesses invaluable reflected exposure.

Of all the intangible benefits the companies receive from their Farm Bureau affiliation, the most important is the identification that comes with the Farm Bureau name. When a Farm Bureau insurance agent knocks on the door in many areas of the country, he immediately has the respectability of the organization working for him. If the man or woman who answers the door is not a member himself, perhaps his father was, or maybe his son is active in a 4–H club which meets in the Farm Bureau building. In any case, the image is not the same as that presented by other insurance companies, and image is all-important in the sale of insurance.

*   *   *

In return for all the financial and intangible benefits the Farm Bureau companies receive from the organization, what does the organization gain from this relationship? Two things—increased membership, as the previous chapter has shown, and money. Much of the revenue from the businesses is funneled back into the organizations. Some is paid in rent. (The IAA alone received nearly $400,000 in rent in 1968 from its affiliated companies.) Some is "earned" as revenue from advertisements in Farm Bureau publications. There are numerous other forms of payment for other services rendered to the companies by the organizations.

One of the most common methods by which the companies funnel money back to the Farm Bureaus is through percentage rebates based on the volume of their business. These are sometimes called "sponsoring fees," or "overriding fees." Between 1950 and 1965, for example, the Nodak Mutual Insurance Company, theoretically "owned" by its policyholders, but controlled by the North Dakota Farm Bureau, paid $324,087 to the state Bureau for its services to the company. This represents 16.5 percent of the total income of the North Dakota Farm Bureau for those years. Nodak also paid another $264,189 during those years to the state's twenty county Farm Bureaus.[15]

Putting aside for the moment the fascinating tax consequences of these transactions, other ticklish problems arise. First, there is the problem of who ultimately bears the burden of these payments from the companies to the organization. They are based on the volume of business, and of course are part of the costs passed on to the purchaser. In effect then, Farm Bureau members in these states who buy insurance from these Farm Bureau companies are making a second payment to the Farm Bureau in addition to their annual dues—a payment of which few are aware.

If the policyholders have little knowledge and less control over these payments, who does? We are told by the North Dakota Farm Bureau: "The amount of such compensation shall be reexamined annually, and may be changed by mutual agreement of parties hereto."[16] Who are the "parties hereto"?—the Nodak Mutual Insurance Company and the North Dakota Farm Bureau. One can imagine the president of the North Dakota Farm Bureau sitting down each year with the president of Nodak, hammering out an agreement after hard negotiation on the value and costs of the services provided by the Farm Bureau to the insurance company. The insurance company, one would assume, would be trying to minimize the costs of these services. The Farm Bureau, on the other hand, would be trying to maximize its charges.

The competing interests of all parties—Farm Bureau members and insurance policy holders—would be properly protected by this process of negotiation. There is one catch, however. The president of Nodak is, in fact, also president of the North Dakota Farm Bureau, and the directors of the insurance company are also the directors of the Farm Bureau. The result is a unilateral decision on the part of the state Farm Bureau leadership on what percentage of the insurance company's income will be paid to the Farm Bureau for services rendered. Supposedly the state insurance commissions, charged with protecting the public's interests, are regulating this sort of thing, but many state insurance commissions are more concerned with the welfare of the insurance industry than that of the public. Besides, any state insurance commissioner who decides to take on a Farm Bureau insurance company must be prepared to face not only the company, but also the political strength of the state Farm Bureau, which—as Mr. Gambrell discovered in South Carolina—can be formidable.

In addition to percentage rebates or "sponsorship fees," there is another method by which the insurance companies transfer funds to the Farm Bureaus. When the affiliated companies are stock companies, as is the case with twenty-three of the insurance companies, most if not all of the stock is owned by the state Farm Bureau or its holding company. In some cases this stock pays dividends to the state organization. Once again putting aside the intriguing tax aspects of this for later scrutiny, these dividends can be a substantial source of revenue for the Farm Bureaus. Since 1951, for example, the Cal-Farm Life Insurance Company, almost all of whose capital stock is owned by the California Farm Bureau, has distributed over $500,000 to its stockholders.[17]

By now it should be clear that the Farm Bureaus and their insurance companies are inextricably intertwined. The leadership is the same. The headquarters are the same. They share directors, officers, staff, office space, expenses, and lobbying. Many of the activities of one have a vital impact on the other. A good portion of the revenue from the businesses finds its way back to the coffers of the Farm Bureau. As things now stand, distinguishing the Farm Bureau from its businesses would be like picking the eggwhites out of scrambled eggs.

In addition to claiming that there is little connection between the Farm Bureau and its insurance companies, the organization's leaders also contend there is no connection among the insurance companies from state to state.[18] They claim the companies in each state operate independently of the others, and therefore, there is no reason to consider them as an integrated group. There is considerable evidence, however, to the contrary. Actually, the Farm Bureau insurance companies are part of a giant, interlocking nationwide network.

The very method by which Farm Bureau insurance spread from one state to another belies the organization's persistent claim today that each company should be considered separately. As Murray Lincoln explained it, "We in Ohio helped the Missouri farmers set up their insurance company, and that sort of friendly, helping hand went in a chain fashion across the country."[19] The decision to keep the network decentralized was made very early, and very deliberately. "Many considerations were involved," relates O. M. Kile in his authorized history of the Farm Bureau, "but one factor influencing the independent state action was the belief . . . that several smaller companies might be more efficient than one large company."[20] And, he might have added, less carefully scrutinized.

The early Farm Bureau insurance companies were launched in several different ways. The Illinois state organization, in order to comply with a state requirement that there be a budget surplus for new insurance enterprises, conducted a campaign for policies which were conditional on obtaining a sufficient number of applicants. The purchaser gave an undated check for $25; when enough applicants had been obtained, the company was licensed and in business. Once the first few companies were in business, the job became easier. The Ohio Farm Bureau Insurance Company advanced the New Hampshire Farm Bureau $25,000 to get its company started. Another variation of this leap-frog technique was to have an existing Farm Bureau company open a branch in a neighboring state. When the amount of business in the new state became sufficient to support its own company, it would then spin off from the neighboring parent as a new venture. In this manner, the Oklahoma and Colorado insurance operations were created out of the Kansas company.

As the system grew, the interrelationships between companies and between states became more sophisticated. But in each case, whether the company had been organized as a mutual company—technically owned by its policyholders—or a stock company, it remained tied closely to the Farm Bureau organizations. By the late 1940s, Kile could state unequivocally about the companies: "All have some legal device to assure Farm Bureau control."[21]

In addition to the active cross-pollination from state to state, cooperative ventures were undertaken jointly by groups of state Farm Bureaus. Even today, several Farm Bureau insurance companies are still jointly owned by more than one state organization. The Southern Farm Bureau Insurance

Companies, for example, with almost $250 million in assets, are controlled by the Farm Bureaus of Alabama, Arkansas, Kentucky, Mississippi, and Texas. In similar fashion, Western Farm Bureau Life Insurance Company is controlled by Farm Bureau Service Companies in Arizona, Colorado, Idaho, Montana, New Mexico, Oklahoma, Oregon, and Wyoming. The 3,000 shares of outstanding stock in the Farm Family Life Insurance Company is divided among Farm Bureau holding companies in Connecticut, Delaware, Maine, Massachusetts, New Jersey, New York, Pennsylvania, Rhode Island, and West Virginia.

Many Farm Bureau Insurance companies operate in more than a single state. Where this is the case, representatives of all participating state Farm Bureaus frequently serve as directors. For example, Cal-Farm Insurance, although based in California, also sells insurance in Nevada, Washington, and Hawaii. The Wyoming Farm Bureau Mutual Insurance Company also operates in Montana.

Personnel frequently move from one company to another within the Farm Bureau network. Indeed, it is difficult to pick up a copy of the AFBF "Official Newsletter" without reading about an employee of one Farm Bureau insurance company who has been appointed to a post in another company in another state. For example, the chief executive officer of the Cal-Farm Life Insurance Company was previously with the Indiana Farm Bureau Insurance Company. The executive officer in charge of Western Farm Bureau Life was previously sales director for Southern Farm Bureau Life, and before that he held the same position with Cal-Farm Life.

*   *   *

Thus far we have concentrated on the $1.5 billion network of fifty-five insurance companies directly controlled by the Farm Bureau. But that is by no means the end of the Farm Bureau insurance story. The Farm Bureau also enjoys a special relationship with another giant insurance complex, Nationwide Insurance. Nationwide itself is a 31-company, billion dollar network with over 4.5 million policies in force in 45 states. It employs 15,000 people, and had a business volume (net written premiums) in 1968 of nearly $500 million. Nationwide Life Insurance was listed by *Fortune* magazine as one of the top 50 life insurance companies in the country in 1968. Its subsidiary companies deal in housing, radio, and finance.

Nationwide is the son of Farm Bureau and the apronstrings have never been completely cut. This giant operation began in 1926, when the Ohio

Farm Bureau Federation launched the Ohio Farm Bureau Mutual Automobile Insurance Company, with $10,000. Under the skilled direction of cooperative architect Murray Lincoln, who was also the executive-secretary of the Ohio Farm Bureau at the time, the insurance company blossomed and expanded its operations into several states. Through the 1940s, the Board of Directors of the insurance company was identical to the Ohio Farm Bureau Board.

In 1947, the Ohio Insurance Department moved to break the connection. As Lincoln described the objections of the state insurance examiners:

The boards of directors of the Farm Bureau insurance companies offered sponsorship fees to various organizations. On the other hand, the same men rushed around to the other side of the table, where they became directors of the boards of the sponsoring organizations and said, "Okay, we accept those fees." The examiners said they felt people should not negotiate with themselves.[22]

Of course, this objection applies equally well today to Farm Bureau insurance companies in many other states. But the public officials in Ohio insisted that this relationship be stopped. In 1948, therefore, a separate Board of Directors was established by the Farm Bureau Insurance Companies of Ohio. Lincoln, and many of this staff, stayed with the insurance companies.

Until 1955, the companies continued to operate under the Farm Bureau name. But because they wanted to expand and were prevented from doing so because most states already had Farm Bureau insurance companies, the Ohio companies chose to adopt a new name—Nationwide. According to an Ohio Farm Bureau brochure, "The change in name and the physical separation of Nationwide from the [Ohio Farm Bureau] Federation and Landmark [the Ohio Farm Bureau Cooperative] have not altered the purpose of the three organizations to maintain their warm and friendly relationship, and to cooperate in advancing each others' interests. . . . The three comprise a broad family group, united by ties of a common origin, strong mutual interests, and an identical social and business philosophy."[23]

Just how warm and friendly is that relationship? "In the final analysis," their joint statement explains, "the Board of Trustees of the Ohio Farm Bureau Federation . . . and the Board of Nationwide determine what this relationship shall be, and on what terms it shall function." This sounds fine, until we discover that the majority of the Board of Directors of the giant

Nationwide complex are "recommended" by the Ohio Farm Bureau Federation. Nothing is more likely to ensure a warm and friendly relationship between two bodies than having the majortiy of one recommended by the other.

Most of Nationwide's "Ohio directors" were themselves former members of the Board of Trustees of the Ohio Farm Bureau Federation. For example, three months after Ohio Farm Bureau president Frank Sollars stepped down from that position, he was elected to the boards of four Nationwide Insurance Companies.[24] Many other top executives with Nationwide have served long tours of duty with the Ohio Farm Bureau. Nationwide's general chairman and executive officer, George Dunlap, was a director of the Ohio Farm Bureau for fifteen years, director of his county Farm Bureau for twenty-five years, director of three Farm Bureau affiliate companies for fourteen years, and an incorporator of the Ohio Farm Bureau Cooperative Association.[25]

The relationship is also warm and friendly because of the mutual benefits that the Ohio Farm Bureau and Nationwide enjoy from it. The Ohio Farm Bureau serves as a "sponsor" of Nationwide Insurance in Ohio. Farm Bureau members account for more than 130,000 of Nationwide's Ohio policies in group hospitalization, tractor and auto casualty alone. "Awareness of the sponsoring relationship inclines Farm Bureau members to look to Nationwide for total account service," says a brochure issued jointly by Nationwide and the Ohio Farm Bureau. Nationwide agents have access to the Farm Bureau mailing list. Nationwide agents come to Farm Bureau meetings. The Farm Bureau's monthly state publication, in addition to full-page ads for Nationwide, frequently carries articles describing the personnel, projects and plans of the Nationwide companies, as well as questions and answers on insurance from Nationwide officials. In addition, the public affairs department of the Ohio Farm Bureau has often worked for passage of state legislation beneficial to the insurance industry.

What has the Ohio Farm Bureau received from this arrangement? The annual payments from Nationwide to the Ohio Farm Bureau Federation provide the organization with no less than 25–30 percent of its operating budget, and over $2.5 million of Nationwide funds are invested in securities of the Ohio Farm Bureau (Landmark) coops. In the course of plying their insurance wares, Nationwide agents also sell Farm Bureau memberships. In fact, awards are given to Nationwide agents partially based on the number of Farm Bureau memberships they have sold. The announcement of the 1969 gains in membership by the Ohio Farm Bureau hailed the contribution of the Nationwide salesmen.[26] The relationship between Nationwide Insurance and Farm Bureau is not confined to Ohio. Aside from Alaska—which has no Farm Bureau—only Vermont, Maryland and Ohio have no Farm Bureau insurance company operating. All have sponsoring relationships with Nationwide, similar to the one in Ohio. The Farm Bureaus in these states have refrained from organizing their own companies, and the fifty-five existing Farm Bureau companies have not entered these three states.

What can we conclude about the relationship between Nationwide and Farm Bureau? First, especially in Ohio, the relationship is deep and ongoing and substantially benefits each. Despite the praiseworthy intention of the Ohio Insurance Department in 1948 to legally and physically separate the Farm Bureau from its insurance companies, the Ohio Farm Bureau still retains considerable influence over the Nationwide network. In addition to the fifty-five company, $1.5 billion insurance network that the Farm Bureau owns, operates or controls directly, there is another billion-dollar network of thirty-one insurance companies over which it retains considerable indirect influence. This combination gives the Farm Bureau an economic wingspan of impressive proportions, $2.5 billion in insurance alone.

The center of this insurance network—at least the fifty-five companies under direct Farm Bureau control—is the American Farm Bureau Federation (AFBF) and its own insurance operation, the American Agricultural Insurance Company. This company, with AFBF president William Kuhfuss at the helm, is primarily a reinsurance company for the state operations. (A reinsurance company is, in a sense, an insurance company's insurance company. In order to back up the risks they assume, insurance companies reinsure these risks with other "reinsurance" companies.) AFBF's American Agricultural Insurance Company now has a contract with each of the other Farm Bureau Insurance Companies to provide for their reinsurance business in one way or another. American Agricultural has current assets of more than $27 million, an increase of more than 50 percent in the past five years.

In 1966, American Agricultural inaugurated a commercial risk division, engaged in writing insurance directly to customers.[27] This business is primarily supplemental to the states, especially for high-risk insurance that the state companies will not write. It is interesting to note that in June 1967, when AFBF Secretary–Treasurer Roger Fleming was telling Congressman Resnick that American Agricultural Insurance Company was only a reinsurance company, it had been directly writing policies for more than a year.[28]

In March of 1969, American Agricultural was reorganized from a mutual to a stock company. "One specific result," we are told by the announcement of the reorganization, "will be that American Agricultural Insurance Company may write both new and more extensive insurance policies."[29] So, despite their protestations to the contrary, the AFBF itself is directly in the insurance business, along with the state Farm Bureaus.

Along with reinsurance, the AFBF and its American Agricultural Insurance Company also offer the Farm Bureau insurance companies a wide range of services referred to as "coordination." Among other things, American Agricultural provides management assistance to the member companies of the Farm Bureau group. At almost any given time, at least one company is in fact receiving such assistance from the national headquarters. Staff members of the AFBF travel around the country providing the state companies with what they delicately describe as "educative counsel." The AFBF purchases professional management training courses for personnel in the state companies, and organizes management workshops around the country for company employees.[30]

The AFBF has also been instrumental in promoting new insurance ventures in states previously not covered by a Farm Bureau company. For example, in 1955 the AFBF assisted the seven eastern states organizations that controlled the Farm Family Life Insurance Company in launching a new casualty insurance company, called the Farm Family Mutual Insurance Company.[31]

In addition to such coordination and promotion from the AFBF, the managers of the individual Farm Bureau companies maintain fairly close contact with each other. Twice a year the executives of all the Farm Bureau insurance companies meet together for a formal management conference. These management conferences establish permanent committees to deal with joint ventures. For example, the Advertising Committee provides for extensive joint advertising done by all fifty-five of the companies. The management conference also operates training programs for staff personnel of the companies. There is also frequent consultation among state managers on individual programs and problems.

The total effect of all these interlocks, overlaps and interconnections between the Farm Bureau companies and each other, as well as between them and the Farm Bureau organizations, shatters any illusion or claims that they are completely separate and independent. Farm Bureau insurance is clearly a single network, and just as clearly controlled by the Farm Bureau organization. Only when the Farm Bureau insurance group is recognized as basically one giant company will it begin to get the attention and scrutiny it deserves from the government and the public.

The Farm Bureau serves two masters whose interests are frequently in conflict. When the best interests of the companies clash with the best interests of the membership, the organization generally supports the interests of the companies. The historical reason for the Farm Bureau to operate these businesses—to serve commercial needs that would not be satisfied otherwise—is a relic of an early era. Today, the Farm Bureau businesses sustain and preserve the organization. In terms of money, policy, and power, they dominate the organization.

5

The Farm Bureau Supermarket

BIG AND PROSPEROUS as the Farm Bureau insurance network is, it is only a part of the Farm Bureau business empire, which ranges from oil to chickenfeed, from advertising to baling twine, from travel agencies to shopping centers. The Farm Bureau cooperative network alone, with assets of more than $200 million, rang up $500 million in sales in 1968. Less than forty retail chains in the country can make that claim.

The four major Farm Bureau regional coops are affiliated with various state Farm Bureaus and, in some respects, with each other. One of the largest of the regional coops is FS Services, Inc., which covers Illinois, Iowa and Wisconsin. With 1968 sales of $164 million, FS serves as the central manufacturing and purchasing organization for more than 150 local coops that are part of the FS system. Like a huge conglomerate, FS controls three large feed mills which manufacture thousands of tons of livestock feed each year; four major fertilizer production plants; two large farm seed processing centers; a transportation fleet with over 150 tractor-trailers and over 100 gas- and oil-hauling vans, as well as a 2.5-million-gallon oil barge; 20 percent interest in a petroleum refinery with a capacity of 40,000 barrels per day; and 5,000 employees.

In 1968, FS sold 34 million pounds of farm chemicals, 825,000 tons of fertilizer, 320,000 tons of feed, 45 million pounds of seed, and 420 million gallons of FS petroleum. What sort of bargain do the FS coop members get when they buy these products from their organization? An Illinois Farm Bureau staff member explains that the price of goods sold by FS generally "follows the industry," except in those cases such as fertilizer, where FS so dominates the market that the rest of the industry looks to them to set the prices. (FS sells 40 percent of the farm fertilizer purchased in Illinois.)

Despite its mammoth size, FS Services is not even the largest of the four Farm Bureau regional coops. The Indiana Farm Bureau Cooperative Association took top honors in 1968 with annual sales of nearly $200 million. Then comes FS in Illinois; Landmark, affiliated with the Ohio Farm Bureau, with more than $100 million in 1968 sales; and Farm Bureau Services, Inc., affiliated with the Michigan Farm Bureau, with 1968 sales of nearly $75 million.

Before examining these Farm Bureau coops in detail, one should know something about the central role farmer coops have played in building rural America and developing agriculture to its unmatched level of productive capacity. Over 8,000 farmer coops with more than 6 million members today move more than a fourth of all farm products to market and sell the farmers about a fifth of all their production supplies. Cooperatives have brought telephone service to more than a million rural residents and lit the homes of rural families in 90 percent of the counties in the country.

The vitality of cooperatives—in the past as well as presently—has been due in no small measure to their adherence to several basic principles which distinguish them from regular corporate enterprises. Coops are essentially non-profit enterprises. They are organized around the mutual economic interests of their members. Risks, costs, and benefits are shared equally among those who patronize the coop. Coops do business primarily with their members, and members have an obligation to patronize their coops. Most importantly, coops are *democratically controlled,* ideally on a one-man, one-vote basis, regardless of the amount of capital stock owned by the individual member. Disregard of this last principle can easily turn the others into empty platitudes for management to recite in its annual report, while the unique characteristics of a "cooperative" erode away. The essence of a true cooperative is increased control by the farmer–producer over the markets for his goods and the sources of his needs.

Recognition of the special characteristics that set cooperatives apart from other kinds of private enterprise has resulted in their special treatment by antitrust and federal tax laws. Although cooperatives are subject to the antitrust laws once they are organized, the Capper–Volstead Act of 1922 permits farmers to form cooperatives without being in violation of antitrust restrictions. And as we shall see later, cooperatives enjoy substantial advantages over regular corporations in their treatment by the Internal Revenue Code.

The great majority of farmer cooperatives has faithfully adhered to these fundamental cooperative principles. Most farmer coops are small and tightly controlled by their farmer members. Two-thirds of all coops do less than a million dollars of business a year and only one in ten has more than 20 employees. While greater size itself does not necessarily result in the abandonment of these operating procedures and guidelines, it does create more potential for it. In the case of the giant Farm Bureau coops, such a change seems to have taken place. Investigation of them indicates that in many important respects,—particularly how they are controlled—it is difficult to distinguish them from regular corporations, except in the tax and other competitive advantages they enjoy from their cooperative characterization.

FS Services, Inc., one of the largest Farm Bureau coop systems, is controlled by the Illinois Agricultural Association, as that state's Farm Bureau is known. Each of the Illinois county coops that make up FS sign a contract with IAA agreeing to issue one share of Class B voting stock to the state organization for each share of voting stock it issues to others. By this device, IAA holds at least 50 percent of the voting stock in each county coop at all times. This Class B stock has no par value in most cases, bears no interest, and receives no dividends. Its sole purpose as voting stock is to keep control of FS in the hands of the IAA. A representative of IAA, proxies in hand, is present at important meetings of the county coop. No action can be taken over this virtual IAA veto-power. Moreover, one member of each of the Farm Bureau Boards of Directors of Iowa, Illinois, and Wisconsin—the three states covered by FS—serve on the FS Board of Directors at all times.[1]

In similar fashion, the Farm Bureau retains control of the other three regional coop systems. The Michigan Farm Bureau holds a majority on the Board of Directors of Farm Bureau Service, Inc., and owns a majority of the voting stock. The Board of Directors of Landmark is identical to the Board of the Ohio Farm Bureau Federation. "The two organizations work together almost as one in many of their activities," they proudly report. Landmark pays the Ohio Farm Bureau Federation an annual sponsorship fee, similar to the one it receives from Nationwide Insurance, amounting to 20 to 30 percent of the Federation's operating budget. (The payments received by the Ohio Farm Bureau from these two major business affiliations—Nationwide and Landmark—constitute more than half of its operating budget.) "In legislation," says a Farm Bureau brochure, "both state and national, the Federation assumes leadership, but often calls on Landmark to supply technical and statistical information. Both organizations benefit."[2]

Perhaps, but does the Farm Bureau or Landmark coop member also benefit? What we see here is a further concentration of operations in the hands of the state organizations, and a further dilution of single-minded representation of farmers. When issues arise in which the interests of the members and the coops are opposed to one another, which side will the organization support?

One striking case in which such divided loyalties were put to the test is that of the "patronage refunds" made to coop members. Patronage refunds are returned to coop members each year based upon the amount they buy. Coops are permitted by federal tax laws to refund up to 80 percent of the patronage refunds in the form of stock certificates, requiring only 20 percent to be immediately returned in cash. Usually these stock certificates are redeemable for cash within a reasonable number of years. Legislative battles over these patronage refunds pose a delicate dilemma for the American Farm Bureau lobbyists. This is a clear case in which their farmer members are affected one way and their businesses are affected in just the opposite way. The individual farmer would like to get as much of his refund in cash as possible, particularly since he must pay federal income taxes on the entire refund—cash and stock—when he receives it. The coop management, on the other hand, has more long-range objectives in mind. They retain the 80 percent cash. Some of this is used to redeem old certificates, and the rest is used to expand their facilities and buy out their private competition. This device is an important and unique source of working capital for cooperatives.

Early in 1969, Congressman Resnick proposed to the House Ways and Means Committee, which was considering general tax reform, that the farmer members be given a real choice between receiving their patronage refunds in cash or stock certificates for up to 80 percent of their refund. He also suggested that a legal time limit be imposed (much the same as has been voluntarily established by many cooperatives) before which the stock must be redeemed for cash.

The Ways and Means Committee incorporated a version of Resnick's recommendations in their bill. These provisions were adopted in full by the entire House on August 7, 1969. The House bill provided that the percentage of patronage refunds required to be paid out in cash be stepped up over a ten-year period by 3 percent per year, reaching 50 percent by 1979. Another provision required all patronage refunds issued in scrip or stock be "picked up"—cashed in by the coop—within 15 years.[3]

How would the Farm Bureau come out on these provisions which seemed to pose such an acute conflict? The drama was heightened since there was no organizational policy on the books, and it unquestionably fell to the Federation's officers and directors to establish the immediate policy. In such a conflict the business interests are organized and geared-up to evaluate with professional expertise the precise effects of such proposals. The membership is diffuse and relies to a great extent upon the organization itself for information and evaluation of such proposals.

The scene shifted from the House of Representatives to the Senate Finance Committee. By the time the Farm Bureau testified before that Committee on September 22, 1969, the leaders had made their choice: they strongly opposed the House provisions to give the coop members a larger share of cash and a guarantee period to redeem their stock. "The proposed changes," they reiterated a few days later in a letter to the Committee, "are unwarranted, and the result of such changes would not only represent further involvement of the federal government into the fiscal affairs of private enterprise, but would benefit neither the taxpayer nor the cooperative and their patrons."[4] The unfortunate final note to the episode was struck on October 17 when the Senate Finance Committee voted to delete the section dealing with cooperative patronage refunds from the Senate version of the bill.[5]

Such conflicts are not isolated and peripheral; they are recurring and of the utmost importance in answering the basic question: Is the Farm Bureau a farm organization or a farm business? Another story illustrates quite dramatically why an organization that is supposed to represent farmers and plead their case should not be the same operation that deals with them on a commercial basis. Near the end of Rep. Resnick's personal hearings on farm organizations in 1967, a witness appeared to testify who made a deep impression on Resnick.[6] Her name was Mrs. Norma Williams, an elderly gray-haired widow who owned and operated a 77-acre farm in north-central Ohio. In order to pay for her trip to Washington, dozens of her farmer-neighbors had chipped in. She brought with her a stack of sworn affidavits from them corroborating her story with their own similar experiences.

For thirty years, said Mrs. Williams, she and her neighbors had been members of the county Farm Bureau, and had been buying their feed, seed and fertilizer from the local Farm Bureau coop, a part of the Ohio Farm Bureau Coop (known as Landmark). Many of them were stockholders in the coop, having been induced to purchase stock by other Farm Bureau members or coop managers. In addition to this regular "ownership" stock, at the end of each year they had been receiving patronage refunds on the purchases they had made during the year. The great bulk of these refunds were not in cash, but in stock certificates.

Through bitter experience, Mrs. Williams and her neighbors had discovered that these certificates were worthless. They paid no interest, and repeated attempts to redeem them for cash were unsuccessful. Even the Farm Bureau coops themselves would not accept them as credit on their own bills. Bankers would not accept them as collateral on loans, laughing at requests to value them. Even upon one's death, Mrs. Williams explained, the Farm Bureau coop would not retire the certificates. Despite their obvious lack of value, however, the farmers who "owned" them had been compelled until quite recently to pay state income taxes on them.

Since Mrs. Williams had given her startling testimony to a nearly empty hearing room, it received little coverage by the press. Realizing this, Resnick issued a press release blasting the "funny money" being issued by some of the Farm Bureau coops in Ohio. The reaction confirmed the vital function of a vigorous press. The *Cleveland Plain Dealer* instituted a thorough investigation on its own to probe more deeply into what these farmers felt to be fraud. Reporters from the paper interviewed farmers, bankers, lawyers, competing dealers, Farm Bureau officials and government officials. The paper's conclusion: the stock certificates were worthless, and were creating severe personal hardships.[7]

Based on his own disclosures and those of the *Plain Dealer,* Resnick wrote on September 13 to William Saxbe, then Ohio Attorney General, and now the state's senior Senator. Resnick outlined his findings and urged

Saxbe to give the matter his careful attention. Two days later Saxbe publicly announced that he would investigate the charges. Several days later Ohio's Assistant Attorney General William Hoiles met with Resnick's staff in Washington to review the information they had gathered.

For the next several weeks, stories appeared almost daily in the *Plain Dealer* adding support to the contention of the Ohio farmers that these stock certificates were worthless. The previous year, the paper revealed, county auditors had questioned the Ohio Department of Taxation about the existing policy of assessing taxes on this stock, "explaining to them that the Farm Bureau refuses to redeem it, and no one wants to buy it, indicating there is no apparent market value." The Department of Taxation ruled that the local assessors should "quit charging tax on it beginning 1967."

The *Plain Dealer* also reported instances where the monopolistic practices of Farm Bureau coops were squeezing out independent competition, where Farm Bureau coops were setting up businesses in competition with their own members and then underselling them.[8]

Local Farm Bureau officials interviewed by the paper did not seem to feel there was anything wrong in issuing unredeemable certificates to members. "These farmers are really not out of pocket on anything," explained one Farm Bureau leader. "They didn't put anything into the stock. They just didn't get the cash dividends it represents, but maybe one of these days they will."[9] Even if this explanation were true—which it was not—it is unsatisfactory. Many farmers had been induced to buy at Farm Bureau coops because they were told that a percentage of their purchases would be refunded. In many cases they paid more for their purchases than they would have at other dealers because of that prospect. Meanwhile, the coop had the use of the money it was not distributing to its patrons for expansion and acquisition.

In fact many farmers *were* "out of pocket" money. Many had been convinced and cajoled into purchasing "ownership" stock in the coop as an investment. These victims were unable to sell or redeem their stock for cash. In one case, particularly illustrative of the personal dimension of these deceptive practices, a middle-aged woman, unable to find work after a divorce, was forced to turn to her 20-year investment in coop stock. Not only could she not realize any gain in that investment after all those years, she was unable to get her original $1000 back.[10]

In light of all this, Resnick and his staff were startled when Attorney-General Saxbe announced on October 16 that he intended to take no further action. He said Resnick's charges were "without foundation and contrary to facts." He explained that he had reached this conclusion because the stock certificates were not "non-redeemable," but simply not redeemed. According to Saxbe, the fact that no one, including himself, could find a single case where the coops under question had redeemed this stock in the past fifteen years did not mean that they were "non-redeemable" (which would have been a violation of law), but just "not redeemed."[11] By seizing upon this strained literal view, he passed over the real question: whether the practices that had been disclosed, in substance rather than form, were a fraud upon the customers and stockholders of the coops. He also neatly avoided the question of whether, even if what had been happening was not a violation of existing Ohio law, he had an obligation as chief law officer of the state to recommend changes in the law to at least avoid such practices in the future. By thus interpreting his job in the narrowest of terms, he got off the hook on what would have been a polit-ically risky investigation for the soon-to-be Senate candidate.

Resnick, however, refused to drop the issue. Each day he received new letters, many enclosing packets of these stock certificates, asking if he could help to get their money back. He decided to go to Cleveland to find out whether "worthless" still means worthless. On November 17, he held a full day of hearings in Ohio. The first witness was Assistant Attorney General Hoiles.[12] It was not an easy day for Mr. Hoiles. He steadfastly held to his office's distinction between "non-redeemable" stock certificates and those which simply do not have a "fixed date of maturity." He side-stepped the crucial question of how long these certificates must go un-redeemed before they are, in fact, non-redeemable. He argued that "if [the coops] were to engage in a wholesale redemption program, I think in almost all instances they would become insolvent." Since it would be illegal for them to redeem the stock if it meant that they would go in-solvent, not only had they no obligation to redeem, but they were forbidden to do so.

Of course, this argument ignores the fact that it is the decision of the management of the coop, as with any business corporation, how much of the retained earnings each year will be used to expand the enterprise—to buy or construct new facilities for example—and how much will be put into a program to retire or redeem outstanding obligations such as this stock. While these coops supposedly had no money to redeem, they had not lacked the capital to expand.

When Hoiles contended that the stock wasn't worthless, his semantic refinements enraged the crowded room of farmers holding handfuls of certificates, some more than thirty years old. When pressed, Mr. Hoiles retreated to the classic bureaucratic position: he is not authorized to discuss the "credibility" of the Attorney General's investigation. He had appeared, he explained, merely to instruct Resnick on Ohio law. His final defense was that some members of the coops were satisfied with the redemption policies. If he was proposing that what is otherwise wrong is less so if some of the victims do not get upset, it is a strange new doctrine, legal or otherwise.

After completing his testimony, Mr. Hoiles, displaying more courage than candor, remained at the hearings to listen to the farmers who had assembled. He was visibly shaken when one of the witnesses, after handing Resnick some of the stock certificates, walked to the back of the room and offered him some. "I am a man of good heart," the farmer explained glaring at Hoiles. "Would you like some for your children's education? Put that away for their college education. I am sure that will help. . . . I will give you some—not sell it, give it to you."

Witness after witness described his repeated and futile efforts to cash in the certificates. There was no doubt that they felt, in the words of one, "defrauded and swindled." They certainly deserved more than the cursory dismissal they had been given by their Attorney General. Despite the lack of concern shown by Attorney General Saxbe, the farmers of Ohio received their vindication, if not their money, when the District Director of Internal Revenue Service proposed in 1968 that the Federal Income tax exemption of the Farm Bureau Cooperative Association of Ohio (Landmark) be revoked for the years 1959 and after. Since the earnings of that giant operation are more than a million and a half dollars a year (on which they paid only $127,000 in federal income taxes in 1968), their liability could amount to millions of dollars in back taxes and millions more in the future.[13]

Farm Bureau leaders in Ohio, instead of leaping to the defense of their outraged members, defended the coop actions in which they were so deeply involved. Not only do victimized Farm Bureau members lose the support of their own organization, the double character of the Farm Bureau tends to scare away elected public officials entrusted with protecting the public. Such officials are more reluctant to press ahead unrelentingly against apparent wrongdoing by such a two-headed monster than they would be if it were purely a business operation engaged in the same practices. The duality of such an operation presents the ever-present danger of reprisals in the name of the organization, using its communications and political power. When the government moves against a purely business operation—say General Motors—there is always, of course, the danger of an outcry from other business corporations similarly situated. Such an outcry, however, is at least easy to interpret in terms of understandable self-interest. But a public official faced with the prospect of taking action against a major business that is linked to a major farm organization must also be prepared to face allegations of being "anti-farmer." It is far more difficult for a politician to deal with this reaction. And the result is that businesses with such a political power tend to be less carefully scrutinized.

These have not been the only occasions when the loyalty of the Farm Bureau to its members has been put to the test and has failed. Another blatant example is the Farm Bureau's steadfast support for the oil depletion allowance. It is almost impossible to find a working farmer who favors this tax bonus for oil producers (unless he happens to have some oil underneath his land, in which case he is more likely to be clipping coupons than farming). Such a tax loophole only throws the general tax burden disproportionately on the farmer and other average Americans who are not oil tycoons. When the AFBF's lobbyists appear before the tax committees of Congress, however, to support the oil depletion allowance, they do not reveal the organization's financial interests in oil.[14]

The Farm Bureau's oil operations in particular are worth close examination. About 40 years ago, the Farm Bureau cooperatives of Ohio, Michigan and Indiana joined together to finance an oil blending plant. Today, greatly expanded to include other regional coops, it is known as United Coops, and sells about $50 million worth of oil products annually. FS Services in Illinois has a $7 million investment—21 percent ownership—in the National Cooperative Refinery Association, with a modern oil refinery in McPherson, Kansas, which can produce 40,000 barrels each day. National Coop Refinery purchased an additional $23 million worth of crude oil properties in fiscal year 1967–1968 alone.

The Farm Bureau Oil Company, a subsidiary of the Indiana Farm Bureau Cooperative Association, operates a totally integrated oil enterprise—from the ground to the tank. It conducts its own exploration; drills its own wells; gathers, transports, delivers and stores crude oil through more than 600 miles of oil pipelines; refines the oil, and then distributes it to its customers. The Farmers Petroleum Coop, Inc. serves one out of every four farmers in Michigan. By 1966, Farmers Petroleum controlled the production of 528 oil wells, and distributed over 40 million gallons of fuel oil. Local Landmark and FS gas stations dot the countryside and the population centers of much of Illinois, Iowa, Ohio, and Wisconsin. None of this is mentioned, however, by Farm Bureau representatives when they testify before Congress in favor of the oil depletion allowance.

Conflicts that arise between serving their businesses and serving their members were also illustrated by the comments of the board chairman of Central Farmers Fertilizer Company. Central Farmers is a large, nationwide manufacturer of basic chemical fertilizer and serves as a cooperative supplier for twenty regional coops in the country, including the Farm Bureau's four major ones. Bemoaning the fact that earnings were down about $2.5 million in 1968, the board chairman, who also happens to be general manager of the Farm Bureau's FS coop, explained that this was caused by recent expansions of manufacturing facilities. "This has resulted in a burdensome build-up of supplies and severely depressed prices," he lamented. The fact that the Farm Bureau coop's farmer-members might benefit from such price decreases either did not occur to this gentleman, or did not concern him.[15]

The lesson to be drawn from all this is that—despite the claim by the Farm Bureau to be speaking on behalf of the American farmer—the Farm Bureau's agri-business managers will not always see things in the same light as the farmers. As Isaac once said, "The voice is Jacob's voice, but the hands are the hands of Esau."

Particular problems arise where Farm Bureau coops have become so dominant that they have the farmers in a virtual economic stranglehold. This is especially true in areas of Illinois, Iowa, Ohio and Indiana. Farm Bureau coops in these states have been expanding so rapidly that they are gradually pushing out or buying up much of their commercial competition. "Here in Ohio," writes one small farmer, "Farm Bureau coop—that is, Landmark—is presently buying up independent local elevators, feed mills, poultry processing plants and taking in poultry producer coops to the point of destroying any choice of outlet for the independent farmer's sale of poultry, livestock and grain." He goes on to explain that in many cases the prices paid by the farmers have subsequently gone up and that he now must truck his goods fifty miles to sell them to anyone other than Farm Bureau. In some areas, the farmers have little choice. They buy from Farm Bureau and sell to Farm Bureau, in the farmer's modern version of the company store routine.

In some parts of the country, Farm Bureau coops have followed the large feed companies and processors into the vertical integration spiral. Under vertical integration in agriculture, the farmer–producers sign contracts, as individuals, to produce a product for the contracting feed company, processor, or other agri-business firm. The conditions of production, prices, and other terms have been determined largely by the company. The grower is paid for a service, not a product. For many years now, farmers have been producing milk, vegetables, fruits, chickens and turkeys under vertical integration contracts that have given them little control over their production or return. Many of the producers believe the system has made them the modern day equivalent of the sharecropper.

At Resnick's Cleveland hearings in November, 1967, one farmer testified: "Farm Bureau officials are consistently following the line that 'the future in American agriculture is farming under contracts, that farmers might as well make up their mind to the fact, that since this is so, farmers might better sign the contracts with their own farmer-owned, farmer-managed coops.' . . . [But] farmers have found that it is harder to resist and attempt to change conditions of production when dealing with [Farm Bureau] coops than when dealing with independent agri-business. How do you fight and change the establishment in your own organization when members have little actual voting or managing power? Farmers have found it takes almost a revolt to change the plans of the managing officials, regardless of the claim of 'farmer-owned, farmer-managed.' "

At Resnick's Omaha hearings, an intense and serious Iowa farmer in his late 40s told a poignant story of how the farmer can suffer under Farm Bureau coop domination:

We had an oil company start up as our own little coop, among the farmers. . . . We were rather proud of it. Whether it was going to make a lot of money, or save a lot of money was very questionable, but it was ours. After World

War II, we suddenly discovered we couldn't get enough fuel oil, because [our coop] was an independent little thing. . . . So we were very short of fuel oil, and the Farm Bureau approached us and said, "We can get fuel oil for you." That sounded good so far, so we entered into that thing. "Of course you will have to sign a few papers," they told us, "a little contract on this fuel oil agreement." [Our] board members should have read the contract, . . . but they were too trusting. They signed it, and it took two years to find out . . . that we had signed the company away. We lost the company. [The Farm Bureau] put in $500, and they controlled the voting stock of the company.

They emphasized that they would not use their voting power unless they thought we were going in the wrong direction. Kind of a fatherly attitude. . . . For simple little things like paying our bills . . . they didn't use their vote. But the idea then started to grow among the farmers, "Why should we let those guys tell us what to do?" So we finally got together and [decided to sell the company]. At the annual meeting the very first motion to come before the group was to sell the company.

[When the Farm Bureau] found out that there was something cooking, they tried to stall this. They said, "You are wasting your time. You know that we don't want to throw in our votes. We don't want to vote you down. . . ." But the motion was finally presented, the vote was taken, and we voted two to one to sell the company. Then the Farm Bureau had to throw in their votes and knock the thing out again.

They had control . . . that was unquestionable. [Later] they presented the idea that we could sell it to [a larger Farm Bureau coop]. There wasn't anything else to do. This included two trucks, a gasoline station, storage house and fertilizer plant, and they bought the whole thing for $12,000. It is now all under [the Farm Bureau coop]. And that's the story of our company.

By means of such tactics, and by mutual arrangements, the Farm Bureau regional coops have achieved tremendous economic power in recent years. Specialized "super-coops" supply much of the oil, fertilizer, farm chemicals, and other farm supplies to the regional supply coops, which in turn supply the local coops. Central Farmer's Fertilizer Company is owned by 20 regional coops, including the four major Farm Bureau ones. Its largest shareholder is FS which owns 30 percent. The general manager of FS serves as Chairman of the Board of Central Farmers, which sells over a $100 million a year in basic fertilizer raw materials to its members. Central Nitrogen, Inc. manufactures nitrogen fertilizer materials. Its nitrogen plant in Terre Haute, Indiana has a productive capacity of 100,000 tons per year. It is owned by three of the Farm Bureau regional coops and Central Farmers Fertilizer. The same general manager of FS is a director and member of the executive committee of Central Nitrogen.

*   *   *

There is more to the Farm Bureau business empire. Through its insurance companies, the Farm Bureau has become a major property owner and real estate investor. Alabama offers an interesting example. Bureau investments in that state include ownership of seven large shopping centers. In 1967, the Farm Bureau insurance companies of Alabama purchased the largest regional enclosed mall shopping center in the Southeast—Eastwood Mall in Birmingham—for an estimated $10 million. Other real estate ventures in Alabama include the purchase of a large Birmingham estate for development into a fashionable subdivision; ownership of several hotels, including the historic Exchange Hotel in Montgomery and the $1.4 million Guest House in Birmingham; office buildings; high-priced residential properties; and a substantial amount of open land for future development and speculation. The companies also do a brisk business in mortgages.[16]

Another example will illustrate just how far afield some of the state Farm Bureaus have wandered in search of profits, all under the banner of servicing their farmer members. One of the companies in the California Farm Bureau group is the California Service Agency. An Agency brochure candidly describes this company as:

an advertising agency, plain and simple, . . . oriented towards agriculture, but handling accounts of all kinds. . . . An advertising agency seeks out clients who essentially have something to sell, be it apricots, insurance, alfalfa, seed, corrugated steel, tax service, petroleum products. . . . In addition to those in the agri-business industry, the California Service Agency handles accounts for a number of commercial firms with little connection to agriculture. . . .[17]

The California Farm Bureau Federation has declared that its purpose is to "accomplish through cooperative effort those things which farmers cannot do for themselves as individuals."[18] There is no argument about whether farmers, by themselves, can run their own advertising agency. But why would they want to? It is hard to imagine any enterprise that would not be justified under such a loose definition of purpose.

As we have seen by now, the search for profit has led the Farm Bureau into areas wholly unrelated to the interests of the farmer. When these business activities get as far removed from agriculture as an advertising agency or a car rental agency (Louisiana), or as unrelated as office buildings and hotels, it becomes difficult to understand the "service-to-member" rationale offered by the Farm Bureau. It seems obvious that many of these affiliate companies exist simply to make money. The question then arises as to whether the resulting conglomerate can honestly be called a farm organization. After all, Standard Oil certainly cannot be called an organization of oil users, and it wouldn't be any more of one if it formed county-level groups and held barbeques for its customers every summer.

The result of this aggressive search for business has led to a vast and rapid expansion of Farm Bureau enterprises in recent years. The fastest region of commercial growth for the Farm Bureau has been the South. A Georgia newspaper recently declared that the Farm Bureau in that state "holds a prominent place on the skyline of Georgia's growing economy."[19] In addition to the basic Farm Bureau ventures—farm supplies, insurance, and a marketing association—Georgia has the Georgia Farm Bureau Investment Company, which serves as a finance company for auto purchasers. After delving into the activities of all ten prospering affiliates of the Alabama Farm Bureau, one reporter concluded: "Farm Bureau in Alabama is far bigger than most people realize. . . . It is big enough to wield a heavy impact on the fact of Alabama business and the fabric of Alabama politics."[20]

Despite the rapid growth of Farm Bureau business in the South, the most prosperous state Farm Bureau operation is that of the Illinois Agricultural Association (IAA). In addition to its several bustling Country Insurance Companies, IAA controls more than a dozen different affiliated companies. All are tied closely to IAA by means of interlocking directorates, overlapping management, and IAA ownership of class B voting stock. These companies include Interstate Producers Livestock Association, the largest livestock marketing association in the United States, with annual sales of nearly $170 million; Illinois Grain Corporation, one of the largest grain-marketing coops in the country, also with sales of more than $170 million a year; the Illinois Milk Producers Association, which represents the producers of 90 percent of the grade A milk marketed in

Illinois; Prairie Farm Dairy, a coop which handles more than 300 million pounds of milk a year and had sales in 1968 of $37 million. Along with these coops, IAA controls Country Capital Management Company, a private mutual fund not restricted to Farm Bureau members. To keep tabs on this huge multifaceted operation, IAA publishes a monthly magazine that reaches about 200,000 homes, and another publication for the 10,000 state and local employees of IAA and its affiliates.

"In our entirety, we are large, and growing," the IAA proudly tells its prospective employees, and no one would argue the point.[21] The combined assets of all 19 IAA affiliates amounts to more than $500 million. Sales in goods, premiums and services are more than $600 million a year, and as the man said, they're growing. Already, the IAA operation alone ranks as one of the largest agri-business complexes in the nation.

All the Farm Bureau commercial activities discussed thus far have been those on a state or regional level, with the parent organization, the American Farm Bureau Federation, merely a shadow in the background. But the AFBF is far more than that. Headquartered in Chicago, the AFBF owns and operates several businesses of its own. In addition to its $27 million insurance company, it also operates the Farm Bureau Mutual Fund, with net assets of about $10 million. Open only to Farm Bureau members, this fund has been vigorously promoted since its inception in 1966, and despite the vagaries of the stock market, it has had considerable success. It is under the professional management of Scudder, Stevens, and Clark, a Boston firm of investment advisors, but the Board of Directors of the Mutual Fund is identical to the Board of the American Farm Bureau Federation.[22]

Another company affiliated with the American Farm Bureau Federation is the International Farmer-to-Farmer Corporation, a world-wide travel agency. Justified as satisfying the educational desires of farmers to observe agricultural methodology around the world, Farmer-to-Farmer plans tours for farmers to such agricultural centers as the Caribbean Islands, invites them to enjoy "twenty-one glorious days of sunshine and relaxation" in the South Pacific Islands, promotes vacations at the Beach Club Hotel in Ft. Lauderdale, Florida, and runs trips to Montreal Expo.[23] Possibly, where there are farms along the way, the travellers stop and look. But obviously the service is essentially a commercial travel agency, simply one that specializes in farmers. This is not to say that farmers should not travel. But there does not seem to be any scarcity of travel agencies in the country, or mutual funds either, for that matter.

In 1965, the American Farm Bureau Federation established the American Farm Bureau Service Company to act as a group buying agent for its members. It has concentrated on the purchasing of tires, batteries, and baling twine which it markets under its own label, "Safemark." By the end of 1968, the American Farm Bureau Service Company was selling its goods through 32 Farm Bureau Service Companies around the country, with more than 1500 participating counties. The products are purchased in large lots from major manufacturers. "Safemark" tires, for example, are manufactured by the General Tire Company. They are then distributed through state companies to local outlets. In some cases, they are sold locally through Farm Bureau outlets, but in many cases an independent local dealer is selected for the franchise. This selection, of course, gives the county organization considerable economic leverage in the community, since nearly $10 million of merchandise is sold through this network. The customers received sizeable savings, sometimes 25–30 percent, and the program has been a strong incentive for new and continued membership.[24] One southern Farm Bureau member—not a farmer—explained: "I figure that a new set of tires every three years for both my wife's car and mine more than pays for my membership."

In at least partial response to the emergence of the National Farmers Organization, with its vigorous and vocal advocacy of collective marketing by farmers, the Farm Bureau has been placing great importance of late on its marketing program. The American Agricultural Marketing Association (AAMA), an affiliate of the American Farm Bureau Federation, coordinates marketing activity in 31 states. The state associations are organized on a general commodity basis, that is, all producers are members of the same association. The AAMA enters into a "joint agency" contract with each state association making them joint bargaining agents for the participating producers. Negotiations with purchasers are usually conducted jointly by the AAMA and the state association, but the AAMA occasionally proceeds directly with the purchaser. According to Kenneth Hood, general manager of the AAMA, the state associations which make up the national system, plus the other Farm Bureau marketing programs, did over a billion dollars worth of business in 1968.[25]

Another operation directed by the American Farm Bureau Federation is the American Farm Bureau Research Foundation. The Foundation, a non-profit, tax-exempt organization, engages in research related to farm production and marketing. The costs of the research are borne by private contributors, while the operating expenses are carried by the American Farm Bureau Federation.[26]

At one time, the American Farm Bureau Federation operated a Trade Development Corporation which was in the international agricultural brokerage business, finding markets for domestic products and charging regular commission fees. This proved to be commercially unsuccessful, and this activity is now conducted by the Trade Development Division of the American Farm Bureau Federation. Nevertheless, "if someone gives us a fee, we will take it," commented one American Farm Bureau Federation official.

The American Farm Bureau Federation also crowns a national network of state record-keeping services. These state companies provide record and tax-preparation services for the organization members. The parent company in Chicago can call the records into Chicago and do the work there, or, in some cases, provide the electronic data processing capabilities to the states. The American Management Board, a corporate affiliate of the AFBF, was set up to coordinate the activities of all the AFBF's businesses.[27]

The importance of the American Farm Bureau Federation in the Farm Bureau's corporate scheme should not be underestimated. In some areas, such as insurance, it has a strong coordinating function, providing re-insurance service, writing certain high-risk commercial policies, and providing direct management assistance. In other cases, the American Farm Bureau Federation takes an active role in promoting state companies. Recently, for example, it placed one of its own staff men temporarily in the New England region to develop enough record-keeping programs to justify a new company there. Indeed, one of its vital business functions is to organize multistate programs in those smaller farming states that cannot support businesses on an individual state basis.

In an Associated Press wire service interview a few years ago, AFBF president Charles Shuman gave a graphic illustration of the gigantic scope of the AFBF's financial resources. Shuman confirmed reports that the national organization was thinking of buying a grocery chain. According to the AP story, the target was thought to be the Great Atlantic and Pacific Tea Company—the A&P—largest grocery chain in the nation with assets at that time of nearly $800 million. Although the deal was never consummated, Shuman admitted that "it would be feasible. It would be possible. It would be easy."[28]

Before making any final estimates about the total size of the Farm Bureau business empire, we must look at one final level of this sprawling organization. Beneath the layers of national and state operations lies a vast network of 2,800 county organizations. Many of the county Farm Bureaus are major property owners in their own right. Many own at least the office building in which they reside, and often rent space to government agencies or commercial enterprises. Many county Farm Bureaus have additional land holdings, often including the county fair grounds. For example, the local member cooperatives of the regional FS system alone have total assets of nearly $150 million.

By now one must realize that the Farm Bureau business empire is one of the largest commercial conglomerates in the country, with nearly $4 billion in total assets. Despite its immense size, however, it has undoubtedly been the least understood. One of the reasons it has received so little scrutiny has been its misleading statements to Congress and to the public when discussing these commercial activities. Despite its leaders' insistence that Farm Bureau businesses are separate and autonomous operations, it is clear that the Farm Bureau and its business enterprises are part of a single interwoven network. The businesses are tightly locked to the Farm Bureau organizations, and substantially linked to each other, both within states and from state to state. Statements to the contrary by Farm Bureau leaders are merely smokescreens.

Finally, unless a bird is to be called a tree, and a tree a stone, it is difficult to accept any longer the notion that the Farm Bureau is even predominantly an agricultural organization. Certainly for some it serves some of the functions of a trade association—it has meetings, there are discussions, and it works for legislative goals. But looking at the total picture, its concern for agriculture is largely as the market for its own goods and services, as the cornerstone of its commercial empire.

The inevitable result of the Farm Bureau's commercial expansion has been to thrust it into the impossible position of responding to two, often conflicting sets of interests: its own, as one of the nation's largest agri-businesses, and those of the individual farmers who buy from and sell to it. The Farm Bureau's record in dealing with this dilemma stands as its own indictment.

6

Representation Without Taxation

THE AMERICAN FARM BUREAU FEDERATION and the county and state Farm Bureaus are tax-exempt. They enjoy this special status along with business associations, labor unions, religious, charitable, educational and fraternal associations, and numerous other non-profit groups organized for the mutual benefit of their members. The Commissioner of Internal Revenue is empowered to reevaluate the tax-exempt status of any organization and revoke it if there are "substantial changes in the organization's character, purposes, or methods of operation."[1] But despite the Farm Bureau's definite shift in recent years from an agricultural to a business organization, it has successfully retained its valuable tax shelter.

Prior to 1950, tax exempt organizations had nearly blanket exemption from federal income taxes. The Internal Revenue Service made numerous attempts to deny exemption to organizations that were extensively involved in profit-making activities, but these usually failed in the courts. The Supreme Court had ruled in 1924 that the ultimate test of the right to an exemption was the destination of the income and not its source.[2]

Many abuses arose. By 1950, numerous tax-exempt organizations were extensively engaged in profit-making businesses in direct competition with tax-paying entities. One of the South's most profitable textile operations was turned into a tax-exempt foundation, involving its $34 million holdings. Union College in New York State purchased all of the properties of Allied Stores Corporation, one of the nation's largest department-store chains. The University of Chicago bought the Encyclopedia Brittanica. And New York University went into the macaroni business, with the profits from the pasta going to the law school. At that point, Congress stepped in.[3]

In 1950, provisions were added to the Internal Revenue Code to tax some of the "unrelated business income" of tax-exempt organizations. Unrelated business income tax is paid by most tax-exempt organizations on certain kinds of income they receive from business activities.

Although the Farm Bureau organizations and businesses are inextricably interwoven, they are legally distinct. The businesses pay federal income taxes like any other comparable businesses. A considerable part of their income, however, is diverted to the tax-exempt state and county Farm Bureaus as "sponsorship fees," rents, dividends and advertising fees. It was to cover such income from unrelated businesses that the unrelated business income tax was enacted.

If all of the money that the state and county Farm Bureaus are receiving from their businesses were in fact being taxed by the federal government via the unrelated business income tax, there would be no cause for outrage, no reason to charge that the federal government is subsidizing this commercial giant. But, unfortunately, all of the business income to the Farm Bureau organizations is not being taxed. Even where the unrelated business income tax is being applied to the Farm Bureau to its limit, there is revenue going untaxed. That special tax is not a blanket tax. It was not designed for an organization with the pervasive business interests of the Farm Bureau. When it is applied to the Farm Bureau, even to the fullest extent possible, there are gaping loopholes which permit the organization to shelter a considerable portion of their income from federal income tax. Furthermore, even where it could have been applied, the unrelated business income tax has not been levied on the Farm Bureau in the past to the fullest extent possible. The tax-free income thereby permitted is available for the Farm Bureau's organizational, political, and legislative activities, despite the fact that it is produced by commercial businesses.

The actual taxes paid by county, state, and national Farm Bureau organizations are, of course, a quiet secret between themselves and the Internal Revenue Service. But we can look at the tax laws themselves to see what income the Farm Bureaus receive tax-free. Assuming for the moment that the unrelated business income tax is being imposed upon the Farm Bureau organizations to the fullest extent possible, what benefits do they still get from their tax exemption? To start with, the first thousand dollars in income received each year by a tax-exempt organization is tax-free, regardless of its source. It does not matter, in the case of the Farm Bureau for example, whether this income comes from rents, insurance company rebates, or advertising revenue. This amounts to over $285,000 a year in potential tax-sheltered income to the Farm Bureau, $1,000 for each state organization and $1,000 for each county organization.

Another category of income which is tax-free to exempt organizations, regardless of its source, is income derived from dividends. Whether received from stock in the organization's own companies, or others, dividends are not taxed. This can be a sizeable windfall. The Cal–Farm Life Insurance Company, for example, has distributed more than $500,000 in dividends to its stockholders since 1951.[4] One of the major stockholders, of course, is the California Farm Bureau. In 1966, the Illinois Agricultural Association received tax-free dividends from its affiliates amounting to nearly $53,000.[5] The twelve Farm Bureau life insurance companies, with total assets of over $1 billion, are stock companies. Most are substantially owned by state Farm Bureaus or their holding companies, and many have paid healthy dividends to their stockholders over the years.

A substantial portion of the rent that many state and county Farm Bureaus receive from their affiliated companies would also not be touched by the unrelated business income tax; the organizations enjoy this money tax free. Intricate tax provisions subject some rent received by tax-exempt organizations to the tax, but leave much untaxed. Essentially, the rent received by the Farm Bureaus from some of their older buildings is not covered by the unrelated business income tax.

Even a provision of the 1969 Tax Reform Act which deals with rental income of tax-exempt organizations will add little tax burden on the Farm Bureau. The new law would tax *all* the rental income received by exempt organizations from companies they "control." But although it is clear that the Farm Bureau controls most of its companies, the definition of "control" used in the new tax law is very narrow, excluding from its reach many of the Farm Bureau affiliates.

Just how does all this tax-free income received by the Farm Bureau affect the average taxpayer? If a Farm Bureau business were dealing with someone other than an exempt organization—for example if its landlord were not exempt or if it were contracting for promotional services from any regular commercial company—the money it paid for those services would be taxable income to the recipient. The landlords would pay taxes on the rent they receive; the advertising and public relations agencies would pay tax on the fees they receive for promoting Farm Bureau businesses. But when the Farm Bureau organizations receive the same money for performing the same services, much of it is tax free. So by making such business arrangements with a tax-exempt organization, the federal Treasury is losing the revenue it would receive if the arrangements were made with a regular commercial operation, or if the organization did not have a tax exemption. Similarly, if the dividends received by a tax-exempt organization were paid to a private individual or a tax-paying entity, those dividends would be taxed as regular income in the hands of the recipient. So the average taxpayer pays more because the Farm Bureau pays less.

The Farm Bureau businesses also benefit from the tax breaks that the nation generously confers upon the organizations. To the extent that the Farm Bureau organizations do not have to pay taxes on the income they receive from business activity, they can provide the services they are offering, for example, promotion and office space, more cheaply than the businesses could provide for themselves or obtain by contracting with a tax-paying outside entity. That saving can either be passed on to customers—giving Farm Bureau businesses a competitive advantage—or can be retained as higher profits. In either case, the businesses benefit from the organizations' exemption, even though they are paying taxes themselves. The Farm Bureau's independent competition suffers.

To this point we have focused on the benefits that the Farm Bureaus receive from their tax exemption even where the unrelated business income tax is fully levied. If it were applied fully to the individual Farm Bureau organizations, it would cover all the rest of the business income they receive, i.e. business income—except dividends—above $1,000, including the bulk of the rental income. Only the Internal Revenue Service can answer the question of exactly where the unrelated business income tax has been applied to the Farm Bureau, and where it hasn't. This much, however, is clear: much of the Farm Bureau's business income has not been covered by that tax in the past.

Let us examine how the Farm Bureau has gotten away with this. In addition to the gaps that we have already seen in the tax, the unrelated business income tax is not levied on an exempt organization's business income unless the business activity which produces the income is: 1) regularly carried on by the organization, *and* 2) not "substantially related" to the exempt purposes of the organization. For example, the money earned by a church from a one-time bazaar would probably not be taxed, because it is not a business regularly carried on by the church. It is perfectly clear, however, that the Farm Bureau businesses are "regularly carried on."

What about the other half of the requirement? What does it mean for the business to be "substantially related" to the "exempt purposes" of the organization? The principal purposes for which agricultural organizations such as the Farm Bureau receive a tax exemption—the "exempt purposes" —are "the betterment of the conditions of those engaged in agriculture, and the improvement of their products and their occupational efficiency."[6] In order for the Farm Bureau to escape from the unrelated business income tax, therefore, it must convince the Internal Revenue Service that its businesses are substantially related to these purposes. That they generate money for the Farm Bureaus to operate is not sufficient. It must be shown that the business activities themselves contribute importantly to achieving these purposes.

What are some examples of where the tax would, or would not, apply? In the case of an organization engaged in rehabilitating handicapped persons, the business of selling the articles made by such persons as part of their rehabilitation training would be a related business, and any income the organization earned from such sales would not be taxed. If a union conducts refresher courses for its members and sells handbooks and technical manuals to those in the course, that income would not be taxable since one of the purposes of a union is the development and improvement of the skills of its members. If a trade association presents a trade show in which its members display their products, the income from the charges to exhibitors for exhibit space and the admission fees charged to viewers would not be taxed since one of the purposes of a trade association is to promote and stimulate interest in the industry's product. On the other hand, the operation of a cinderblock plant by a university would be an unrelated business; it would pay unrelated business income tax on the income it received. The operation of a bar and cocktail lounge by an agricultural organization would also be an unrelated business.[7]

An important factor in determining if the business is related or unrelated is the size of the business in comparison to the size of the exempt organization. For example, the operation of a wheat farm is related to the exempt activity of an agricultural college if the wheat farm is operated as a part of the educational program of the college and is not disproportionately large when compared with the educational program.[8]

The question in the case of the Farm Bureau, then, is whether the businesses affiliated with the Bureau—the insurance companies and the regional cooperatives and the travel agencies and the accounting services—are related businesses. If the Farm Bureau can convince the IRS that they are, *all* of the income transferred to the organizations from the businesses, regardless of whether it is in rents or dividends or sponsorship fees—escapes taxation. For years, Farm Bureaus in many states took exactly that position, particularly regarding their rental income, and they paid no taxes on it. And for many years, the Internal Revenue Service let them get away with it. The Illinois Agricultural Association for example, earned nearly $400 thousand in 1968 from renting space in its office buildings to its own companies. This was not the kind of rental income we saw before which is automatically free from the "unrelated business income tax." But the IAA paid no tax on this income.[9]

In 1968, however, the IRS balked. In reviewing the IAA's tax returns for 1962 and 1963, the IRS representative contended that a "portion of the rental income received by the Illinois Agricultural Association from affiliated companies is subject to Federal Income Tax." He proposed that the IAA pay back taxes and penalties of more than $125 thousand just for those two years.[10] The IAA, naturally, contested this position, claiming that this rental income was not taxable. But in 1970, the Internal Revenue Service ruled that, when considering whether or not the rent received by an exempt farm organization is to be taxed, the subsidiary companies that sell insurance or farm equipment or provide marketing and other business services for the members are not related businesses. Therefore, an exempt farm organization can no longer escape paying unrelated business income tax on the income it receives from renting to these affiliated companies.

"Although the subsidiaries are providing goods and services for farmers," explained the Internal Revenue Service, "these activities do not advance and improve the condition of farmers in their agricultural pursuits within the meaning of the [Internal Revenue] Code. These activities are carried on primarily for the production of income. They have no [causal] relationship to the achievement of the exempt purpose of the agricultural organization nor do they contribute importantly to the accomplishment of such purposes."[11]

This long-overdue decision is certainly correct. Much of the Farm Bureau business enterprise serves individuals who have little relation to farming. Many Farm Bureau members are not farmers, and a sizeable portion of Farm Bureau products and services is sold to those who are not even members. Insurance is sold to member and non-member alike. Someone driving up to an FS or Landmark gas station is not asked if he is a Farm Bureau member. His tank is quickly filled, even if he doesn't know the difference between an ox and an oat. By what theory is selling gasoline to salesmen, or insurance to Chicagoans, or farm supplies to farmers who are not members of the Farm Bureau "reasonably necessary" to the performance of the function for which the organization was granted an exemption?

In the case of the income derived from selling to people who are both Farm Bureau members and farmers, the case for the Farm Bureau was much stronger in the days when it was providing business services that the farmer could not otherwise obtain. But as we have seen, this is far less true today, and many of the Farm Bureau businesses are openly competitive with their private competitors.

The unrelated business income tax on exempt organizations has serious holes when applied to an organization like the Farm Bureau. But the minimum step to be taken in relation to the Farm Bureau is to extend the unrelated business tax over the organization to the limits of that tax's reach.

Another major source of income to the Farm Bureau organizations from their affiliated companies is the insurance company rebate or "sponsorship fee." In some cases, this amounts to a quarter or a third of the state organization's revenue. Is this income subject to the unrelated business income tax?

The Internal Revenue Service faced this issue earlier than the rent issue. Where an agricultural organization renders services to an insurance company, for example, by assigning a part of its administrative and secretarial staff to an insurance program for its members, and receives in return an overall fee from the insurance company, this income will be taxed as from an unrelated business. Services of this type, rendered in connection with an insurance program for its members, explained the Internal Revenue Service, "are activities which constitute business of a kind ordinarily carried on for profit. Such activities are not usually associated with the functions of an agricultural organization and normally would not be carried on by such an organization in the furtherance of its exempt purposes. Therefore, these activities are not related to the organization's exempt purposes other than through the use it makes of the net earnings it receives. . . ."[12]

It would seem, then, that after this ruling by IRS the money that the Farm Bureaus get from their insurance companies in fees or rebates would now be taxed. But like most tax problems, it is not that simple. The IRS ruling dealt with only one type of arrangement made between the Farm Bureau organizations and their insurance companies. It specifically covered only the service contract arrangement, where the insurance company gives the organization an overall fee for certain specific services that the organization provides for the company. In some states, however, the payments to the Farm Bureau organization are not specifically geared to the services rendered but are based on a percentage of the total premiums paid by members of the organization who buy insurance. How the Internal Revenue Service treats this income is less clear.

Moreover, a recent federal court decision gives some hope to agricultural organizations who want to contest being taxed on all or some of this insurance revenue. A federal court in Oklahoma during 1970 granted a refund to an agricultural organization for the taxes it had been assessed on rebates it received from a cooperating insurance company. The company wrote a group insurance policy for members of the organization and gave to the organization a percentage of the premiums. The court ruled that making the insurance available for its members was, in this case, a related business.[13] As long as the Farm Bureau has its tax exemption, such avenues of relief are always open to them.

There are other channels through which income earned by the Farm Bureau's wide-ranging business ventures is returned to the organizations for their use. Until recently, an important money-maker for the organizations was the revenue from advertisements in its numerous publications. But, in 1967, the Treasury Department—parent to the Internal Revenue Service—declared that exempt organizations would have to pay taxes on much of the income they received from advertising in their publications. The Department acted after thorough investigation had shown that a number of exempt groups conducted "active and competitive advertising businesses" in connection with their publications. Spokesmen for the Treasury

Department asserted that "the matter is one of fairness to commercial publications which have to pay a tax on revenues from the same sort of advertising. . . . There has been evidence of some tax-exempt groups openly soliciting advertising on the basis that the rate for their magazines is less than competing commercial magazine rates."[14]

A heated controversy followed the issuance of these regulations. Some organizations angrily contended that the IRS had overstepped its authority. Congress entered the fray with the recent tax enactment to settle the validity of the regulations. To the extent that these magazines such as the AFBF's *Nation's Agriculture* show a profit, they will now be taxed on their advertising revenue.

Shifting from the Federal to the state and local tax scene, one of the most important tax advantages for the Farm Bureau, at least in the past, in many areas has been its exemption from the real property tax. As we have seen, the Farm Bureau is a large property owner, with county office buildings throughout the country and splendid state office buildings to serve its commercial affiliates as well as itself. In many areas, especially in those states where for many years the Farm Bureau was recognized by law as a "public" institution, these office buildings have been exempt from property taxes. Exemption from the costly property tax has extended not only to buildings occupied jointly by the organization and the business affiliates, but in some cases has spilled over to buildings used purely for commercial purposes. Publicity generated by Resnick's 1967 investigation prompted the Attorney-General of Iowa to rule that, at least in one case where a Farm Bureau-owned building was being used to store fertilizer and other products offered for sale, "any part of the structure used for commercial purposes is taxable. . . ." He went on to rule that "if it proves difficult for the county assessor to determine which part is used commercially, all of the building should be listed as commercial."[15]

In some cases where Farm Bureau property is not totally exempt from property taxation, it is treated most graciously. One midwestern businessman, in competition with the Farm Bureau, was curious about its tax load in his community. The Farm Bureau owned a half a block of land near the town's business center. Local Farm Bureau officials had turned down an offer of $40,000 to purchase the building and property, he claimed. In checking with the assessor's office at the county court house, he discovered that the Farm Bureau was paying only $64.74 a year in property taxes. "I then asked the assessor to figure up with the valuation they had on the property what the property tax would be if the property were owned by an individual. At the present levy, the individual would be paying $808.14."

In addition to receiving such gentle tax treatment—both federal and local—the Farm Bureau has extended its business operations into fields smiled upon by our tax system—oil, insurance, and cooperatives. Probably no sector of our economy has been as pampered by the tax system as the oil industry. The infamous oil depletion allowance has permitted oil producers to deduct 27.5 percent from their gross income, regardless of the costs incurred in their operations. (In 1969, Congress reduced this allowance to 22 percent.) The depletion allowance, although the most notorious of the oil industry's tax bonuses, is not the only one. Certain development costs, such as those for exploration, can be deducted entirely in the year incurred, where the equivalent costs in other industries would have to be deducted over several years. Oil companies further decrease their tax burden by selling oil production payments to investors.

The combined effect of these devices is an unusually favorable tax climate for the oil men. In 1964, for example, the five largest U.S. oil refiners paid effective tax rates of 0.8 to 8.6 percent of their gross income. (In 1964, the tax rate for corporations earning more than $25,000 a year was supposedly 48 percent.) The combination of tax advantages conferred upon the oil industry permitted the Atlantic–Richfield Co. of New York to pay no federal income tax from 1962 to 1967, while earning nearly $500 million in net income.[16]

If the oil industry has been the favorite child of the tax system, the insurance industry has been treated almost as well. With $336 million in net premiums earned in 1968, and another $15 million in investment income, the forty-two Farm Bureau property-liability insurance companies paid Uncle Sam a total of only $2.2 million in federal income taxes. The twelve Farm Bureau life insurance companies were nearly as fortunate. With a total premium income in 1968 of more than $157 million, and another $46 million in net investment income, they paid only $4.8 million in taxes.[17]

Many of the Farm Bureau businesses are organized as cooperatives. Because of the unique characteristics of farmer cooperatives, a profusion of special tax benefits have been conferred upon them. When properly qualified under the tax laws, farmer coops can receive a tax exemption. The earnings of exempt coops, whether paid out as patronage refunds or as dividends to stockholders, are exempt from corporate income tax. However, because exempt purchasing coops are required to sell 85 percent of their goods to those who are both farmers and members of the coop, many coops prefer not to be tax exempt.

Whether or not a cooperative is exempt, it has notable tax advantages over non-cooperative corporations. Simply stated, a regular corporation pays corporate income tax on its yearly earnings at a rate of about 48 percent. If it then distributes some of its income after taxes to its stockholders as dividends, these dividends are once again taxed in the hands of the stockholders as part of their gross income. Farmer cooperatives avoid this so-called "double taxation." They can exclude from their income, for tax purposes, all their patronage refunds, leaving this to be taxed solely in the hands of the customer.

The most obvious consequence of this tax advantage is the ability of the cooperative to compete on very favorable terms with the prices of their non-cooperative competitors. The tax saving can be passed on to their customers, either by reducing prices or by making refunds at the end of the year. But there is another more subtle and probably more crucial advantage for cooperatives lurking in the tax laws. As we have seen before, the entire patronage refund need not be returned to the customers in cash. Indeed, in most cases only 20 percent of it must be paid in cash; the rest is distributed as scrip or stock certificates, redeemable some years in the future. Meanwhile, the cooperative has the use of these non-taxed earnings to finance its own expansion. In other words, the cooperative can deduct 100 percent of its patronage refunds from its income for tax purposes while retaining 80 percent of it to supply needed capital. A true case of having your cake and eating it too, at least most of it.

In most cases the outstanding stock certificates will have to be redeemed, or cashed in, at some time in the future. There is currently no legal time limit imposed during which they must be redeemed, but most coops have their own regular schedule. It is important to remember, however, that the stock certificates issued in any given year will be redeemed years later out of future earnings, earnings which in part will be generated by the use of the customer's money in the interim for expansion, financing new facilities, and general growth. The constant source of capital made available by the use of most of the coops' distributions to their customers has enabled many Farm Bureau coops to expand rapidly in recent years.

The most graphic way to illustrate the effect of these tax provisions for coops is to look at some of the operating figures from one of the Farm Bureau coops. The Indiana Farm Bureau Cooperative Association had nearly $4 million in "savings" (or net income) before federal income taxes in 1968. Had it been a non-cooperative corporation, it would have theoretically paid regular corporate taxes on this—as much as 48 percent, or nearly $2 million. As a cooperative, however, the Indiana Coop could deduct about $3.5 million as patronage refunds and dividends to preferred stockholders, leaving only $400,000 of taxable income instead of nearly $4 million. And because of other standard adjustments to which it was entitled, the Indiana Farm Bureau Coop paid a total of only $10,000 in federal income taxes in 1968.

Although the Indiana Coop deducted $3.2 million as patronage refunds, only 20 percent of this was in fact paid out in cash, leaving $2.5 million in the hands of the company. In 1968, however, only $2 million worth of outstanding stock certificates from previous years' patronage refunds (1956) were actually retired for cash, leaving the company a neat $500,000 untaxed, available for expansion and improvement.[18]

The numerous tax advantages flowing to the Farm Bureau business operations—because of the favored industries in which it deals and the privileged modes through which it operates—have played a large role in the previously described business success story. Taking the Illinois case once again for illustration, the fourteen Farm Bureau companies in that state which published their income figures had a total net income in 1968 of more than $19.5 million before federal income taxes. Yet they paid only about $3.2 million in federal income taxes—an effective rate of little more than 18 percent.[19] To say that this was all done within the letter of the law is little consolation. We must be doing something wrong.

Thorough consideration of what needs to be done in the oil, insurance, and cooperative areas is beyond the scope of this inquiry. The oil-tax mess periodically surfaces in Congress only to be ultimately beaten back by one of the best-financed lobbies in Washington. Congress made loud noises about the oil depletion allowance during the deliberations over the 1969 tax bill, and finally cut it back somewhat, but this is only a beginning of what needs to be done. The oil area is one part of the tax laws that Congress would better attack with a saber than a scalpel.

A movement has been growing recently to bring the insurance industry under closer federal supervision. Under the prodding of such people as Senator Warren Magnuson of Washington, Congress is being asked to take a close look at various aspects of the industry. It can only be hoped that when the public probe is launched, the tax treatment of the industry will be simultaneously studied.

The cooperative problem is a slightly different one. As indicated before, a cooperative which is truly a cooperative has certain unique values worth preserving and even fostering. But it appears that in the case of many Farm Bureau coops at least, it is stretching the imagination to call these enterprises cooperatives in any meaningful sense of that term. More critical examination into the character of these operations is essential. True cooperatives should be encouraged, and the tax laws are certainly an appropriate means to do this. Precisely because they are so generously favored they should be scrupulously supervised.

The basic question, however, remains: Is the Farm Bureau itself entitled to any tax exemption? Although the provision of the Internal Revenue Code under which the Farm Bureau is exempt dates back to 1909, it is probably the most inadequately defined of all the provisions granting exemptions. While the grants of exemption to civic and business leagues, clubs and fraternal associations spell out with some detail the criteria for exemption, an exemption is granted to "labor, agricultural, and horticultural organizations" without further explanation of what those terms mean.

What qualifies as an agricultural organization for purposes of tax exemption? The Treasury regulations tell us only that in order to qualify for exemption under the provision pertaining to agricultural organizations, the organization must: "(1) have no net earnings inuring to the benefit of any member, and (2) have as their objects the betterment of the conditions of those engaged in such pursuits, the improvement of the grade of their products, and the development of a higher degree of efficiency in their respective occupations."[20] Two things should be noted about these requirements: unlike the specifications for other similar organizations, they do not explicitly prohibit the organization itself from being profit-making; and they define the organization in terms of its purposes rather than its membership.

Although business leagues, chambers of commerce, fraternal and civic associations are specifically restricted by law from being organized for profit, agricultural associations are explicitly prohibited only from having any of their earnings going to members. It is puzzling why such a distinction has been made. But even though tax-exempt agricultural organizations are not specifically prohibited from being organized for profit, such a limitation would seem to be implicit in the very motion of tax-exemption. The Internal Revenue Service, for example, denied a tax-exemption to an organization composed of agricultural producers whose principal activity was to market livestock for its members. Its central purpose, claimed the Service, was to act as a sales agent for its members, and such an organization does not qualify for exemption.[21]

Treasury Department regulations state that being non-profit *alone* is not sufficient for an organization to obtain a tax-exemption, which implies that it is, however, a prerequisite. Is the Farm Bureau "organized and operated for profit"? In light of the extensive and interconnected commercial empire described in the preceding chapters, this question is not as simple as Farm Bureau officials would like Congress and the public to believe. We have seen that it is virtually impossible to define the boundaries between organization and business in all but the most formal and artificial sense. Recognizing this, the question becomes: How does one characterize this multifaceted giant?

What is the Farm Bureau? Certainly the Farm Bureau is meetings, election of officers, committees and policy positions. But it is also insurance and oil, real estate and communications, fertilizer and feed and seed. And the relative proportions of these two components—in terms of energy expended, space used, resources employed—overwhelmingly favors the multibillion dollar business side. The center of gravity of the Farm Bureau rests comfortably in its commerce. Its *principal* purpose is no longer "the betterment of the conditions of those engaged in agriculture and the improvement of their products and their occupational efficiency," except insofar as selling insurance, fertilizer, gasoline and seed to farmers achieves those purposes. But that is the same purpose of John Deere or International Harvester, or the agricultural division of any major insurance company, which do not share the Farm Bureau's financial privilege of tax exemption.

Finally, in considering the validity of the Farm Bureau's tax-exempt status, we must look to the character of its membership. Other provisions of the tax laws granting exemptions to other kinds of membership organizations have defined the organizations in terms of who the members are. In order for a business league to be entitled to exemption, for example, its members must have "some common business interest."[22] Not so with agricultural organizations. The Internal Revenue Service has taken the position that "it is not mandatory that the organization's members be engaged in agricultural pursuits." The Service permitted a group organized to "encourage the breeding, proper development, and care of better types of breeds of horses" to retain a tax-exemption even though only about 25 percent of its members owned horses or had any connection with their breeding or development.[23]

The case of the Farm Bureau strongly pleads for a change in this policy, bringing it in line with the requirements for most other trade associations. Attention to the common economic interests of the membership of agricultural organizations is essential as a protection against abuse. Such a safeguard does not even require a change in the law, but simply a change in the regulations issued by the Treasury Department to amplify the tax laws. Such a change would add to the requirements for tax exemption as an agricultural organization the provision that the members of the groups— or nearly all—must be engaged in agricultural pursuits.

Extending the full range of the unrelated business income tax over the Farm Bureau network would not eliminate the tax benefits the organization now enjoys. As long as it is permitted to retain its tax exemption, it will be receiving a sizeable subsidy from the federal government. Because the unrelated business income tax was designed to deal with universities, charities, hospitals, and membership organizations that are primarily serving their members, it is not an all-encompassing tax blanket. As long as the Farm Bureau has its tax exemption, some of the income it derives from its business operations will not be taxed.

Clearly, as the Farm Bureau is currently structured, its organizational aspects cannot be separated and isolated from its business enterprises. To permit the Farm Bureau's tax exemption to continue, then, is to provide a sizeable national subsidy to this corporate hybrid, a subsidy it neither needs nor deserves. As urgent public needs press more heavily on our resources, and as the individual taxpayer views with increasing antagonism the inequity of his tax burden, we can no longer tolerate the misuse of tax privileges by self-interested organizations like the Farm Bureau.

The Farm Bureau's tax exemption should be withdrawn. This would hardly destroy the Farm Bureau. It would simply be forced to pay its own way. It can certainly afford that.

7

The Rock Against Radicalism

BORN OUT OF WEDLOCK early in the century, the Farm Bureau was fathered by big business in reaction to the spread of more radical farmer movements, and mothered by the federal government as part of its new policy to bring modern agriculture to the farmer.

The chronic problem of American agriculture—surplus production—began to emerge following the Civil War. Technology stimulated by the War, and the acquisition of vast new tracts of agricultural land, greatly expanded the country's agricultural output. Industrial depressions in the 1870s and 1890s severely aggravated the problem by dampening the demand for agricultural products.

The first modern farm organization—The Grange—was founded in 1867 by Oliver Hudson Kelly, a government clerk from the state of Washington. The Grange movement of the 1870s, fanned by the farmers' bitter resentment of the discrimination practiced by the railroads against them, resulted in a head-on clash between the monied railroads and the aroused farmers. Although the independent political parties that this grassroots movement spawned were not themselves particularly successful, the antirailroad forces achieved a stunning victory in 1887, with Congressional enactment of the historic Interstate Commerce Act, imposing governmental control over the railroads.

With these victories, however, the farmers' political strength began to be co-opted by the major political parties. The Grange turned to the task of stimulating economic cooperation among farmers. Its energies created the first agricultural cooperatives in the country. But the national depression of

1876–77 struck a major blow at these efforts, with bitter consequences for the Grange. Its membership plunged from 858,000 in 1875 to 124,000 two years later.

The Populist movement that erupted among rural people at the end of the 1800s was bitterly hostile to concentrations of power in corporate hands. It was a farmer revolt against industrialism and a movement for democracy, as manifested in its demands for referendum, recall, income tax, and direct election of Senators. The Populist wrath exploded in 1892 with the angry campaign of William Jennings Bryan for the Presidency. Bryan's defeats in 1892 and again in 1896 contributed to the decline of the Populist movement, but not before much of its program had gained wide popular acceptance.

The disastrous conditions in much of agricultural America at the close of the 1800s gave birth to another movement, in a sense the legatee of the Populist tradition. In 1902, an impoverished editor named Newt Gresham, from Emory, Texas, founded the Farmer's Educational and Cooperative Union of America. The Farmers Union, as it became known, initially stressed the economic and cooperative necessities of farmer organization. A system of warehouses in the cotton states and cooperative stores outside the South launched the Farmers Union into the arena of cooperative buying and selling for the farmer.

During the first two decades of the 20th Century, the general farm population experienced a relative prosperity unknown before or since. The rate of the nation's land acquisition slowed after 1900. Demand for agricultural products quickened. Growing industrialization swelled the cities, stimulating the farm economy. Surplus was not a problem, at least for the time being.

The government's agricultural policy during this period turned to educating farmers in the techniques of scientific farming. The Department of Agriculture had been created in 1862, with a role that was primarily educational. The Morrill Act of that year had granted land to the states for the establishment of "land grant" colleges "to teach such branches of learning as are related to agriculture and the mechanic arts . . . without excluding other scientific and classical studies, and including military tactics."[1] The Hatch Act in 1887 had provided government aid to these colleges to establish and maintain experimental stations for agricultural research.

By the early days of the 1900s, many colleges were carrying on active off-campus agricultural research. It was a natural step to hire professional agents to spread the new scientific developments to the farmers. The first such agricultural agents appeared about 1907, in the South, and gradually spread throughout the country. By 1914 there were 881 county agents. At first these positions were established on an ad hoc basis, as an outgrowth or "extension" of the land grant colleges. Gradually this movement became known as the "Extension Service."

Initially this new service was financed partly by counties, and partly by the U.S. Department of Agriculture. Soon, however, it received a boost from the dominant business interests of the day. The country was still largely rural, and business feared another Populist-style revolt. Such industrial giants as John Deere, International Harvester, the Great Northern, Pennsylvania, and Rock Island Railroads, and the Chambers of Commerce saw the county-agent movement as a safe antidote to more radical farm movements.

O. M. Kile, in his officially sanctioned and saluted history of the Farm Bureau, has explained: "The coming of the county agricultural agent, around 1910, injected a new and potent element in farm affairs. The first county Farm Bureaus grew directly out of the county agent's activities, and from the county units it was but a logical step, first to state federations, and finally to the national federation."[2]

The first Farm Bureau was born in a Chamber of Commerce. The Broome County Chamber of Commerce, based in Binghamton, N.Y., formed a committee on agriculture in 1911, and with some financial assistance from the Lackawana Railroad, hired a county agent. The county agent soon found it difficult to cover the entire Broome County area by himself, so he appointed community chairmen, "from among his best cooperating farmers." In 1914, the "Broome County Farm Bureau" was established as a separate entity, assuming the affairs of the Chamber of Commerce's agriculture committee, and continuing a close relationship with the Chamber. The name "Farm Bureau" had the connotation of a public body, which has created untold confusion ever since, all to the Farm Bureau's benefit.

Throughout the country, similar organizations of farmers grew up around the county agents, providing them with an "organized clientele." These early Bureaus received a potent transfusion from the business world. The Chicago Board of Trade, looking over its shoulder at the simmering Non-partisan League in North Dakota, reportedly sent $1000 each to the first one hundred Bureaus organized.[3] The Farm Bureaus—first known as "councils of agriculture" in the South—were also promoted by many state legislatures. Laws were passed in several states requiring that before a county agent could be approved or receive state funds, a county organization of farmers—sometimes specifically designated a "Farm Bureau"—had to be established on a dues-paying basis and pledge partial funding of the agent.

In 1914, Congress passed the landmark Smith–Lever Act providing federal matching grants to the states to support county agents. "The Smith–Lever Act of 1914," wrote Christiana McFadyen Cambell in her excellent history of the Farm Bureau during the New Deal, "is almost as much a charter for the Farm Bureau as it is for the Extension Service."[4]

The county agent idea had thereby become national policy with federal funding, and it spread rapidly. World War I, with its heightened food demand, produced the Emergency Food Production Act in 1917, placing a heavy emphasis on the county agent and providing a healthy financial commitment to his development. By 1924, 93 percent of the cost of county agents was publicly financed.

The county agent gradually became the publicly paid organizer of the Farm Bureau. "Since more members meant more funds to work with and greater interest throughout the county," explains official chronicler Kile, "membership campaigns were pushed and the county agent at that time frequently took an active part in membership solicitation."[5]

The establishment of statewide federations of county Farm Bureaus grew out of the practice of inviting the county Farm Bureau presidents to the state meetings of county agents at the university. The next logical step was to organize the state federations into a national unit, and after a preliminary meeting in Ithaca, New York, the American Farm Bureau Federation was created in 1919. At the close of its first year, there were 317,108 paid-up members of the American Farm Bureau Federation and more than twice that number in county organizations around the country.

Its inextricable link with the publicly financed government agents gave rise to the notion, not entirely laid to rest today, that the Farm Bureau was a public institution. Indeed, in some states, the courts ruled that the Farm Bureaus actually were "public institutions." This view of the organization was encouraged in these early days by statements from officials of the Department of Agriculture. "I do not believe it is going too far to say," said one such officer, "that the United States Department of Agriculture and the office with which I am connected is responsible for the development of the Farm Bureaus in this country."[6]

From its beginnings, the Farm Bureau was mainly an organization for wealthy farmers. The underlying principle of the Extension method is "demonstration," and in spreading new developments it naturally tended to focus on the more prosperous farms. The farmers that joined together to sponsor the agents' work, who could afford the time and the $10 dues in 1910, were relatively well-off. According to historian Eric Goldman, "The [Farm Bureau] organization concentrated its drives among the more successful farmers."[7]

Because such members naturally had little desire for radical social or economic change, the Farm Bureau soon became a bulwark against the radical farm movements then growing among farmers who were suffering as a result of the depression following World War I. In an address in 1919, the Secretary of Agriculture, David Franklin Houston, called upon farmers to join the Farm Bureau in order to "stop bolshevism." The Farm Bureau itself actively promoted the idea that it represented an alternative to radicalism. "I stand as a rock against radicalism," proclaimed the American Farm Bureau's first president, James Howard.[8] Such statements certainly did not displease the organizations' business benefactors and they did little to quell the "early rumors circulated against the Farm Bureau—that it was a creature of Wall Street; that it was controlled by big business, particularly the packers; and that it represented only big business."[9]

The drying up of foreign markets and the revival of European agriculture following the end of World War I left the overexpanded domestic producers once again facing a surplus problem. Farm prices began to slide, but the prices of the non-farm goods needed by the farmer remained high. Severe farm depression set in. In 1919, a bushel of corn bought five gallons of gasoline; the following year it bought one.

The early Farm Bureau legislative program focused on packer control measures, higher tariffs for imported farm products, and antitrust exemptions for the growing cooperative marketing movement. There were early legislative failures, but the strength of the united farm lobby coalesced during the 1921 Congress. A bipartisan Farm Bloc in both Houses, strongly backed by a united farm lobby, enacted most of the farm program: packer controls, higher tariffs, and the Capper–Volstead Act—the Magna Charta of cooperatives. The Farm Bureau justifiably claimed partial credit for much of this legislation. But the implications of a private organization, heavily sponsored by the government, trying to influence the policies of that government did not seem to perplex the Farm Bureau or Congress.

The Farm Bureau's early political strength was enhanced by its close relationship to President Warren Harding's Secretary of Agriculture, Henry Wallace, father of Franklin Roosevelt's first Agriculture Secretary. The elder Wallace had been active in establishing the American Farm Bureau Federation, and worked closely with his old associates during his term of office. Kile also gives the Farm Bureau credit for the selection of Wallace's successor in 1924. In fact, a close cordial relationship to most of the successive heads of the Agriculture Department, particularly in the earlier years, has been one of the sources of the Farm Bureau's political strength.

Despite its origin as an educational organization, the Farm Bureau's major goal during the first half of the 1920s was developing its economic muscles. At the organizational meeting of the American Farm Bureau Federation in 1919, there had been a split between the advocates of an education-oriented organization who saw no need for big budgets and heavy fees, and those, particularly the midwesterners, who favored major business operations. Although a compromise was nominally reached, it heavily favored the Midwest view since that region represented about 90 percent of the early Farm Bureau membership.

Enlisting the valuable help of the county agents, the Farm Bureau began to undertake cooperative buying and selling. "Usually the state Farm Bureaus did not enter directly into these activities," explains Kile, "but organized state and county cooperative groups for that purpose and kept varying degrees of control. . . . Holding to this principle has saved embarrassment to the underlying farm organization when some one line of its business operation goes bad."[10]

The impetus for these early business ventures was genuine. Existing business enterprises were unwilling to venture into rural areas. The practical difficulties of distribution and the prevailing view that the farmer was a high credit risk kept business away from the farm. "Farmers in those days generally were having a hard time getting decent feed," explains Murray Lincoln, the driving force behind both the giant Ohio Farm Bureau operation and Nationwide Insurance. "Most of the stuff that was being sold as feed was little more than ground-up leavings off the grain elevator floors—pure rubbish."[11]

Obtaining insurance was another problem for the farmer. Explains Lincoln: "The farmer wasn't getting a fair break in automobile insurance rates. The rates were geared to the number and kind of accidents and claims of urban drivers and really bore no relationship to the experience of rural car owners."[12] Similarly, it was difficult for the farmer to obtain insurance on his investment—his crops and barns—and on his life. So, the Farm Bureau went into the insurance business.

During the last half of the 1920s, the farm crisis deepened, and the attention of the Farm Bureau focused on Congress for relief. The problem was surplus production; their program was passage of the McNary–Haugen bill. This bill would have established a government corporation to dump the surpluses of certain commodities abroad, with the Farm Bureau working as a kind of broker for its members. Congress passed McNary–Haugen but President Coolidge vetoed it. The farmer outcry following the veto contributed to Coolidge's decision not to seek reelection in 1928. The contest that year between Republican Herbert Hoover and Democrat Al Smith provided the clearest choice for farmers since the Bryan–McKinley race in 1896. Smith endorsed the McNary–Haugen bill, and although the American Farm Bureau Federation avoided an official endorsement, many of its leaders campaigned actively and vigorously for Smith. His defeat signalled the demise of the drive for McNary–Haugen.

Hoover's approach to the farm crisis did not differ drastically from his general approach to the collapse throughout the economy. His Federal Farm Board tried to revive agriculture by supporting farmer marketing cooperatives. Although the coops became big business during this period, Hoover's effort to get farmers to voluntarily cut acreage and production was a failure, and the farmers continued to strangle on their own productive skills.

In 1931 the Farm Bureau's third president, Sam Thomson, resigned to accept an appointment to Hoover's Farm Board, and Ed O'Neil, a salty and dapper southerner, began what was to be a most successful seventeen-year presidency. Economist John Kenneth Galbraith, then an editor of *Fortune* magazine and a former staff economist for the American Farm Bureau Federation, described O'Neil near the end of his tenure:

Ed O'Neil was not reared as a dirt farmer and despises the breed of farm politician that so describes itself. He is the grandson of a colonel in the Army of the Confederacy, the owner of the family plantation near Florence, Alabama —in short, a southern gentleman. Educated in natural sciences and law at Washington and Lee, he traveled abroad after graduation in the best tradition of the well-born young Southerner. He still smokes a blend of imported English tobacco, which he mixes to his own taste; he loves good food, good company, and good Scotch whiskey. Many farm audiences have heard him declare that his suit of clothes cost $125 and that other farmers should be privileged to pay as much.[13]

Despite, or perhaps partly because of his flamboyance, O'Neil proved to be one of the most effective political orchestrators in the history of Washington lobbying.

The situation inherited by O'Neil and his powerful vice president, Earl Smith of Iowa, was bleak. Membership had plummeted from about 400,000 to an all-time low of 162,246 by 1933. Gross farm income had fallen to little more than $5 billion in 1932, a drop of $12 billion. Hoover's Farm Board was failing. The farm community was divided by the sectionalism which had flared in conflicts between the South and Midwest on tariffs and the McNary–Haugen bill. O'Neil set out to organize a united farm front and to put together what was to be called the "marriage of corn and cotton."

Although the Farm Bureau did not take an official position on the presidential race in 1932, its preference was clear beyond doubt. A Farm Bureau delegation met with FDR on October 1, 1932, and upon emerging from the meeting O'Neil declared to reporters that "Governor Roosevelt has shown a very sympathetic understanding of the whole farm problem."[14] Roosevelt was the first candidate ever to unequivocally advocate "equity" of income for the farmer compared to his city cousins. Farmers, along with the rest of the country, overwhelmingly supported him on election day.

Conflicting viewpoints have been voiced on the importance of the Farm Bureau's role in shaping the agricultural legislation and policy of the early New Deal. It is clear that O'Neil regarded himself as Roosevelt's agricultural tutor during these days, and FDR at least let him believe so. The official Farm Bureau view, as expressed by Kile, is that the organization was the architect of that early New Deal farm policy. According to Kile, Farm

Bureau special counsel Fred Lee was given the principal responsibility of drawing up the Agricultural Adjustment Act of 1933. In a later and more objective study of the Farm Bureau role in the New Deal, Christiana McFadyen Cambell disputes the notion that the Farm Bureau was an originator of New Deal policy. Its importance, she contends, was that of a unifier of the sectional and interorganizational splits among the farm forces, and the most potent political force behind the wide-ranging farm legislation of the 1930s.

A rising wave of radicalism was building again in farm country, serious enough to prompt Farmers Union President John Simpson to declare that a rural revolution was imminent. The Farmer's Holiday movement, growing in 1933, called for direct action by the farmer—withholding of produce and a general strike. Many spontaneous strikes were erupting, and bank officials arriving to foreclose farm properties were often turned away by angry mobs of farmers. Something had to be done quickly. After encamping friendly Henry Wallace (the younger) in the office of Secretary of Agriculture, the Farm Bureau threw its energies behind the Agricultural Adjustment Act of 1933. O'Neil spearheaded the National Agricultural Conference, a united farm bloc including all the major farm groups, which solidly and strongly supported the emergency measures.

The farm legislation that Congress passed in 1933 was the most ambitious economic planning effort in the country's peacetime history to that date. The Agricultural Adjustment Act gave the Secretary of Agriculture broad powers to raise prices by reducing output. Farmers were to receive cash payments for cutting the acreage used to produce basic commodities, and these payments were to be financed by a tax levied on food processors. Farmers were not *required* to take land out of production, but they were given strong inducements to do so. The goal was to increase the prices received by farmers by reducing production and, accordingly, surpluses. In order to bring immediate benefits, millions of acres of cotton were plowed under and more than six million hogs were slaughtered.

Congress also set up the Commodity Credit Corporation in 1933 to provide federal loans to farmers who had only their farm products as security. By this mechanism, the government acted as a guarantor of a fair return for the farmer: if the market price for his goods went above the value of the loan, the farmer sold his produce and repaid the government, pocketing the difference; if prices fell below the value of the loan, the Commodity Credit Corporation sold the commodities and absorbed the loss. In the meantime, the commodities were placed in government storage.

The Agricultural Administration Agency (AAA) was set up to administer this new program. But because of strong resistance by the Farm Bureau forces and the need for quick implementation, the idea of a strong central agency was abandoned. O'Neil insisted upon decentralized administration of the program, placing major responsibility with the Farm Bureau-favored Extension Service. The AAA proved to be a new lease on life for Extension and correspondingly an anticipated windfall for the Farm Bureau.

As Kile explains: "The strong local Farm Bureau units soon became the logical clearing-houses through which the county and township production-control associations were organized. In hundreds of communities, the local Farm Bureaus, being the only organized group nearby to act, literally took over this job of getting local AAA committees organized, and mobilizing farmer support and participation."[15] Once again, as with the activity of the government in promoting the county agent, the periods of greatest government involvement in agriculture have been the periods of the Farm Bureau's greatest growth.

The new responsibilities under the AAA resulted in a vast expansion of the Extension service. By the end of the decade, only eighty of the country's three thousand counties were without an agent. The Farm Bureau's membership mushroomed along with the Extension service. The AFBF launched a membership drive in the South to capture some of the three million AAA participants before they could be organized into a rival group. The Bureau received considerable support in this effort from the Extension Service. The director of Extension in Alabama granted leaves of absence for members of his staff to work on Farm Bureau membership drives and he used his influence with Extension Directors in other southern states to facilitate smooth working relationships between the Farm Bureau and the Extension Service. The southern membership campaign based on the AAA lifted the southern region of the Farm Bureau from the weakest to the second largest section of the organization. It is now the largest.

The Farm Bureau quickly exploited its unique relationship with the Extension Service, the administering agency of the massive AAA farm program. In some cases, it took credit for the government AAA check itself. On June 1, 1939, the *Washington Daily News* published a letter sent to farmers by a county agent in Alabama using the Extension mailing frank. The letter advised the farmers that their AAA checks were awaiting them in his office and urged them to join the Farm Bureau, implying that the Farm Bureau was responsible for the AAA benefits. Violent protests by the other farm organizations and demands for a Congressional investigation had no effect. By 1934, Farm Bureau leaders were proclaiming that "the Farm Bureau and the AAA are inseparable."[16]

The Farm Bureau's appropriation of the AAA was as much defensive as offensive. Conscious from its own experience of how a government farm program could spin off a national farm organization, the Farm Bureau acted swiftly to avoid such potential rivalry. For example, when a spontaneous movement sprang up among farmers in 1935 to hold a massive demonstration in Washington in support of embattled AAA legislation, the Farm Bureau quickly moved in to seize leadership of the march and head off the formation of an alternative power center.

On January 6, 1936, the Supreme Court handed down its controversial decision in the *Hoosiac Mills* case, declaring the AAA to be unconstitutional. Congress, said the Court, did not have the power to control agricultural production. That was a local matter, for the states. It struck down the federal government's asserted right to enter into voluntary control contracts with the farmers and invalidated the processing tax used to finance the program.

Reaction to this challenge was swift. Within six weeks, with the strong support of the Farm Bureau and with O'Neil still wielding an effective coalition of farm groups, Congress passed the Soil Conservation and Domestic Allotment Act. The Soil Conservation Act, clearly a stop-gap measure to fill the void created by the Court, hung the same kinds of acreage controls and government payments on a new peg—soil conservation. Farmers were given payments not for cutting production, but for cutting the acreage of "soil-depleting crops." An acre by any other name would smell as sweet.

The Soil Conservation Act predictably proved to be another boon to the Farm Bureau. The more than 4,000 local production-control committees —the basic units of the AAA of 1933—were now consolidated into 2,711 "county agricultural conservation associations" along general rather than individual commodity lines. This network was even more suited to the Farm Bureau's organizational pattern than the old AAA program. The county Farm Bureaus, with the ever-obliging assistance of the county agents, quickly gained control of the program at the local level. The Extension agents' activities during this period, in the words of historian Grant McConnell, were "conducted at the end of a leash."[17]

By 1938, the New Deal craftsmen had constructed a more comprehensive replacement for their fallen AAA—the Agricultural Adjustment Act of 1938—the touchstone of all subsequent farm legislation. The soil conservation program was continued under the AAA of 1938, which also authorized establishment of acreage allotments and quotas limiting the quantity of a product which might be marketed if two-thirds of the producers of the commodity favored the quota.

For the first time, the new law formally adopted the term "parity" of income for farmers. Parity is one of those terms—like carburetor, DNA, and the Monroe Doctrine—that you hear but only vaguely understand. As it relates to agriculture it simply reflects the farmers' purchasing power, the relationship of the price of what he sells to the price of the non-farm goods he buys. Parity is useful as a standard to compare how well the farmers are doing from year to year. In order to make this comparison, a basis for comparison is chosen. In the New Deal legislation the period 1909–1914 was chosen as the base since it was a relatively prosperous period for farmers. Full parity then (or 100 percent) is the price the farmer must receive for his goods to give him the same ability to buy non-farm products as he had during the base period. The AAA of 1938 authorized direct payments to the farmers to support this parity.

"Parity" became the Farm Bureau slogan in the 1930s much like McNary–Haugenism had been the decade before. But although the Farm Bureau supported the final legislation in 1938, it urged that parity be achieved by price supports through the commodity loan mechanism, rather than by direct payments from the government to the farmer.

Farm Bureau resistance to direct payment stemmed at least partially from its growing fear that the Department of Agriculture was beginning to assert itself more aggressively in the administration of the government's farm programs. These early fears presaged a deep and eventually open split between the Farm Bureau and the Roosevelt Administration.

The seeds of the struggle between the Farm Bureau and the Department of Agriculture were sown in 1936, with the early efforts of the Department to centralize the sprawling farm program, and consequently deemphasize the role of the Extension Service. By the early 1940s, over the vociferous opposition of the Farm Bureau, USDA had taken over control from the Extension Service of the Rural Electrification Administration, as well as the functions of the AAA.

The split between the USDA and the Farm Bureau was a deep one. Certainly there was a strong element of self-interest in the Farm Bureau's opposition to removing these programs from the purview of the Extension Service, fearing the erosion of a primary source of the Bureau's power. But the deeper reasons for the break lay in the shift in emphasis of the New Deal during the late 1930s. In the closing days of that decade and the early days of the next, a new breed of administrator took over the direction of the Agriculture Department. Younger, often not farmers, their view of the Department of Agriculture's role and the basic direction of the New Deal differed from that of their predecessors. They saw the constituency of the Department as not only commercial farmers, but consumers, other rural people, and subsistence farmers as well. They set out, in McConnell's term, to "democratize" farm programs by dealing directly with farmers, which would obviously decrease the influence of the Farm Bureau. Notes McConnell, "The Department of Agriculture was on its way to emancipation."[18]

With this new activist approach came a new perspective on policy goals. The early New Deal had been an emergency reaction to a dangerous crisis. With the immediate crisis to some extent passed, the New Dealers sought more fundamental social reforms. In the Department of Agriculture, this took the form of the Farm Security Administration. The FSA was the Roosevelt Administration's most extensive effort to face the problems of the rural poor, the subsistence farmer, and the rural black man, particularly in the South. The Farm Bureau claims and deserves credit for destroying the Farm Security Administration.

The FSA, launched in 1937, was a promising and far-reaching social experiment, outside the mainstream of the general farm policy. The basic thrust of the New Deal agricultural policy had been rehabilitation—restoring the depressed landowner to his pre-Depression level through the existing framework of price and credit mechanisms. There had been some activity aimed at those who had been down-and-out even before the Depression, namely the Resettlement Administration which set up some subsistence homesteads, but this was small in scale and chiefly for the urban poor.

The Farm Security Administration was created as a "poor man's Department of Agriculture," directed toward the lower third of the country's population. FSA attempted to change the existing social order somewhat by giving tenants and sharecroppers what we would call today "a piece of the action."

The FSA sought to assist existing subsistence farmers through the use of loans supervised by FSA local personnel (note the decision to avoid the Extension network). It encouraged farm ownership by seeking Congressional authorization for long-term (40-year) loans at 3 percent to tenants and sharecroppers to enable them to buy family-size farms. It went to work to improve conditions for migrants. Its most controversial undertaking, and the one that was to be its undoing, was the organization of "resettlement projects," cooperative agricultural operations for the poor. The FSA focused on the South and on the blacks, a departure which called for no little political courage, especially at that time. The Farm Bureau, fearful of the attempt to root farm workers on their own land and anxious about the emergence of a rival power base, launched a multiple warhead against FSA. It undertook a hasty investigation in 1941 calculated to discover a scandal. It particularly seized upon the "resettlement projects" (only 9 percent of the FSA financially), and characterized them as socialist schemes, comparing them to Russian "kolkozes." And it perpetrated the argument that FSA's clients should not be helped: "The two million smallest farms consumed (themselves) on the average of about one-half of their production . . . and sent only $100 worth of products to market. The group produced only about 3 percent of the marketed crops. They do not have the land, facilities, or labor to produce large quantities of food."[19] The Farm Bureau kept up an incessant barrage against FSA in Congress until, by the mid-1940s, it had successfully destroyed it.

As long as the New Deal had been aimed at recovery and relief, and stayed within the old traditions, the Farm Bureau went along. Even the most prosperous farmers were suffering from the depression, and the seemingly drastic measures of the early New Deal simply restored their position. When the New Deal turned the corner toward more fundamental reform, the Farm Bureau got off. "Worry increased," explains Kile about the Farm Bureau attitude in the closing days of the 30s, "over what Farm

Bureau heads called unsound banking and a tendency toward charity and social objectives—as exemplified by the loans being made by the Farm Security Administration." The Farm Bureau became disturbed over what it termed, "the confusion and loss of confidence created by an impractical and wasteful bureaucracy more concerned with social experimentation than the production of food."[20]

The battle over the Farm Security Administration was part of a larger war to resist the new direction of the Agriculture Department. At the 1940 American Farm Bureau Federation convention, a formal resolution was passed calling for decentralizing of the USDA. Essentially, the proposed plan would have divided the Department of Agriculture and the government's farm policy into 48 separate fiefdoms. The Farm Bureaus' plan called for committees in each state to coordinate the AAA, the commodity loan program, the soil conservation program and the federal crop insurance program. Each state committee was to be composed of individuals selected by a federal board from nominations by the state director of Extension "after consultation with statewide membership farm organizations." The purpose of the Farm Bureau's proposal was obvious to James Patton, president of the Farmers Union. The Farm Bureau plan, he said, "would turn the [Agricultural Adjustment] Administration into a company union for the Farm Bureau, especially in the eleven states where the county agent and the Farm Bureau are officially linked together."[21]

The Farm Bureau's assault on the Agriculture Department had other targets besides the Farm Security Administration. Blitzes were launched against the network of land-use planning committees which might provide the nucleus for a rival organization, and the Farm Credit Administration and AAA, both of which had been taken over from the Extension Service by the Agriculture Department. The Farm Bureau's success in slowing, if not crippling these programs during the early 1940s was stunning. "Their remarkable success was possible," says McConnell, "only because of the single-mindedness of Bureau leaders at a time when most of the other people in the country were preoccupied with a quite different war."[22]

Their success was also due in part to the organization's mastery of the lobbying art and O'Neil's political craftsmanship. Kile describes the scene of an O'Neil performance before a Congressional committee:

President O'Neil is headline witness and the master of ceremonies. Before taking his seat at the long, shining mahogany conference table, and before the

Chairman had called the committee to order, Mr. O'Neil had shaken hands and passed a few pleasantries with each of the Committee Members present. These are mostly old friends, or at least acquaintances, even though some of them may not be friendly to the particular proposal O'Neil is bringing before them. Without exception, all committee members are fully aware of the strength of the Farm Bureau in their home states, and of the personal power of the Farm Bureau head should he care to exercise it in their respective states.[23]

About this time, Washington observer William Kipplinger called the Farm Bureau "the smartest, best turned-out lobby in Washington." According to *Fortune* magazine at the time, "it nearly always gets what it goes after."[24]

Much of the Farm Bureau's legislative success during this period was the result of O'Neil's success in forging a compromise between previously warring interests—both commodity and sectional—within his organization. The high point of this fusion was reached in 1941, with the Farm Bureau-inspired enactment by Congress of a fixed loan rate at 85 percent parity for the basic crops. O'Neil masterfully engineered a united front between the cotton South, which favored tighter production controls and high loan rates, and the corn-producing Midwest, which was less concerned about higher market prices but strongly opposed controls on production.

The new unity between corn and cotton also produced a shift from the Farm Bureau's traditional high tariff policies. The South had always been generally internationalist (cotton is sold widely on the world market), but the Midwest had been historically isolationist in its farm policies (corn is primarily sold domestically). With the increasing problem of surplus and the easing of the midwestern domination of the Farm Bureau, O'Neil was able in the 1930s to ease the farm group toward a more internationalist position. The shift was capped by Farm Bureau support for Secretary of State Cordell Hull's Reciprocal Trade Agreements. By the end of World War II the Farm Bureau had become unabashedly internationalist. During the 1940s it endorsed the United Nations and International Monetary Fund. The Bureau had become increasingly aware (and remains so today)—that the health of the farm economy was inextricably bound up with conditions—agricultural and otherwise—around the world.

The Farm Bureau also maintained its exquisite cross-ruff with the Extension Service throughout this period. Utilizing the strength it had derived largely from its long association with the Extension programs, the Farm

Bureau labored endlessly on behalf of that program in Congress. Its string of victories in this area further strengthened the hand of the county agent, which in turn strengthened the Farm Bureau even more. "The land grant colleges and extension services expressed their appreciation," says Kile, "of the big increases in funds made possible by Farm Bureau efforts."[25]

With the end of the War, the Farm Bureau revived its campaign to wrench control over the farm programs from USDA, and place it in the hands of Extension. In 1946, encouraged by its ultimate triumph over the Farm Security Administration, and its successes in limiting the land-use planning committees, the organization turned its fire on the Soil Conservation Service, which, like the Bureau's other targets, had the audacity to deal directly with farmers. By this time, however, hostility to the Farm Bureau–Extension alliance was growing, and Bureau leaders were less successful with these new demands.

Nevertheless, the Farm Bureau continued to treat the government-financed Extension Service as its own palace guard during the 1940s. In 1943, faced with a scarce wartime labor market, the Farm Bureau succeeded in bringing the farm labor program under the control of the Extension Service, thus placing itself at a considerable advantage over other farm groups. In 1947, in a pattern that has been repeated in substance since, the Farm Bureau demanded a 20 percent cut in all government spending, including the Department of Agriculture, with the notable exception of the Extension Service.

As the Farm Bureau and the Roosevelt Administration grew further apart during the 1940s, a basic realignment of political interests was taking place. Although never particularly enthusiastic about the labor movement, the Farm Bureau had maintained a loose coalition with it in the mid-1930s based on the pragmatic principle of non-interference with each other's vital interests. Urban labor votes in Congress had passed the AAA in 1938, in exchange for Farm Bureau agreement to limit its opposition to the Wage and Hours Act to exacting an exception for farm labor. A parity payment appropriations bill in 1939 had been dramatically saved from defeat by the eleventh hour intervention of New York City Mayor Fiorello La Guardia. In return, he received Farm Bureau support for a labor-backed measure to eliminate the $50,000 limit on WPA projects. During the early post-War years, however, the Farm Bureau shifted to active opposition to labor's interests, strongly supporting the Taft–Hartley Act in 1947. The organization has emerged today as a vocal and powerful anti-union force.

Bureau support was generally regarded as crucial to the passage of the other major union-restricting legislation since Taft–Hartley—the Landrum–Griffin Act. It has been a bulwark against repeal of section 14b of the Taft–Hartley Act—a perennial demand of organized labor which would remove from the statute books the authorization for states to pass "right to work" laws prohibiting the union shop. The Farm Bureau has bombarded state legislatures calling for such "right to work" laws. Shuman and former-president Allan Kline have both been members of the Citizens' Committee to Preserve Taft–Hartley, organized to resist repeal of 14b. Most recently, the Farm Bureau worked feverishly to defeat the provisions of the Postal Reform Act of 1970 which authorized the union shop for postal workers.

AFBF opposition to such other minimum indices of 20th century industrial enlightenment as the minimum wage, fair labor standards and child labor laws has not endeared it to organized labor through the years. Nor has its resistance to compulsory unionism, industry-wide bargaining, secondary boycotts, or the National Labor Relations Board, whose functions it seeks to shift to the courts. The most explosive battleline between labor and the Farm Bureau today is the unionization of farm workers and the Farm Bureau's fight against it.

At the same time that labor was suing the Farm Bureau for divorce in the late 1940s, the united farm front, so effective during the 30s, was beginning to break up, a split that has lasted to the present. The National Farmers Union vigorously supported the Farm Security Administration as well as other agencies coming under Farm Bureau attack. The Bureau's exploitation of the Extension service, always a thorn in good relations among the farm groups, increased the tension. The Farmers Union, more sympathetic to labor, also broke with the Farm Bureau over the latter's demand that price controls during the War be linked to wage controls. A realignment of interests gradually emerged, pitting the Farm Bureau against the Administration, the Farmers Union and the labor unions; the Grange, at this point, still sided with the Farm Bureau more often than not.

With the end of Ed O'Neil's long stewardship in 1947, the Farm Bureau had come a long way from its Depression nadir. It now had more than a million members, compared with 160,000 in 1933. It was organized in all but three states. Most of its state units were well financed, and already had full-time staffs. The Farm Bureau's hold on the county agent was still firm.

Although the primary thrust of O'Neil's administration was legislative, the business side of the organization also grew tremendously during these years. What had started in the late 1920s as a bootstrap insurance operation in a few states had grown into a network of insurance companies with more than $100 million in assets by the end of O'Neil's reign.

With the election in 1947 of Allan Kline, a conservative Iowan, the Farm Bureau's generation of agri-business executive leaders took charge. Writes Kile: "Iowa being at or near the top of Farm Bureau membership and scope of Farm Bureau sponsored business, Mr. Kline acquired extensive experience in the business side of farm organization activities. In fact, his office in Des Moines was credited with being one of the largest in point of dollar volume of business handled, and certainly one of the most diversified in interests, of any in that city."[26]

One of president Kline's first actions in 1947 was to establish a separate insurance department in the parent American Farm Bureau Federation, which soon spawned the AFBF's own American Agricultural Insurance Company. Kline was also an agri-businessman with a world view. In a postwar economy, he recognized the need to develop the country's world markets for agricultural products. During his presidency and later, he travelled widely in the interest of expanding U.S. agricultural markets.

The 1948 convention in Atlantic City proved to be a turning point in Farm Bureau history. Although the organization had been edging away from support of the government's general farm program for some time, after strenuous debate a clean break was made. This decision caused a rupture in the Farm Bureau's relations with other farm groups which has not healed to this day. It also marked the beginning of the Farm Bureau's continuing crusade to purge the federal government from agriculture, to return the farm economy to the "free market."

The Farm Bureau proposed a halt to the high fixed-price supports that had been enacted in 1941 and extended into the post-war years. In their place, the Bureau advocated a variable price support program. Essentially, variable price supports are intended to work like this: As production increases, surplus increases. When this happens, supports will be decreased in order to discourage production, and cut surpluses. The process is intended to work in the reverse also.

Congress, with strong support from the Farm Bureau, flirted with such flexible price supports in 1948, but ultimately extended the high rigid supports to the end of the 1940s. In 1949, President Harry Truman's Secretary of Agriculture, Charles Brannan (later general counsel to the National Farmers Union) proposed a drastic shift in government farm policy. The "Brannan Plan" would have scrapped the concept of parity price and computed price supports on an income standard, providing direct payments to some farmers instead of commodity loans. It called for higher supports and tighter production controls, involving the government more deeply in agriculture. This scheme was so repugnant to the Farm Bureau that it put aside its variable support policy for the time being and backed the rigid supports in order to defeat the proposal.

With the election in 1952 of President Dwight Eisenhower, and his appointment of Ezra Taft Benson as Secretary of Agriculture, the Farm Bureau regained an influence over farm policy unknown since the early days of the New Deal. Benson was a strong advocate of the Extension Service, and its role expanded during his tenure. Some of the farm action programs —SCS, REA, and FHA—were circumscribed, to the benefit of the Extension Service and the Farm Bureau.

Relations between Benson and the Farm Bureau could not have been warmer. According to former AFBF vice president Walter Randolph, Benson was "the greatest Secretary of Agriculture in history." Benson proclaimed that his policies "are closely in line with those long advocated by the American Farm Bureau Federation." Or, as one of his aides put it: "We try to start out with our programs being independent of all the farm pressure groups, but we usually end up buying just about what the Farm Bureau advocates."[27] That they bought what the Farm Bureau advocated is clear; that they started out independent of farm pressure groups is open to some question.

In 1954 the Benson–Farm Bureau alliance succeeded in dumping high, rigid price supports for the Farm Bureau-favored flexible ones, to sink as low as 60 percent of parity. The general argument put forth during the 1950s for the Benson–Farm Bureau campaign to sharply curtail acreage controls and price supports went as follows: All the major difficulties in agriculture can be traced to government intervention. High fixed price supports encourage unmanageable surpluses, price our goods out of the foreign market, and keep the farmers from adjusting to market demands. If government restrictions on production were eliminated, farmers would adjust their output to meet the needs of the marketplace.

The argument proved to be wrong. Despite lower price supports and eased production controls, output actually increased, and by 1960 there was enough wheat in government storage bins to meet the needs of the country for two years. Government-owned stocks of farm commodities increased from $1.3 billion in 1952 to $7.7 billion in 1957. In the meantime, tens of thousands of farmers were "adjusted" out of business.

During the Kennedy–Johnson Administrations, the Farm Bureau's role shifted back to that of the vocal opposition, as Secretary of Agriculture Orville Freeman attempted to increase price supports and production controls in order to cut the increasing surpluses. Sliding further to the right, the Farm Bureau began to blast the government programs as "socialist" schemes. Freeman himself came under a constant barrage of bitter and often personal attacks from the Farm Bureau.

The most dramatic confrontation between the Kennedy Administration and the Farm Bureau occurred over the 1963 wheat referendum. Frustrated by an ineffective voluntary production control program, under which farmers were not required to participate and limit their acreage, the Kennedy Administration proposed mandatory controls for wheat and feed grains. By law, such a step required a referendum and approval by two-thirds of the producers of the affected commodities. The Administration campaigned strenuously for the proposal; President Kennedy went on television to personally urge farmers to approve it.

The Farm Bureau mounted a massive campaign against the proposal. Predicting the loss of individual freedom at the hands of an overbearing and omnipotent government, the Farm Bureau effectively turned the vote into a crusade for freedom, and defeated the proposal. Farmers later reported receiving literature, for example, showing a picture of Russian leaders seated around a Kremlin table, and carrying the unmistakable message that a vote for the Administration proposal was an invitation for this kind of totalitarianism. It was a stunning and typical victory for the Farm Bureau. Typical in that the Farm Bureau counted its successes during the Kennedy–Johnson years more in terms of what it stopped than what it began.

Much of the credit for the defeat of the referendum goes to the president of the American Farm Bureau at that time, Charles Shuman. Elected to re-place Kline in 1955 Shuman stepped down in December, 1970. He describes himself as a "freedom fighter for American agriculture." His fight takes on the trappings of a crusade. Between 1955 and 1970, Shuman traveled widely around the country, and during most of the 1960s his role was that of unqualified critic of the Kennedy–Johnson farm policies. His intensifying attacks on Freeman prompted one farm journal, the *Nebraska Farmer,* to comment: "We're getting to the place where we wonder about Charles B. Shuman's purpose in life. As head of the nation's largest farm organiza-tion, . . . Shuman should be fighting for farmers, it seems to us. But Shu-man's actions seem more and more to be aimed primarily at fighting Secretary of Agriculture Freeman, the Kennedy Administration and the Democrats in general."[28]

Shuman is a pleasant, deliberate man who neatly straddles the worlds of business and farming. An honors graduate with a Master's degree from the University of Illinois, he is comfortable talking the language of the agri-cultural economist. He can also talk easily with business executives, since he headed seven national business operations as president of the Farm Bu-reau. His homespun manner and craggy face are a constant reminder of his farm roots, and he frequently emphasizes his points with "in my county," or "on my farm." His farm—to which he returned after his resig-nation—is a thousand-acre spread, about 170 miles from AFBF's Chicago headquarters. A *Time* magazine cover story a few years ago portrayed Shuman dressed in denim overalls, wading through the cornfields.[29]

Shuman is a deeply conservative American. He neither smokes nor drinks, and at one time taught Methodist Sunday school. A confirmed ideo-logue, he traveled more than 75,000 miles a year as AFBF president, speaking several times a week in his "crusade" to save no less than the very freedom of the American farmer from an encroaching government. He calls the Farm Bureau staff "agriculture's freedom fighters."

"The competitive market price system is based on the survival of the fit," preaches Shuman, "which is one of the fundamental laws of the uni-verse." He traces most of the country's ills, including the "moral decay in America," to the continuing shift of responsibility to the government. He writes off the entire New Deal, Fair Deal, New Frontier, and Great Society as "ridiculous" attempts to "remake the world," as "welfare state planning programs based on the false 'new economics' theories that the economy could be 'fine tuned' and managed by Washington bureaucrats." "Planning," he contends, "is often a favorite tool for the left-wing liberals who want to replace the market system with socialistic management of production, prices and people." Indeed, Shuman's adherence to Adam Smith has taken him to the point of declaring that a free market economy is a God-given moral law, and that "when we turn to government to negate economic truth, and to avoid adjustments that are demanded by changing conditions, we are, in reality, rejecting God's law in favor of man's law."[30]

One of God's laws that seems to be revolutionizing argiculture today is contract farming, and the Farm Bureau has become a true believer. This may be because the National Farmers Organization, which is organized around the idea of collective bargaining for farmers, has been cutting into Farm Bureau membership lately. Or it may be because of Farm Bureau estimates that by 1979, half of all farming in this country will be done by contract.

The clearest example of contract farming today is the poultry business, which previously consisted of independent poultry farmers. Now, the giant companies that supply the feed to the poultrymen—Pillsbury, Ralston–Purina, and a few others—control the whole process. They have vertically integrated the industry. The farmer becomes a contract grower by agreeing ahead of time to sell his chickens to the company according to standards supplied by them. The company supplies the capital, the chicks, the feed, the veterinary care, and the equipment. About 90 percent of the broilers sold in the United States today are raised under such contracts with only five giant companies.

This arrangement begins to look very much like an industrial operation, with the farmer as employee, instead of entrepreneur. For many of these contract farmers, as well as for thousands of unorganized producers with little power, the Farm Bureau is attempting to assume the role of bargaining agent. "We are convinced," wrote AFBF secretary-treasurer Fleming, in his annual report for 1968, "that producing under contract on the basis of specification is the wave of the future, and the contracting producers need to be organized to strengthen their bargaining power."[31] To president Shuman, this means a call for greater expansion of the Farm Bureau: "We are only in the kindergarten stages of our marketing effort," he claims modestly.

With the election of President Richard Nixon, the Farm Bureau believed that an administration more closely attuned to its farm policy had come to Washington. Farm Bureau leaders were convinced that the battle over the government farm program was won and that all that remained was the question of how long it would take to sweep away the debris. They were encouraged in this belief by the increasing weariness of urban liberals in Congress—the group that had traditionally helped to carry the farm programs—with the annual agricultural outlays which they now felt could be better spent in the cities.

But despite some early statements which appeared to align the Administration with the Farm Bureau on this issue, Nixon's Secretary of Agriculture Clifford Hardin ultimately backed what was essentially an extension of the existing programs for three more years. Such an extension was passed by Congress in 1970. The legislation was strongly backed by most of the country's farm organizations except the Farm Bureau. However, as long as the fundamental split exists in the farm lobby between the Farm Bureau and the other organizations, while the farm constituency continues to shrink, future prospects for Farm Bureau victory on basic farm policy remain bright. The Farm Bureau leadership envisions the government farm program as eventually withering away. A victory by attrition, they feel, is no less a victory.

The Farm Bureau enters the 1970s with a new national president. After 16 years of leadership, Charles Shuman resigned as president of the American Farm Bureau Federation at the end of 1970. He told the Federation convention that "the major battles are over and it is time for old generals to just fade away."[32] The new general is William Kuhfuss, who rose to the top position by same route as Shuman, stepping up from president of the powerful Illinois state organization. As president of the Illinois operations, Kuhfuss effectively directed the affairs of that half-billion dollar business network and his business experience played a large role in his selection.

The 58-year-old Kuhfuss, who looks like he just stepped off the train from a 35th-year Princeton reunion, is the seventh president of the giant organization. With his election, the Farm Bureau has shed even the denim overalls.

8

Divorce, Farm Bureau Style

THE HISTORY of the Farm Bureau is so interwoven with the history of the Extension Service that it is impossible to sketch the evolution of one without some discussion of the other. For fifty years the Farm Bureau has enjoyed a comfortable symbiosis with the public program, supplying some of its funds and unwavering political support in exchange for the services of the county agents. Decades after specific direction from Washington to the contrary, the county agents still aided Farm Bureau membership drives, edited its publications, promoted its businesses, and resided in its offices. In return, the Farm Bureau supplied millions of dollars to the county agents and campaigned actively each year in county, state and national legislatures for healthy government appropriations for Extension. Today, despite almost fifty years of effort on the part of critics of the relationship, and repeated edicts from generations of Department of Agriculture and Extension officials, the Farm Bureau continues to enjoy a favored relationship with the government Extension Service in large parts of the country.

This unique arrangement, of course, thrust the county agent into an untenable double role for many years. He was a public employee with a duty to serve all farmers equally. At the same time he was receiving some of his salary from a partisan, private farm organization that was competing with other farm organizations for members and with other businesses for the farmer's dollars. Frequently, when his two masters differed on policy, the county Extension agent found himself in an impossible dilemma. Even messages from the national Farm Bureau leadership to local bureaus calling on them to exert pressure on their Congressmen were sometimes transmitted through the Extension agents.[1] As a result, generations of farmers in many regions of the country grew up believing that the county agent was an adjunct to the county Farm Bureau, and that government-sponsored programs like the popular 4–H groups for farm youth were actually Farm Bureau programs.

By the 1920s the Smith–Lever Act and World War I had combined to stimulate the institution of county agents in nearly every rural county. In those early days the county agent was so busy building his Farm Bureau constituency that he had little time for members of other farm organizations, or the resolutely independent. The mounting chorus of dissent to this practice resulted in an agreement signed in 1921 by Dr. A. C. True, head of the State Relations Board (predecessor of Federal Extension Service) and American Farm Bureau President James Howard. The "True–Howard" memorandum stipulated that county agents were

to perform service for the benefit of all the farming people of the country, whether members of the farm bureau or not. . . . They will not themselves organize farm bureaus or similar organizations, conduct membership campaigns, solicit memberships, receive dues, handle farm bureau funds, edit and manage the farm bureau publications, manage the business of the farm bureau, engage in commercial activities or take part in other farm bureau activities which are outside their duties as extension agent.[2]

The exhaustive enumeration of forbidden acts underscored the degree of existing involvement by county agents in Farm Bureau affairs. This mutual understanding should have been the end of the story. The official pronouncement, however, was only the first of a long stream of disregarded statements that formed a paper curtain around the alliance. The following year, 1922, Secretary of Agriculture Henry C. Wallace enshrined the "Understanding" in departmental regulations which applied to all county agents. Those regulations carefully pointed out, however, that they were not intended to prevent contributions from private organizations to the Extension Service, nor to discourage Extension from accepting them.

In 1923, the present structure of the Extension Service began to take shape with the creation of a national office of Extension under a Director of Extension Service. That office, however, as it was created and has evolved, is one of the weakest in Washington in terms of its ability to control its constituent parts. It operates under a "Memorandum of Understanding" with the Land Grant colleges dating back to 1914, and providing for "joint supervision" of the Extension program. Through the years there has been far more attention to "joint" than to "supervision." The attitude is only slightly different from what it was in the 1930s when an Extension official explained: "Rarely, if ever, is pressure exerted by the federal government on the state to adopt the federal viewpoint on extension work. . . . It is believed better that a state learn by its mistakes than for the federal government to insist on a piece of work or a method the state does not believe in."[3]

This is not to say that the federal authorities lacked the powers needed to enforce their policies if they had so desired. The Smith–Lever Act authorized the Secretary of Agriculture to withhold funds from any state misapplying or misusing them. The Secretary has the power, routinely exercised, of approving the appointment of state Extension directors who are initially selected by the governing boards of the state colleges. And although the county agents are appointed by the local sponsoring body upon recommendation by the state Extension office, the Federal Director of Extension has the rarely used power of final review. He also reviews and approves state programs and budgets. As a practical matter, however, these powers are encrusted by years of non-use, and the center of gravity of the Extension Service is still safely embedded at the state and local level.

As we have seen, the Farm Bureau and Extension marched hand in hand through the 1920s and 30s, overwhelming the AAA program, and turning their fire toward the Department of Agriculture when Extension was threatened. The 1930s, with the overlap of the Farm Bureau, Extension and the AAA, produced particularly blatant abuses: misuse of the Extension franking privilege for pro-Farm Bureau mailings; taking Farm Bureau dues directly out of AAA checks; and widespread recruitment of Farm Bureau members by county agents.[4]

Then came the widely publicized "Alabama incident" in 1939. A Washington paper reprinted a letter from a county agent strongly implying that the farmer should show his appreciation for his government check by joining the Farm Bureau. Opponents of the relationship between the Farm Bureau and Extension were appalled. The Grange demanded action. The federal Extension Director said he had no power. He requested that the state Director investigate. In the end, the agent was "reprimanded."

The Grange turned to Congress for more meaningful action to separate the Farm Bureau from Extension, but its efforts failed because of insufficient support.

As the Farm Bureau intensified its attacks on the Farm Security Administration, the government administration of price supports, and the reorganization of the Agriculture Department, new allies were gradually converted to the cause of separation. During the 1940s, they concentrated mainly on preventing the Farm Bureau–Extension alliance from overrunning the entire farm program.

In 1945, Secretary of Agriculture Clinton Anderson called for a national study of Extension by a joint committee named by himself and the Association of Land Grant Colleges and Universities. Over the protests of some Farm Bureau supporters, the study Committee concluded: "It is not sound public policy for extension to give preferred service to any farm organization." It recommended that the "formal operating relationship . . . be discontinued." However, the Committee went on to recommend that the "initiative" on the matter be left to the Farm Bureau leaders and the Extension officials in the states. The report was duly adopted by the Land Grant college association, but the sentiment of one Extension director present at that session was doubtless widespread: "When we get all through, each state will do as it pleases until Congress or some other authority forces a change."[5]

During the time of Secretary Anderson's study committee, the Agricultural Activities Task Force of the Hoover Commission was also conducting an examination of the Extension Service. The chairman of this committee, however, was Dean H. P. Rusk, of the University of Illinois, a prominent advocate of the Farm Bureau–Extension tie. Rusk wrote the entire committee report himself, seeing to it that the report completely ignored the Farm Bureau's domination of Extension.

In the late 1940s, support for separation began to appear within the Federal Extension Service itself and among some of the Land Grant colleges. The Washington headquarters of Extension, as well as some of the colleges, began to grow more sensitive about their affiliation with a private organization that was becoming increasingly embroiled in partisan disputes. In 1947, the Federal Extension Service became at least a nominal supporter of separation. In a report that year, it described the extent of the problem: in nearly 400 counties in 13 states the county agents were being paid at least in part by the Farm Bureau and were collecting Farm Bureau membership dues or keeping membership records. In 56 other counties, the agent did similar kinds of work for the Farm Bureau, although he reportedly did not receive any remuneration from the group. In 177 reported counties, the sign over the Extension office read, "Farm Bureau office."[6] This was the situation in 1947—twenty-six years after the True–Howard agreement had called for an end to such activities.

The Farm Bureau's fight against the Brannan Plan and its active support of Taft–Hartley led many urban liberals in Congress to support the movement to cut the Farm Bureau off from Extension. In 1949, the liberal Americans for Democratic Action joined forces with the separationists. This fresh support was marshalled by the other farm groups in a renewed campaign for Congressional action in 1950. Representative Walter Granger of Utah introduced a bill to separate the two entities. The bill detailed the particulars: no private donations to Extension that bestow personal benefits on the donor; no non-governmental activities by the agents; no farm organizations serving as cooperating bodies; no preferential treatment among farmers; no political activities for county agents.

But the emerging coalition was still no match for the Farm Bureau. The organization rolled out its arsenal. Armed with a resolution passed the previous year by its delegates which advocated that "the relationship of Extension to farm organizations should be left entirely to state determination,"[7] the Bureau's political strategists trooped twenty state presidents before the committee hearing testimony on the bill. Nearly every state represented on the committee was represented in the parade of Farm Bureau presidents. Each president, as he started his testimony, undoubtedly cited the Farm Bureau membership in that state. It was probably unnecessary; the Congressman from that state knew. The bill was shelved.

In the early 1950s, a new and significant development began to emerge. Some of the state Farm Bureaus, faced with old state statutes declaring them "public institutions" because of their tie to Extension, found that these regulations now had the effect of prohibiting certain of their business activities, or preempting their right to be included in state or national federations. Some of these state Farm Bureaus began to move away from rigid opposition to separation, taking a neutral position. Some even supported it. With the Farm Bureau obstacle removed in these states, their legislatures in many cases revoked the statutes that required Extension to be tied to the Farm Bureau, thus freeing the Bureau to pursue its business interests without hindrance.

The realization that the relationship might be a liability for both parties began to creep into Washington with the administration of Ezra Taft Benson at the Agriculture Department. Benson was only slightly less enamored with Extension than he was with the Farm Bureau. It seems paradoxical, at first, that total separation, on paper at least, was ordered by such a partisan. But Benson, and ultimately the Farm Bureau itself, came to believe that the tie was doing more harm than good.

Benson's efforts to decentralize the Department of Agriculture and place more responsibility with Extension were meeting angry opposition because of the advantages many felt would thereby fall to the Farm Bureau. It was now thirty-three years after the first official declaration prescribing fair treatment for all farmers, nine years after the Department of Agriculture had adopted separation as official, if toothless, policy. But the other farm organizations continued to allege that fair treatment and separation were bureaucratic illusions. Roy Battles of the Grange charged in 1954 that "in some states these two groups are practically synonymous. Where this is the situation, farmers who do not belong to the Farm Bureau receive mighty little, if any help from Extension workers. . . . Women in these areas are not permitted to sing, or are unwelcome, in Extension choral groups unless their Farm Bureau dues are paid."[8] According to James Patton of the National Farmers Union: "The aggregate of time devoted by publicly paid Extension Service employees to membership campaigns, sale of insurance, promotion of livestock, commission houses and other business enterprises, writing and editing columns, attending and carrying delegates to meetings and other improper activities on behalf of the Farm Bureau unquestionably aggregates hundreds of thousands if not millions of dollars annually."[9]

This bitter and intense feeling on the part of the other farm groups, supported by a widening base of non-farm liberals, presented Benson with a troublesome obstacle to his plan to reinforce Extension. The Farm Bureau itself, particularly because it had a sympathetic administration in power, eased away from rigid opposition to separation. Benson–Farm Bureau programs, such as flexible price supports, were in jeopardy because of the emotions aroused over the organization's ties to Extension. Moreover, the growing Farm Bureau business empire decreased the dependence of the organization on Extension for its strength. The entire issue was becoming the Farm Bureau's Achilles heel and, as one historian concluded in his study on the separation movement, "a minor and already diminishing objective was sacrificed to the major goal."[10] In 1954, the AFBF's John Lynn told the House Agriculture Committee that the Farm Bureau approved the recent separations in some of the states, thus signaling the end of the Farm Bureau's long and successful opposition.

Any lingering hesitation on Benson's part vanished with the 1954 Congressional elections. The Democrats gained a majority in both Houses, and Congressmen who favored separation would be ascending to the chairmanships of some key committees. Unless the Secretary of Agriculture acted soon himself, the initiative would have been taken by Congress.

Thus, in November 1954, Benson issued Memorandum #1368, which applied to all employees of the Department of Agriculture. It stipulated that no employee should: accept the use of free office space or travel expenses from a farm organization; advocate a particular organization; advocate that activities of any particular federal, state or local agency should be carried out by a particular farm organization; or solicit membership for an organization, directly or indirectly.[11]

The reaction of the other organizations to the announcement of the Memo was guarded. After all, this was beginning to take on the aura of an old movie seen again and again on the late show. The Farm Bureau was not terribly flapped; Charles Shuman, at that time president of the Illinois state organization where Extension and Farm Bureau were the most closely linked, confided that "it went a little farther than I anticipated, and farther than I wished it would. If this eventually results in the complete separation of Farm Bureau and Extension in Illinois, then the first question I would ask is who is going to put up the one million dollars the ninety-nine county farm bureaus are supplying annually. I haven't heard any suggestions along that line yet."[12]

The reaction of the rest of the Farm Bureau organization was generally conciliatory. Perhaps they could foresee that they would have their cake and eat it, with the Memo taking the sting out of the opposition while being enforced as timidly as its long line of predecessors. They were reinforced in this view by Benson himself who pointed out the absence of deadlines in the Memo and admitted that "there is no disposition to make it hard on anyone . . . since there is no hurry involved and no deadlines.

... I am sure it will work out all right."[13] Not a particularly two-fisted attitude to bring to the enforcement of a policy already on the books for more than thirty years. In fact, Mr. Benson's confidence was misplaced. Today, seventeen years after his Memo, although the situation has been corrected in some states, the Farm Bureau still retains special ties to Extension in several other important farming states.

To see what has happened since the Benson Memo, let us focus on Illinois, the home of the AFBF's headquarters. Illinois has the largest state Farm Bureau membership, with more than 190,000 family members, and historically it has been the most intertwined with Extension. Not surprisingly, the immediate reaction on the part of the Illinois Extension officials charged with implementing the Benson Memo was to establish a committee to study it. From the beginning, it became clear that Illinois Extension had no intention of more than token compliance. At an early meeting of Illinois Extension to discuss the issue, the only specific alternative to direct private contributions from the Farm Bureau brought up was "possible contributions by farm organizations to the College of Agriculture."[14] The college would then "reassign" the funds to support Extension programs.

This device, a transparent evasion of the Memo, was eventually adopted in Illinois to circumvent the ban on direct payments to Extension agents from local Farm Bureaus. The University of Illinois organized "County Councils" to replace the local Farm Bureaus as sponsoring agencies, but these councils usually remained dominated by Farm Bureau members. All funds from county Farm Bureaus were thus channeled to the University as "grants."

The slipperiness of this transaction is evident when viewed in its entirety. County agents, called "farm advisors" in Illinois, remained housed in Farm Bureau-owned buildings. The county Farm Bureaus, forbidden by the Benson Memo from supplying free office space, "charged" the University rent for the office space used by the agents. A portion of the county Farm Bureau's grant to the University was returned to the county Farm Bureau to pay for this rent. This was their solution to the "no free rent" directive. In this case, the Farm Bureau and the Extension Service in Illinois were partners in an obvious conspiracy to circumvent the official policy of the federal government.

In a similar manner, local officials handled the matter of the Farm

Bureau's control over the county agents. A former Illinois farm advisor sent Representative Resnick a series of letters in which he related in detail his experiences after the Benson Memo. He was notified during the 1955–1956 period that he was being released after six years as an Extension agent because the county Farm Bureau would no longer pay part of his salary. The county Farm Bureau president came to him and told him that the organization had decided to dismiss him at a special meeting. A few days later, he received official word of his release from the University of Illinois. He explained: "The University made a big fuss (because of Benson's memo . . .) about how they did all the hiring and firing. But the truth is somewhat different. The University of Illinois would send a number of qualified . . . men to a given county and the local (county) Farm Bureau would take the guy they liked and could come to terms with on salary. When it came to firing, the official word came to the advisor from the University of Illinois, but only after the decision had been made by the Farm Bureau board."

In 1961, E. T. York, Jr., Administrator of the Federal Extension Service, journeyed to Illinois to investigate reports of non-compliance. After his investigation, he concluded: "I have seen and heard enough to be convinced that there is a serious lack of compliance with the Secretary's Memorandum No. 1368 on the part of the Illinois Extension Service— some six and one half years after the memo was issued." In a letter to the Director of Illinois Extension, York criticized the fact that farm advisors were still housed in Farm Bureau-owned buildings in every county in the state, citing the "mere paper transactions" by which Bureau and state college leaders were deliberately circumventing the prohibition on free office space. He enumerated other blatant violations of the letter and spirit of the regulations: in some cases the advisor had no separate phone and could only be called through the Farm Bureau; the letterhead of some county Farm Bureaus still listed the farm advisor as one of the organization's services; the Farm Bureau continued to use Extension mailing lists; "Extension agents have been accused of supporting the Farm Bureau's fight against the Omnibus Farm Bill (introduced by President Kennedy)." York then revealed one of the worst-kept secrets in history. "It has been suggested," he confided, "that the Farm Bureau benefits directly by the fact that many people are brought in direct contact with their varied commercial interests as these people visit county Extension offices housed in Farm Bureau buildings. With the implied close association between Farm Bureau and the county farm advisors, many people feel that the Farm Bureau benefits through increased business from services rendered by Farm Advisors."[15] Such a sweeping indictment from national headquarters doubtless would have moved men of less resilience, but the Illinois Extension people had refined procrastination to an art.

In 1963, the Department of Agriculture felt compelled to issue an "Interpretation of Secretary's Memo No. 1368." Perhaps the Secretary's meaning had not been clear enough. The new guidelines declared that "services of the Government which the Department of Agriculture is responsible for rendering shall be made available to all people on an equal and impartial basis." It prohibited Department employees, including Extension agents, from maintaining "close relationships" with those farm organizations which have as an important purpose the influencing of legislation affecting the Department of Agriculture. This was an official recognition of the incestuous character of the relationship between a publicly aided private organization and the government it seeks to influence.[16]

The "Interpretation" of 1963 of the "Memorandum" of 1954 which was an amplification of the Department policy declared in 1945 which was merely a restatement of the incorporation into Departmental regulations in 1922 of the "True–Howard" Agreement of 1921, went on to define the prohibited "close relationship." "In general, conditions of 'close relationship' would be those where reasonable charges of discrimination could be raised by any organization, group or persons regarding services provided by Extension Service personnel to any other organization or group." The Interpretation concluded on an interesting note. Funds given by an organization to Extension, it declared, must be given through the University and without specification as to use. Of course, this is precisely what the Farm Bureau and Extension in Illinois professed to be doing. That the Department felt compelled to specifically enumerate this requirement would indicate that even this minimum subterfuge was not being universally practiced.

In 1964 the president of the University of Illinois and the Secretary of Agriculture set up still another "Task Force" to study the problem and recommend what action needed to be taken. This time, the group hired professional consultants to survey the extent of the identification of Farm Bureau and Extension in the minds of Illinoians. They discovered, to no one's surprise, that the Cooperative Extension Service has a "mixed" identification in the minds of the public. Sixty-one percent of the farm advisors acknowledged that farmers more commonly think of the Extension farm advisor's office as part of the county Farm Bureau, as did 70 percent of the vocational agricultural teachers in the state's schools, and nearly 60 percent of the farmers themselves. "It would appear," the task-force study group concluded, in a marvelous display of understatement, "that the efforts made by the University to create an image of separate identification in the eyes of the public has not been entirely successful."[17]

The study group also discovered that "the leadership of the Illinois Agriculture Association [The Illinois Farm Bureau] feels strongly that the situation as it now exists is satisfactory. . . . They felt that many county Farm Bureaus would withdraw funds if Extension moved out of the building." The Farm Bureau leaders obviously felt that having the agent housed in the same building as their headquarters was the significant factor warranting large annual contributions. Without this proximity, the benefit to the Farm Bureau from an active county agent system apparently would not be sufficient to justify continuing financial support.

Ninety of the 99 farm advisors in Illinois, the study group discovered, were still housed in buildings owned and occupied by the Farm Bureau. About 15 percent of the Illinois Extension budget of more than $4 million was derived from Farm Bureau contributions. (Interestingly enough, 60 percent of the farmers interviewed dismissed one of the major reasons given for delaying separation—financial and administrative difficulty in moving. They felt that if the farm advisers were moved, private investors would be willing to build or lease adequate space for the agents.)

It was painfully clear that Extension in Illinois was still part of the Farm Bureau fiefdom. As long as official demands to separate were accompanied by nothing stronger than the odor of ink, it was apparent that the University of Illinois–state Extension Service–Farm Bureau triumvirate was prepared to do nothing more than make the little concessions necessary to cloud the visibility of the relationship. But to overcome this well-established resistance, the study group recommended, and the sponsoring groups adopted, only more window dressing.

The course prescribed by the study group called for a re-emphasis of the educational role of the Extension Service and a renewed effort to establish its identity among Illinois farmers as independent from an unnamed "general farm organization." To accomplish this, farm advisors were to be located in "physical facilities which emphasize to the public they serve, their close association with the University of Illinois and the United States Department of Agriculture and [do] not imply close association with any general or specialized farm organization." In addition, clear identification of the farm advisors as members of the University staff was called for.

The attitude of the Illinois Extension officials in carrying out this mandate was clearly reflected in its response to inquiries by the Resnick investigation about their progress. "An aggressive publicity program" wrote J. B. Claar, Director of Illinois Extension in 1967, "has been conducted to make certain the attentive public understands that services of Cooperative Extension are available to all. However, it is doubtful that this is a problem of any significance."[18]

In August 1965, the University of Illinois Board of Trustees adopted the objective of "altering as quickly as possible without damage to the effectiveness of the [Extension] Service, the present predominance of locations in buildings of a single farm organization."[19] However, since 1965, only about forty farm agents have been moved out of Farm Bureau buildings. More than fifty Extension offices remain comfortably lodged inside buildings owned and occupied by the Farm Bureau organization and its business affiliates. The policy of "separate identity" was deemed to be accomplished, in many cases, merely by adding a partition between the two offices or by opening a new entrance to the Extension office.[20] The benefits to the Farm Bureau of having the government's farmer education program and the popular 4–H headquarters nestled within its own county headquarters and close to its insurance salesmen have not been impaired by a few inches of plywood.

"There's no place else for them to get what they get here," one Illinois county Farm Bureau executive-secretary explained about his Extension Service tenants. "Of course, the cooperation we get from them is not as good as when we were paying $16,000 to $18,000 a year to them—we are only paying about $4,000 to $5,000 a year now—but it is still good." The Extension agents in that county use all the facilities of the well-equipped Farm Bureau building—the auditorium for large meetings, the cooking and dining facilities for dinners. When asked if the closeness encouraged favoritism of the Farm Bureau over other farm organizations in the county, the executive-secretary smiled and admitted that agents are only human and that it is really impossible not to be extra cooperative to someone working so close to you each day.

The major emphasis of the Illinois Agricultural Association today in its continuing relationship with the Illinois Extension Service is on the active 4–H program. Where the Extension offices are housed in the Farm Bureau buildings, 4–H clubs often meet in the Farm Bureau auditorium. Many of the county Farm Bureaus in Illinois sponsor the annual 4–H fair, the highlight of the youth group's yearly program and the culmination of months of work on the part of the farm youth. These fairs are often jointly planned and managed by the county Farm Bureau and county Extension personnel. In some Illinois counties, the Farm Bureau actually owns the fair grounds itself. A board of Farm Bureau members serves as the official operating committee of the fair, yet the fairs remain known simply as 4–H fairs. The annual contribution from the county Farm Bureau (most county Farm Bureaus in Illinois are still paying Extension several thousand dollars a year) not infrequently goes toward the salary of an assistant Extension agent, whose responsibilities include managing these fairs. The value of having 4–H youth come to Farm Bureau meetings to receive the awards they have won represents an excellent long-term investment by the Farm Bureau.

A farm organization leader in Illinois, testifying at Resnick's Chicago hearings in August 1967, reported another windfall to the Farm Bureau from its association with 4–H and the county fairs. The 4–H youth in one Illinois county, he testified, conducted a fund-raising campaign to build some new buildings on the fair grounds—Farm Bureau-owned property. The title to the new buildings wound up with the county Farm Bureau.

The advantages of the Farm Bureau's continued association with 4–H and other Extension activities have not been lost on the other farm organizations. In a joint statement, the Illinois branches of the Farmers Union, Grange, and National Farmers Organization, accused Dr. David Henry, president of the University of Illinois, of "discriminatory use of Federal Agricultural Extension funds, and an obvious bias for the perpetuation of a specific agricultural interest in the state."[21]

The special relationship that the Farm Bureau continues to enjoy with the Extension Service is not, unfortunately, confined to Illinois. An enterprising reporter for the Buffalo *Courier–Journal,* in upper New York state, discovered the reverse situation. In at least seven counties in New York state, the Farm Bureau rents offices for its organization and businesses from the Extension Service. It is the only farm organization, and the only private organization except for the American Cancer Society, to rent space from this public agency.[22] The respectability of the public landlord undoubtedly rubs off on its commercial tenant.

The latest report released by the federal Extension Service shows that the Extension Service rents offices from the Farm Bureau in eleven states —Illinois, Iowa, Kentucky, Missouri, Tennessee, California, Florida, Indiana, Kansas, Ohio, and Rhode Island. It also indicates that in the fiscal year ending June 1967, of the more than $200 million spent on Extension during that year, $3.8 million still came from private sources, almost $1 million from the Illinois Farm Bureau alone.[23]

Until the Extension Service is completely independent from the Farm Bureau—independent in reality as well as in fanciful studies, reports, and directives—it cannot function without the suspicion of serving a special interest. A trickle of private money, unique among federal programs, has been allowed to pollute the necessary independence of a vital government activity. Membership in a special private group as prerequisite for equal service by the government is a denial of the most fundamental liberties on which our society is based.

Until the Extension Service and the Farm Bureau are separated physically as well as financially, a cloud of confusion will hang over the independent character of the Extension Service. It is unacceptable to cite the financial and administrative problems of moving; sufficient evidence exists that these are self-serving arguments put forth by those who, for other reasons, do not wish to see a move. And it is inadequate to claim that knocking out a new door or nailing up a new partition is, in any meaningful sense, separation. As one indignant farmer put it, "If a man and his wife tell me they are divorced, but they're still living in the same house, I ain't likely to believe 'em."

The story of the fifty-year battle to pry apart the Extension Service and the Farm Bureau is more than a classic case of the "implementation gap" in administrative policymaking. It is a dark episode—not yet closed—of a public program gathering its own constituency, the constituency becoming an institution, the institution becoming self-serving and swallowing the program itself, turning it into a powerful tool for its own perpetuation.

9

"Do I Have to Agree to Belong?"

IN THE HIGHER ECHELONS of the Farm Bureau there is a great deal of talk about the democratic processes of the organization. There is much less of such talk from the membership. Despite all the claims about grass roots policy-making and popularly elected leadership, the style of democracy practiced by the Farm Bureau is closer to autocracy.

Farm Bureau leadership has never been very happy at the prospect of a groundswell of farmer opinion beginning either within the organization or outside it. The leadership derives its political power from its ability literally to speak *for* the American farmer. Through the years the organizational hierarchy has moved quickly to quash any threat to its self-proclaimed status as spokesman for the farmer, even when it meant squelching popular uprisings of farmer sentiment in the process.

As we have already seen, during the New Deal the Farm Bureau attempted to thwart the Department of Agriculture's efforts to reach out for direct contact with farmers. These efforts presented a special danger for the Farm Bureau: the prospect of a rival farm organization arising from the constituency of a government farm program. Since the New Deal, the organization has strongly resisted a series of attempts by the Department to "go to the farmer" directly, even when the asserted purpose of such excursions has been merely to determine farmer sentiment on proposed government policies.

In 1949, President Truman's Secretary of Agriculture, Charles Brannan, proposed a series of "Family Farm Policy Review" meetings around the country, in which he and the Department's top officials were to sound out farmer opinion and give farmers an opportunity to discuss how "farm policies should be improved to help family farms and farm families make their full contribution to the strength and security of a free America." Farm Bureau President Allan Kline strongly denounced the plan to get "grassroots" sentiment. The plan was "fraught with dangers" he proclaimed. "It is the sort of procedure which would recommend itself to an authoritarian government. . . . It does not seem to us to be consistent with true democratic processes or with the local responsibility, without which self-government cannot be expected to survive." Despite letters from the national organization to the local Farm Bureau officials telling them to boycott the meetings, the sessions were held, although not without some dampening effect from this demonstration of democracy, Farm Bureau style.[1]

In 1953, a group of beef farmers, angered over sagging prices under the regime of Agriculture Secretary Ezra Taft Benson, organized a "Cattleman's Caravan" to Washington to protest their situation. Benson denounced the proposed demonstration and was quickly joined by the American Farm Bureau Federation, somehow fearful of farmers speaking for themselves.[2]

One of the more recent attempts by the Farm Bureau to protect its members from direct dialogue with government administrators of the farm program was its campaign against the "shirt sleeve meetings" of Agriculture Secretary Orville Freeman in 1967. Freeman, a favorite Farm Bureau dartboard during his eight year tenure under Presidents Kennedy and Johnson, proposed a series of direct meetings with farmers in the Midwest to discuss the Administration's farm policy. Once again, in order to save democracy the Farm Bureau urged its members to boycott the meetings.

In a remarkable document—a letter sent to all the Nebraska county Farm Bureau presidents and others—the Nebraska Farm Bureau president set forth a series of irrelevant or inaccurate reasons why Farm Bureau members should not attend the meetings: 1) the Secretary of Agriculture is a "political appointee"; 2) he is not part of the legislative branch of government; 3) "Farmers and ranchers can get together without being called by the Secretary"; 4) public forums are not a suitable method of determining farmer opinions. In the closest approach to the real underlying reason for the Farm Bureau's opposition to the meetings with individual farmers, the letter stated: "The Secretary can receive any justifiable help he wants from the bonafide agricultural groups in this country"—i.e., the Farm Bureau.[3]

If the Farm Bureau has tried to stifle farmer expression outside the organization, no one can accuse it of not practicing what it preaches. There is a noticeable lack of internal democracy throughout the Farm Bureau organization. This organization is largely controlled from the top. Its leadership is self-perpetuating, and its policy, although nursed through an elaborate procedural labyrinth, is rarely permitted to wander very far afield. "The Farm Bureau's cherished belief that its policy was made at the grass roots and adopted by a democratic process turns out to be partly illusion," concluded Christiana McFadyen Cambell in her study of the organization's New Deal period.[4] There appears to be no reason to change that assessment today.

Tightly held control has been maintained largely by means of internal decision-making procedures guaranteed to produce leaders thoroughly familiar to those currently in power and to generate policies in line with the leadership's views. The people who actually enact Farm Bureau national policy and select the leadership of the national organization are themselves selected by a careful process of distillation designed to insure that only the purest spirits reach the top.

National policy is sent down from above. The newsletter of the American Farm Bureau Federation, sent weekly to local officials, periodically presents "Farm Bureau Policy Development Features," posing issues to be considered in policy-making. Agricultural and non-agricultural issues are presented. With each feature, there is a discussion of the pros and cons of a particular stand. Selection of the issues is itself an important aspect of policy-making; and although other issues are not precluded from consideration, at least the ones that the leadership wishes to see presented are guaranteed to be put on the table.

The lower stages of national policy-making vary from state to state. Some counties simply devote one or more of their meetings to adopting local policies and passing on recommendations for state and national policies. In other states, elaborate mechanisms have been established including "county forum committees," "tentative resolutions committees," "district report forums," ad infinitum.

Only a small percentage of Farm Bureau members actually participate even at the local stage of policy-making. One county executive-secretary put the figure at 10–15 percent. A state Farm Bureau staff member conceded that probably only about 10 percent actually take part in policy-making. This is apparently no accident. A Midwestern journalist, having observed Farm Bureau politics for many years, commented: "The annual 'Policy Development Meetings' are a cynical farce. Frequently less than a dozen people attend such meetings because they know they will have to listen to a lot of 'background material' and 'basic facts' which are so slanted as to presuppose the answers in the very way the questions are asked." Or as a lady who used to be a county Farm Bureau officer remarked, "Most people talk to convey a meaning; the Farm Bureau talks to keep you from figuring out the meaning."

The crucial phase at the county level is the selection of delegates to attend the state convention. There, state policies will be enacted and resolutions on national issues will be formulated for submission to the national convention. The Farm Bureau does not go in for broad-based democracy; it prefers the indirect variety. Delegates to state conventions in many cases are not selected by the membership directly, but by the county leaders, themselves elected. These chosen delegates attend the state convention, vote on state policies, and themselves select the handful of people to represent the state at the annual American Farm Bureau Federation convention, where national policy is determined and national leadership selected. The process is much like skimming the cream off the top of the barrel, putting it into a smaller barrel and skimming the top off again. Such a system is not calculated to stir things up. Nor is what you wind up with necessarily representative of the whole.

The end product for the Farm Bureau is about two hundred voting delegates at the national convention who are at least two, sometimes three steps removed from the membership base. The six voting delegates to the national convention from Ohio in one recent year, for example, were the president and the vice president of the Ohio Farm Bureau Federation, the president and the vice president of the (Ohio Farm Bureau) Landmark Coop, and two state board members. So, to be precise, the AFBF's president, its board of directors, and the national policy platform are chosen by a *few hundred men* selected by the *delegates* to respective state conventions, themselves chosen by the membership, or by the county leaders.

Such a process is unlikely to produce results distasteful to current leadership. Delegates to the state conventions, whether elected by membership or appointed by county leaders, are usually organization stalwarts being rewarded by their county for dedicated service. Similarly, since the state convention can only select a handful of voting representatives to the annual national convention, those most familiar—usually officers and directors—are selected. The faces change little from year to year among the voting delegates at American Farm Bureau Federation conventions.

Even in such a self-perpetuating system, however, there are no absolute guarantees against discord. Despite the "marriage of corn and cotton," there are still regional differences in the organization. Often, however, the leadership manages to stifle dissent. "It seems when you send a group (to the state convention) to vote the way you want," explained a former Farm Bureau member at one of the Resnick hearings, "the pressure gets so great that they will vote right down party lines." A farmer from another state relates: "one time a few years back a neighbor of mine was voted in as a so-called voting delegate to a state convention. Before leaving for the convention he was called in to county headquarters and asked how he would vote on certain proposals that were to come to a vote at the meeting. It so happens he would not vote the way the higher-ups wanted him to vote, so he was told he would have to be replaced as a voting delegate to the convention. He quit the so-called farm organization right then and there."

In another case and another state, a farmer once quite active in Farm Bureau affairs tells the story of his truncated trip to the state convention. He was duly elected as a delegate by the membership of his county Farm Bureau at a meeting at which he spoke against two particular state policies. Shortly after the meeting, he received a letter from the county Farm Bureau board of directors, signed by the county Farm Bureau president. "We understand you are a member of two other farm organizations, consequently, it is a decision of the . . . County Farm Bureau Board that you be replaced as a delegate, since there would be a conflict of interest for you to represent Farm Bureau policies as a delegate to the Farm Bureau State Convention."[5] His demands to know how the county board had authority to overrule his election by the membership, or why farmers' interests weren't farmers' interests no matter how many farm organizations he belonged to went unanswered. He disagreed; he was eliminated. It was as simple as that. Perhaps this is what AFBF secretary-treasurer Fleming had in mind when he claimed proudly in 1967: "Organizational discipline is on the basis of cooperation rather than dictation. Farm Bureau's only discipline is self-discipline—which is the very best kind."[6]

Because of this process of selecting delegates, national conventions of the American Farm Bureau Federation seldom produce many surprises. The policy program, developed largely in yo-yo fashion—dropped from the top of the organization down to the bottom and then hauled back up again—is trimmed into shape. Reports are given on the inevitable gains from last year. The venerable veterans of the organization are honored. And the officers and directors are elected or, as is most often the case, re-elected.

The more or less routine nature of these conclaves forced historian Grant McConnell to conclude that they are "mass meetings to generate enthusiasm, not a deliberative body."[7] This is even more true today than when McConnell wrote in the 1950s. Partly in response to the fuss being made by Resnick's investigation about the lack of internal democracy within the Farm Bureau, and partly in response to widely publicized mass meetings being held by other farm organizations, the AFBF has, since 1967, invited representatives from the county Farm Bureaus to the annual national convention. Over 5,000 attended the 1970 convention. These new participants, however, were not permitted to upset the apple cart; they cannot vote on policy or people. They just increase the decibel level.

Like those of the national organization, state Farm Bureau presidencies have a low turnover. The same men are usually re-elected year after year, serving long terms until they retire or die. The Board of Directors of the American Farm Bureau Federation is made up of twenty-two state Farm Bureau presidents, the AFBF president and vice president, the chairman of the AFB Woman's Committee, and the chairman of the AFBF young farmers and ranchers advisory committee. The AFBF president and vice president are elected for one year terms by the voting delegates at the annual convention. The twenty-two state presidents are elected to the board for two year terms by the same body. There is only about a 15 percent turnover each year; most directors are re-elected when their term expires.

If this all sounds pretty rigid, it should. As Kile has written, "The line of succession up from the ranks is now well defined, and few reach the top except through that course."[8] Indeed, few reach the top at all. The Farm Bureau has had only seven national presidents in its fifty-two years, and only three in the nearly forty years between 1933 and 1970.

The result of such inbreeding over the years has been to solidify the Farm Bureau into an autocracy, often unwilling and unable to tolerate any "disloyalty" or criticism from within. During the Resnick investigation, several people reported that Farm Bureau members had lost their insurance, along with their Farm Bureau membership, when they became too active in other farm organizations. Some years ago, the *St. Louis Post Dispatch* reported that the Farm Bureau of Wayne County, Illinois, "has notified seven members, some also belonging to [the National Farmers Union] that their membership is being terminated January 1. The ouster action stems from a public meeting last January at Wayne City when the seven criticized both the Bureau and the Agricultural Extension Service."[9] However frequent these surgical operations are, they certainly do not promote an atmosphere of free-swinging democracy inside the organization. And they further discredit claims by the Farm Bureau's entrenched leadership that it truly represents the rank and file American farmer.

The same authoritarian tactics used within the organization have often marked the Farm Bureau's strategy toward its rivals. The Farm Bureau has not managed to destroy the NFO and NFU, but this failure is hardly due to a lack of effort. Back in 1950, in the heat of the controversy over the Brannan Plan, which pitted the Farm Bureau against the more liberal NFU, the Farm Bureau attempted to link both the NFU and the Brannan Plan with Communism. The attack began in the Senate with a two-hour tirade by the late New Hampshire Senator Styles Bridges, former secretary of the New Hampshire Farm Bureau, and then a director of one of its insurance companies. Bridges charged that the NFU was a "communist-dominated" organization (and was immediately and vigorously challenged by a long line of his colleagues, including the Senate's chief communist hunter, Joe McCarthy). Down the line, in the course of the reelection campaign of Rep. Walter Granger of Utah (the Congressman who had introduced legislation to separate the Farm Bureau and Extension), the Utah Farm Bureau linked Granger and the Farmers Union and then echoed the "Communist" charge against the NFU. That provoked a successful libel suit by the NFU, which cost the Farm Bureau a judgment for over $25,000.[10]

By the early 1960s, the more activist National Farmers Organization emerged as a threat to the Farm Bureau's predominant position. In mid-August of 1963, a major strategy meeting was held in Chicago, presided over by President Shuman, to draw up a blueprint for crippling the NFO. A memorandum later sent to the participants summarizing the "major conclusions developed" at the meeting, outlined several steps to be taken: "obvious and continuing linkage of NFO with industrial labor unions [should be exposed]; . . . farm leaders should recognize that some persons may envision NFO as a vehicle for a political alliance of farmers and industrial workers," the statement warned. (This apparently is something which must be fought at all costs.) The memo suggests that farm organizations consider dropping from membership "those persons who transfer their principal allegiance to NFO," which could mean any NFO and Farm Bureau member who disagrees with Farm Bureau policies. It also urges vigilance lest control of county organizations be seized by "NFO representatives." As protection against this possibility, county leaders are told to ensure that "informed" members are on hand to vote at elections.

The memo goes on to recommend the use of existing legislation or, if necessary, new legislation to curtail the NFO. Newspaper editors and publishers, radio and TV station broadcasters and owners must be contacted, according to this plan, to warn them of potentially "libelous" attacks by NFO on others "who do not submit to NFO control." Finally, it urges that politicians, federal government administrators, industrial union leaders, and "others who promote NFO" should be "neutralized." "Special attention should be given to religious leaders who are economically uninformed but highly partisan and articulate proponents of NFO." It is not explained what "neutralization" involves.[11]

With such a reaction to a threat from the outside, one might imagine how the Farm Bureau leadership reacts to any suggestion of rebellion from within, or any open break by local groups with the organization's national policy. The most blatant and dramatic example of this intolerance is the case of the Webster County Farm Bureau in Nebraska. Beginning in 1960, members of this county group set out to change two central policies of the Nebraska Farm Bureau: one calling for 50 percent parity for wheat and feed grains, and the other advocating a hike in the interest rates of the Rural Electrification Administration.

Repeated unsuccessful attempts to bring about some change at the state level convinced the Webster County Farm Bureau members that the organization's procedures were stacked against them, and that the problem was more basic. What was needed, they decided, was a genuine reform of the decision-making apparatus of the Nebraska Farm Bureau, to make it more responsive to rank and file opinion. "When you vote on the county level," explained the Webster County's president Alfred Schutte, "everything looks good. It usually is. From there on, your votes are all delegated to someone else, someone who is brainwashed by state and national officials, someone whose vote you can never check on to see if he represented you." So at the annual meeting of the county organization in 1961, the members passed a series of resolutions to be presented at the state convention. The proposals were aimed at giving the membership more voice in making policy. "Since the structure of the Nebraska and American Farm Bureau is such at this time," announced Schutte to the local press after the meeting, "that the individual members have little or no say in final Farm Bureau policy, the Webster County resolutions for the coming year were aimed at eliminating present methods of having policy set by a few farmers."[12]

Responding to reports about this meeting in the newspapers, the president of the Nebraska Farm Bureau dispatched a letter to all county Farm Bureau presidents in the state telling them that they were no longer to release recommendations on state and national issues until they had been formally adopted. "As regards recommended changes in the procedures within the organization," he added, "there is little that can be accomplished by involving the public in such discussions."[13] The Webster County group was not silenced. "We ask that we be allowed to exercise some of this freedom of which Farm Bureau preaches in our own organization," answered Schutte. He charged that the state organization was attempting to intimidate them and suppress their Constitutional right of free speech.[14]

For the next few years, the Webster County Farm Bureau vigorously battled the leadership of the state and even national organization, even pulling AFBF president Shuman himself into the fray by calling for his resignation for "anti-farmer interpretations of Farm Bureau policy." Stung by the publicity caused by this small but vocal county group, the organization soon retaliated. "I found out later," says Schutte, "they had contacted some of our members with the hope of them . . . getting me out of the president's office." Rumors began to circulate to the effect that Schutte and other members of the Webster County Farm Bureau had "communist leanings."[15]

When a letter to the editor of a Nebraska farm journal asked why Schutte remained a member of the Farm Bureau when he found so many things wrong with it, Schutte replied:

First, maybe because I want to keep my insurance with them. Second, I find not "many" but one thing wrong with the Farm Bureau. That is the way they arrive at their farm policy stand. . . . I do not want to be antagonistic, but do I have to agree with F.B. to belong? When F.B. leaders did not agree with our farm program, they severely crticized our democratic government, and leaders. Surely when we produce facts and criticism of F.B. and President Shuman, this can be no worse.[16]

The climax came in 1964. To rebut the impression left by Farm Bureau's Congressional lobbyists that "the American farmer" opposed the pending wheat bill, the Webster County Farm Bureau sent its representatives to Washington to testify to the Senate Committee on Agriculture on behalf of the bill. They argued that in opposing the bill the Farm Bureau did not represent its grass roots members. Retribution was swift and total. Within 90 days, the Board of Directors of the Nebraska Farm Bureau had met and adopted resolutions recommending that the entire county be thrown out of the organization. The "grounds for the expulsion," which also called for the individual ouster of Schutte, the vice president and the public relations director, were that the county organization "has openly and continuously opposed principles, policies and programs of this federation and has violated agreements between such federated member, and this federation . . . ." The resolution went on to enumerate the county's offenses, which included opposing the policies of the state and national organizations and securing "the publication of material tending to discredit the Nebraska Farm Bureau Federation and the American Farm Bureau Federation." Most ironic of all, the resolution of the state board charged that the county "has accused the Nebraska Farm Bureau Federation of preventing Farm Bureau members from exercising their freedom of speech. . . ."[17]

A committee of Farm Bureau officials was appointed to "conduct a hearing." It did its work, and the county was expelled. Some of the members of the county group, fearful of the consequences of losing their insurance, had slipped into other county organizations while the expulsion was looming. Others in the group have reconstituted themselves as the Webster County Farmers, and have since then devoted themselves to fighting the Farm Bureau. Their dedication is perhaps explained by Schutte's recent comment: "We used to sell Farm Bureau membership, and we know what it is like. We still blush when we think about how we took our own farmers when we didn't know any better."[18]

The crime of the Webster County Farm Bureau had been two-fold: it had dissented, and it had dissented publicly. The state and national Farm Bureau apparently did not feel that the embarrassing spectacle of having to throw out an entire county for disagreeing with the organization's policies was too high a price to pay for orthodoxy.

The Farm Bureau's inner workings tend to produce a self-perpetuating leadership group, increasingly unresponsive and unresponsible to the rank and file membership of the organization. Kept in power by such procedures, Farm Bureau leaders are not likely to change them in order to make the organization more representative. Despite their fulminations on freedom, the leadership has at least tolerated suppression or, as in the case of Webster County, "neutralization" of dissenters. Lacking an infusion of new vision, the Farm Bureau is clearly suffering from a hardening of the democratic arteries.

10

The Right Wing in Overalls

THE RURAL WARRIOR of the radical right is what the Farm Bureau has become in many parts of the country. Its established reputation as a national farm organization, its extensive communications network, its association with rural youth, and its considerable economic reserves make it an especially valuable ally.

The radical right in the country is an amorphous, shifting mass at the far end of the political spectrum. Its fate over the years has ebbed and flowed, reflecting to some extent shifts in the center of gravity of the general population. The terms "right wing" and "radical right" falsely imply a monolith. In fact, what has been called the radical right in this country spans a broad spectrum: from what Professor Alan Westin has called the "hate" right, including the anti-black, anti-Semitic and anti-Catholic elements in the country, to what he has termed the "semi-respectable" right, composed of groups like the Daughters of the American Revolution.[1]

At the risk of generalization, several characteristics distinguish the so-called radical right from the more moderate conservative elements in the country. The movement generally views the last twenty-five years of our foreign policy as "appeasement, treason, and treachery," at the hands of the communists. It is obsessed with the communist threat, external and internal, and tends to view the American establishment—the churches, the unions, the media, to some extent the business community—as part of a giant leftist conspiracy which has also seized control of large parts of the government. A recent issue of *American Opinion* magazine, the voice of the John Birch Society, contends, for example, that communist control of

government and all other aspects of American life increased from 60 to
80 percent in 1969.[2]

The far right generally attributes our racial and student troubles to the
agitation of communist instigators. It rejects the last forty years of domestic reforms, including in some cases the personal income tax, as welfare state socialism or worse. It resolutely believes, in the name of individual
initiative and self-reliance, that the plight of those who have not shared
in America's wealth—the poor, the black, the other minorities—should
not in any major way be the concern of government. "Inevitably—and
beneath most of it—", suggests writer Peter Schrag in a recent look at the
country's far right, "there is the vision of a smaller, simpler world, of
less government, of a lost innocence, and—at the same time—of a nation
so powerful that only treason and conspiracy could have created its con-
temporary problems."[3]

The Farm Bureau has aided the far right in many ways. The Bureau
has provided a conduit for right-wing propaganda to many areas of rural
America. It has consistently given platforms to itinerant peddlers of right-
wing propaganda, lending respectability to their views. It has helped to
disseminate some of this extremist polemic by selectively lending out Farm
Bureau membership mailing lists. A growing number of state Farm Bureau
leaders openly promote the far right line. And they have not been reluctant, where they felt it necessary, to engage in a little, old-fashioned "red-
baiting" of their own.

The philosophical drift in the Farm Bureau, definitely more pronounced
in some states than others, has brought the Bureau into closer ideological
harmony with the groups on the far right. The national organization believes that the centralization of power in Washington "has led us far into
socialism which is the stepping stone to communism"; that the welfare state
is based on this centralization; that "the redistribution of the benefits of our
economic system by political means . . . is akin to socialism and communism"; and that "Communists as well as other subversive elements" are at
the forefront of civil and student disorders. Or as former President Charles
Shuman put this latter point more succinctly, "when university presidents
and faculties capitulate to communist-led gangs of beatniks, they demon-
strate how freedom ends when courage disappears."[4]

Some of the states are even more unequivocal about the source of all
evil. The Missouri Farm Bureau believes that "any deviation from private

ownership of property and individual responsibility can only carry civilization back to the stagnation of primitive communism." The chairman of women's activities of the Missouri organization recently wrote in the organization's paper that the anti-war and civil rights protests and disturbances "are being backed by the Communists." The Idaho Farm Bureau believes that communism is a "Godless conspiracy to control the world," and "in light of recent developments," calls for a congressional investigation of the subversive activities in the United States State Department (Joe McCarthy is alive and well in the Idaho Farm Bureau). The Texas Farm Bureau urges the state legislature to "declare illegal and of no effect in Texas usurped authority not constitutionally granted the Senate in its surrender of U.S. independence to the U.N. World Government." It suggests that it be made a crime, a felony no less, for federal agents to "attempt any enforcement of U.N. controls over the lives of Texans."[5]

One of the Farm Bureau's special targets is the power of the Federal government and its role in the social reforms of the last few decades. The Farm Bureau juggles such terms as "centralization," "planned economy," "socialism," and "communism," using them in some cases almost interchangeably. Given the charged character of some of those terms among rural and farm people, this subtle semantic manipulation is particularly insidious. When Farm Bureau leaders decry, as they so often do, a government program as a "welfare state expedient," or attack a government official as an "advocate of big government," they do so within a framework in which such charges assume far more significance than they do on their face.

Occasionally a Farm Bureau leader is careless in his name-calling. Late in the Eisenhower administration, the AFBF's general counsel, Frank Wooley, was testifying to the House Agriculture Committee and suggested that communists were behind the government's argicultural production payment plans. Having approved those plans himself, Committee Chairman Robert Poage (Dem.–Tex.) shouted: "We'll go no further into this up here. But if you want to discuss it further, I'll meet you in the alley."[6]

Many state Farm Bureaus have launched vigorous and often elaborate campaigns to proselytize both their own membership and rural communities of their area with their views. Such efforts fall loosely into what is called their "American citizenship" program, with the women's groups often carrying the banner. One of the most common features of these programs is the attempt to give wide circulation to some of the basic tracts of the right wing—both books and films. One of the most popular and most distorted films distributed by the Farm Bureau is "Communism on the Map," a production that comes out of Harding College, in Searcy, Arkansas, known as the "West Point of the far right." The *New York Times* described this bill of fare as "a forty-five minute technicolor production, done with professional skill, that presents an impression of the United States lying helplessly in the closing jaws of a world Communist conspiracy." This film received very wide circulation through the Farm Bureau network; the Michigan Farm Bureau alone showed it to over 150 audiences.[7]

Even more important than the films is the promotion, particularly by the women, of books carefully selected for their reactionary message. Called "Freedom's Bookshelf," the list includes such titles as *The Naked Communist,* and *Peaceful Coexistence—A Communist Blueprint for Victory.* The authors include such noted right-wingers as Cleon Skousen, John Noble, Dr. Fred Schwarz, who runs the prosperous Christian Anti-Communist Crusade, and Ezra Taft Benson, former Secretary of Agriculture under Eisenhower, who thought the Civil Rights Act of 1964 was part of the pattern of communist take-over of America. To balance the fanatics, the Farm Bureau women also push the works of such well-known liberals as J. Edgar Hoover, Herbert Philbrick, and Russell Kirk.

The Freedom Bookshelf is one of the first things to confront a visitor when he enters many county Farm Bureau headquarters. County Farm Bureaus which engage in the most vigorous of these "citizenship" campaigns on a local level are rewarded by the state organization with more books. The Bureau has a cooperative relationship with Bookmailer, Inc., a prominent publisher of ultra-conservative works. The "citizenship chairmen" in Nebraska were told at a meeting that books for the Freedom Bookshelf could be obtained from Bookmailer at a 20 percent discount if they were for a Farm Bureau project.

One of the most important projects of many of the women's groups has been to stock local public school libraries with this impressive booklist. The Antelope, (Nebraska) County Farm Bureau, for example, presented a copy of *The Naked Communist* to every high school in the county, and the Tennessee Farm Bureau women placed Dr. Fred Schwarz's *You*

Can Trust the Communists (to be Communists) in all the Madison County high schools.[8]

Lest anyone think for a moment that the Farm Bureau's purpose in this program is merely to assure the children's exposure to differing points of view, they have been as dedicated in trying to remove books from the school library shelves as in putting them on. During the tenure of Governor Ross Barnett at the Mississippi Statehouse, the Mississippi Farm Bureau, in concert with the American Legion, the White Citizens Councils, and the DAR raised a furor over the textbooks in the public schools, brought about a legislative investigation, and hammered through a new law empowering Barnett to appoint eight textbook-screening committees. The president of the Mississippi Farm Bureau was duly rewarded by being appointed to one. The Idaho Farm Bureau took a stand against the use of certain books in classrooms in that state, and the Wyoming Farm Bureau called on its Board of Education to check all reading lists in the school for books with "immoral contents" and to eliminate any such books when found. The Texas Farm Bureau calls for local public hearings on the textbooks used by the state-supported colleges and universities as well as the public schools. "Freedom Bookshelf" apparently means freedom for Farm Bureau-approved books to be on the shelves.[9]

Farm Bureaus not only have been vigilant in guarding our country's bookshelves, they have also tried to purify our airwaves of any voices to the left of Attila the Hun. The Missouri Farm Bureau accused NBC generally and Messrs. Huntley and Brinkley specifically, of a "pattern of socialist and communist sympathy" for their presentation a few years ago of an interview with the ousted Russian premier, Nikita Khrushchev. The documentary, which won high praise from the viewing public generally, didn't impress the Missourians. In its monthly magazine a few years ago, the Wisconsin Farm Bureau criticized businessmen for placing advertisements with such newspapers as *The Washington Post* and *The St. Louis Post Dispatch,* and for supporting, through advertising, such TV commentators as Huntley and Brinkley, Howard K. Smith, Charles Collingwood, and Edward R. Murrow. They decried "top level management," for being "guilty of turning over thousands and even millions of dollars to their advertising departments and not even taking the time to set up philosophical groundrules of the media selection game. . . ." They urged company executives "to be certain that their funds were not supporting left-wing propagandist . . . ," and recommended instead that they "support the newspaper editor who has gone out of his way to print a sound editorial page."[10]

One of the most important means by which the Farm Bureau spreads right-wing propaganda is through the annual youth conferences held by state Farm Bureaus around the country. These gatherings go under a variety of names, but most are called "citizenship seminars," or "freedom forums." At least twelve states sponsor these annual seminars, lasting from one to five days. In each state, the county Farm Bureaus select a total of several hundred outstanding youths as county delegates. In some cases the students are selected by their school principals or teachers, in others by the county Farm Bureau. Whatever the method, it is a great honor for students to be selected to attend the state-wide gathering. In many counties their pictures appear in the newspaper with articles announcing their selection. The cost of sponsoring each student is generally underwritten by the county Farm Bureau, either alone or in cooperation with local businessmen or civic groups like the Chamber of Commerce. The attending students are urged to return home to their communities as "leaders" to conduct similar programs on their own.

The conferences themselves consist of a series of lectures and discussions, augmented by a wide variety of visual aids including slides, films, charts, and literature. Who does the Farm Bureau select to give these lectures? Political scientists? Historians? Prominent journalists? Recognized experts on government? Government officials? Politicians? And what kind of lectures are given? What views of our society are presented? Are these true seminars, which promote thought and discussion by the students, after they are given a balanced picture representing different shades of opinion? Do these seminars deal with our nation's pressing social, economic, environmental and political problems? Is there debate and discussion about this country's goals and needs?

If even one of these questions could be answered affirmatively, it might be possible to accept these so-called "citizenship seminars" or "freedom forums" for what they are claimed to be: efforts to promote better citizenship. But the answer to every question is "no."

The Kansas City Star has described the seminars as "a cram course in anti-communism and free-enterprise Americanism and political conservatism." Even the organizers of the forums admit that they seek a conservative viewpoint in lining up speakers. In fact, these seminars are high-powered platforms for some of the country's most active and best-known far-right speakers. These sessions give them an opportunity to promote some of the grossest political bunk to some of the most promising and impressionable rural youth.[11]

Far from being a balanced group, the same half dozen speakers keep showing up together, year after year, in state after state. Let us take a close look to see who the Farm Bureau is using to mold the minds of thousands of rural youth, using tax-exempt money. The most popular member of the Farm Bureau travelling lecture team is John Noble. Since 1965, he has been an official speaker for the John Birch Society's speakers bureau. In 1968, when George Wallace campaigned for the Presidency of the United States, Noble headed the Wallace for President Committee in Pennsylvania.

Noble has appeared at more than 25 Farm Bureau youth conferences in seven states during the past 10 years. His claim to fame is that he was a prisoner of the Communists in East Germany and Russia after World War II. He has been telling his story in books, lectures, recordings and videotape ever since. He also operates the Faith and Freedom Forum, which sells his books and records. Among his works are *I Was a Slave In Russia,* and *I Found God in Soviet Russia.* He describes his imprisonment ordeal in great and gory detail to his young audiences. "The Communists aren't 'dumb' or 'divided'," he explains. "They are playing a 'chess game' with the rest of the nations. Only the United States can stop them, so the drive is on to weaken us morally, militarily, and in almost every way. We stand in their way of world conquest." Noble believes we should break off diplomatic relations with the Soviet Union and ban trade relations. "God cannot approve our seeking coexistence with a nation determined to destroy belief in God," he contends.[12]

In addition to his expertise in international affairs, Noble also ventures occasionally into domestic issues in his talks. He believes, for example, that the income tax is destroying initiative in America. He also claims that "socializing welfare programs are violating the Bible, which says if someone is in need it is the responsibility of the relatives or the church to take care of them—never the government."[13] Noble does not cite a specific reference for this point.

Another favorite on the Farm Bureau circuit is W. Cleon Skousen. Skousen, also an official speaker of the Birch Society's speakers bureau,

reports that he was an FBI agent for sixteen years, serving as special assistant to J. Edgar Hoover, and that he served for several years as Chief of
Police of Salt Lake City. He does not report however, that he was fired
as Chief of Police by Mayor J. Bracken Lee, former Governor of Utah
(who had at one time endorsed the John Birch Society himself, which
hardly makes him a flaming Liberal).[14]

Skousen claims he delivers more than 300 lectures a year, to 200,000
people. He has addressed more than a dozen Farm Bureau youth citizenship conferences in at least six states. His specialty is the "historical presentation" of communism. Hopefully his grasp of the past is better than his
accuracy about the future; he has been predicting internal collapse in
Russia for some time now. Another master at the semantic shell game, he
tells the assembled students "how the 'Socialists' and the 'Modern Liberals'
are trying to change our form of government from a 'Democratic Republic'
to a 'Presidential' or 'Centralized' form of government."[15]

Skousen is author of *The Naked Communist, The Naked Socialist* and
So You Want to Raise a Boy, the first of which is a special favorite in
right-wing circles. When Skousen isn't able to attend one of these "freedom
forums," they sell his books anyway.

Boasting even more return engagements than Skousen is Dr. George S.
Benson. From 1936 until a few years ago, Benson was President of Harding
College, the so-called academic center of the right. He is still the driving
force of the National Education Program at Harding which churns out a
torrent of pamphlets, films, tapes, speeches, newspaper columns and other
propaganda material. Benson served on the policy committee of "For
America" under the co-chairmanship of Dean Clarence Manion, a prominent John Birch leader, and General Robert E. Wood; received an award
from the right-wing Congress of Freedom in 1959; has received at least
nine awards from the ultra-conservative Freedom Foundation at Valley
Forge. Although Benson denies membership in the Birch Society and claims
to deplore its extremist views, Birch head Robert Welch has praised Benson. "Down in Searcy, Arkansas," wrote Welch, "Dr. George Benson and
his associates at Harding College have long been in the forefront of those
most ably promoting better understanding and support of the Americanist
philosophy and sociological system."[16]

Benson has addressed at least fourteen Farm Bureau-sponsored youth
forums in six states. His columns have appeared in Farm Bureau papers

in several states—including Missouri, Pennsylvania, Oklahoma, Virginia, Kansas, and Tennessee. Now over 70, he is no longer as active on the Farm Bureau circuit.

Another regular freedom speaker has been Dr. Nicholas Nyaradi, director of the School of International Studies at Bradley University, Peoria, Illinois. Publicity distributed by the Farm Bureau in reporting the forums describes Nyaradi's background as "former Hungarian Minister of Finance and Ambassador to Russia prior to the Hungarian uprising." "After fleeing Hungary," it continues, "he came to the United States and became an American citizen."[17] In fact, Nyaradi left Hungary in 1949, seven years before the Hungarian uprising.

Nyaradi has addressed at least 10 Farm Bureau-sponsored citizenship forums. He tells his student audiences that "Today's socialism is being 'spoon-fed' to the American people in daily doses, and even sugar-coated, so that they do not know what they are swallowing—and by the time they discover it, then it will be too late." He constructs in great detail a depressing image of life in Moscow and then proclaims: "this is exactly the kind of life you would lead if the goals of the Kremlin succeeded. It is what they are planning for each and every one of you."[18]

According to the *Kansas City Star,* Nyaradi told the 1968 Missouri Freedom Forum: "I can guarantee you will witness the explosion of Soviet and Red Chinese bombs over United States cities," and criticized the "mellowing of values" among Americans which he claimed was exemplified by "the country's desire to negotiate its way out of war when in the past unconditional surrender was demanded."[19]

In 1960, Nyaradi announced: "I came to an amazing piece of literature which I can call the plan, the scheme, and the schedule of establishing Socialism in our country." He was referring to a 1947 article by Dr. Arthur M. Schlesinger, Jr., soon to be appointed special counselor to President Kennedy.[20]

Among Nyaradi's other more notable utterances was a speech delivered at Seattle's Boeing plant in 1961: "Well, gentlemen," he remarked, "last year in the fall of 1960, 26 so-called new African nations were admitted to the membership of the UN, with a total population of 170 million backward, uneducated, uncivilized, primitive people—well, let's call it by name, basically second-generation cannibals. . . ."[21]

Rising in popularity among the freedom teachers has been Dr. C. L. Kay, vice president for public services at Lubbock Christian College in Texas. Kay explains to the Farm Bureau seminars that "on the one side is Christianity with its free enterprise system . . . on the other is Communism . . . . We cannot live in peace. In the end, one or the other of us will conquer." Kay told the Montana freedom seminar in 1969 that "the Communists, counting on inner subversion, have set the take-over date as 1973."[22]

This list is only partial. Virtually all the speakers come with the same kind of portfolios and the same kind of message. Dr. Clifton Ganus: Benson's successor as president of Harding College. Melvin Munn: former Texas grocery clerk now heard daily over more than 435 radio stations on H. L. Hunt's "Life Line." Fulton Lewis, Jr.: former staff member of the House Un-American Activities Committee, now director of the stridently conservative Young Americans for Freedom and a member of the Advisory Assembly of the American Conservative Union. Robert LeFevre: one of the more bizarre right-wingers, once active in the mystical "The Great I Am Movement," now operating Rampart College and the Freedom School in Santa Ana, California. (LeFevre is responsible for causing a rewrite of the Girl Scout Handbook which he attacked "because of its political slant and because of its unqualified endorsement of the United Nations and the League of Women Voters.")[23] Herbert Philbrick: well-known subject of TV's "I Led Three Lives" series based on his experience as counterspy for the FBI, now anti-communist lecturer, author and national director of United States Anti-Communist Congress, Inc. This parade of citizenship experts is trotted out each year before groups of rural youngsters assembled and sponsored by the Farm Bureau. These men are touted by the Farm Bureau as "recognized authorities on the subjects with which they deal," and as "outstanding lecturers on the American way of life."

These annual platforms also provide a steady source of income for these characters and their causes—fees range up to $600 for the afternoon.[24] Far worse, they offer primed audiences of young, eager high school leaders. The message they hear at these seminars is the same: pervasive distrust of government; deprecation of civil liberties; a frozen, conspiratorial view of world affairs; a sense of futility about the possibility of easing world tensions and pursuing disarmament; and a laissez-faire attitude toward our serious domestic problems. The Farm Bureau's right-wing speakers twist and pervert notions of self-reliance and personal freedom into clubs with which to beat down the destitute.

One should not assume that the absurdity of some of the diatribes described above reduces these sessions to burlesque. The same speakers return year after year because they are good: they are clever, often dynamic, and disturbingly effective at their trade. The students who attend the forums leave impressed, sometimes convinced. As one young participant remarked at the 1969 Montana seminar: "Dr. Kay . . . was an inspiration to our group because he didn't talk to us as if we were a group of teenagers, but as young adults." One girl, praising a speaker at the 1968 Missouri Freedom Forum said, "It's a good thing they are for our side and not the other. They'd have us all brainwashed."[25]

In addition to showing up at the youth conferences, these missionaries of fear also speak at state and county Farm Bureau functions for adults. At these regular organization meetings other lecturers appear, including Reed Benson, son of Ezra T., and director of public relations for the Birch Society; and Willis Stone, head of the Liberty Amendment Committee, the chief pressure group trying to repeal the federal income tax. One of the speakers at Farm Bureau gatherings, particularly in the south, is Tom Anderson, a council member of the Birch Society, owner and editor of a large chain of farm magazines, and one of the foremost reactionary figures in the country. Anderson opposes immigration, federal income tax, the United Nations, diplomatic relations with all communist countries, coexistence, federal aid to education, obligatory integration of the schools, and government control of public utilities. The Farm Bureau of Alabama has promoted Anderson's books in their monthly magazine, and a review of one of his latest works by the *Missouri Farm Bureau News* described Anderson as speaking "clearly and vividly with wisdom, warmth, and moral awareness."[26]

Farm Bureaus also interlock in other ways with the far right's distribution network. In 1949, *New Republic* reported that Farm Bureau members were receiving literature from Pappy O'Daniel's Christian American Association stamped "Your name obtained by Arkansas Farm Bureau."[27] A woman at Resnick's hearings in Omaha testified that after she became women's chairman for her county Farm Bureau, she began to receive letters from a group called Citizens Womens Council, addressed to her exactly as was her Farm Bureau mail—using her first name rather than her husband's—a form she used only on her Farm Bureau membership. The literature contained "bizarre propaganda, stickers that looked like eyes, red spots that said, 'I see red' which were supposed to be attached to the letters we wrote to Congressmen who didn't fit the ultra-conservative pattern." Senator Gale McGee said a few years ago that: "The extreme conservative . . . Farm Bureau in Wyoming is said to act as a kind of clearinghouse in Wyoming for the right wing political drive. It distributes, among other things, tracts of an extremist outfit called Americans for Constitutional Action."[28] The ACA is an operation that rates Congressmen and aids the most conservative. Strom Thurmond is the ACA's idea of a perfect Senator.

Another symptom of the Farm Bureau's reactionary metabolism is its involvement in the Liberty Amendment movement. The Liberty Amendment, endorsed by seven state legislatures, would repeal the federal income tax. Delightful as that may sound to harried taxpayers, its necessary corollary is retrenchment to a romantic view of post-Revolutionary War America. Liberty Amendment partisans demand that the national government cease all activities not specifically mentioned in the Constitution, including any role in education, welfare and social security, research, agriculture, health, flood control, parks, land reclamation, *ad infinitum*. As recently as 1959, the American Farm Bureau Federation at its national convention voted unanimously for a proposal to repeal the individual federal income tax. Farm Bureaus in several states have supported the Amendment at one time or another; a few still do.

One of the most controversial aspects of the Farm Bureau–right wing axis is the organization's connections with the John Birch Society, pacesetter of the hard-core extreme right. In 1969 the Society claimed to have between 60,000 and 100,000 members, a full-time staff of 77 and a part-time staff of 15. It is reported to have an income of five to six million dollars a year. The Anti-Defamation League of B'nai B'rith concluded recently that the Birch Society "has an imposing network of front groups and 'ad hoc committees' that help to give it a reach and a thrust far out of proportion to its actual members, and that enlist thousands of non-Birchers in the activities of the Society itself." Investigator Schrag concluded in 1970 that there was a "new vitality" in the Birch Society.[29]

Although probably best known for the charge by Birch head Robert Welch that President Eisenhower was a "conscious and dedicated agent of the Communist conspiracy," the Birch story doesn't end there. The Society has been at the forefront of the drive against the poverty program, spearheaded the "Impeach Earl Warren" agitation, and is currently committed to linking sex-education in high schools to the "Communist Conspiracy." Among other targets for its anti-communist campaigns, conducted either directly or through one of the front groups that sprout like weeds in a garden, has been the civil rights movement ("Fully expose the Civil Rights fraud and you will break the back of the Communist Conspiracy"), UNICEF, the grape and lettuce boycotts, and recently "sensitivity training" which apparently is also a communist plot.

As early as 1962, Professor Alan Westin reported that the Farm Bureau was facing "ideological penetration" by the Birch Society. In 1964, Senator Milton Young (Rep.–N.D.) charged that there was "clear evidence" that there had been considerable infiltration of the North Dakota Farm Bureau by the Society, and the Springfield, Missouri *Leader-Press* reported that "The . . . Farm Bureau has worked hand in glove with the John Birch Society in several states." In 1967, the *New York Times* reported that "In several states . . . there is an increasing identity of interest and an apparent overlap in membership between the Farm Bureau and the Birch Society." It went on to quote the president of the North Dakota Farm Bureau as stating: "We have, of course, something in common in philosophy with several organizations, including the Birch Society." In response to these reports, President Shuman replied: "I suppose that anytime anyone opposes the socialist policies of the present [Johnson] Administration in agriculture, you immediately get tagged as a Bircher, right-winger, or McCarthyite."[30]

Occasionally more formal links between Farm Bureau groups and the Birchers have surfaced. In 1964, the John Birch Society *Bulletin* reported:

In our last bulletin we mentioned that such a resolution [for Chief Justice Earl Warren's impeachment] had been passed by the Texas Farm Bureau. We did not have the details at that time, but this action had taken place at the state convention held on November 12 and 13 at Fort Worth. The original resolution had been drawn up by one of our good members in Houston, who had already pushed it through the community and county conventions, before thus getting it sent to the state body. There were 808 voting delegates at the state convention and the resolution was passed by a voice vote.[31]

The same publication, during the wheat referendum, referred Birch members to "any office of the FARM BUREAU" for more information.[32]

The parent American Farm Bureau Federation itself has generally avoided formal links and endorsements of right-wing groups and individuals, except insofar as it is singing their song. There have been some exceptions to this, however. At the national convention in 1961, it passed a resolution expressing regret that retired Major General Edwin A. Walker had been censured "for encouraging and conducting pro-American education." Walker, who had admitted he was a member of the Birch Society, had been reprimanded by the Army for indoctrinating his troops with right-wing political views. In 1963, the American Farm Bureau Federation was listed as a "cooperating organization" by the American Security Council, a military-industrial pressure group that *Newsweek* classified as part of "the military right."[33]

Just as the AFBF generally has carefully avoided formal endorsements of particular groups or individuals, most of the AFBF's top men and staff have avoided formal connections. There have, however, been notable exceptions here as well. Two of the AFBF's chief Washington lobbyists during the Eisenhower years—Frank Wooley and Kenneth Ingwalson—have been active in ultra-conservative movements. Ingwalson was credited by the Missouri Farm Bureau with being "one of the builders of the Farm Bureau's American citizenship program which is by far the most comprehensive and effective conducted by any membership organization in America."[34] Apparently building on that experience, he left the Farm Bureau to become the first executive director of Americans for Constitutional Action; left ACA to work for H. L. Hunt's "Life Line" radio network; and is now active with the Education for Freedom Foundation—a conservative tax-exempt foundation which, among other things, is investigating "campus anarchists." Wooley, who is now Chairman of the Foundation's Advisory Board, went from the Farm Bureau to the ACA and then on to the American Medical Association. He is currently executive-director of the ultra-conservative Association of American Physicians and Surgeons.

Former AFBF President Allan Kline also became more openly active in such groups after stepping down as president in 1955, remaining active until his death in 1968. He became a trustee of the ACA. He supported the principles of the Liberty Amendment movement, stating at one time that "you will find in Karl Marx that he is for most of the things we are now doing. . . . He was for the graduated income tax—steeply graduated— and for the inheritance tax. Why was he for them? . . . in order to destroy private capital."[35]

Kline also became a sponsor of the "1976 Committee," organized to promote Ezra Taft Benson for President in 1968, with Strom Thurmond as Vice President, on a platform to end "the nightmare of insanity and subversion which is today the central fact of our lives . . ." and to uproot "the poisonous vines of collectivism now slowly suffocating all freedom and all individualism on the American scene." According to the Milwaukee *Sentinel,* the group was headed by industrialist William Grede, a council member of the Birch Society who was quoted as saying that "about half the 30 persons who organized the committee . . . were Birch Society members."[36]

The current crop of AFBF barons has generally followed the pattern of avoiding public endorsements of organized right-wing groups and leading conservative figures. Nevertheless, Shuman is a trustee of the Foundation for Economic Education, Inc. at Irvington-on-Hudson, New York, an "education and research" operation which campaigns against nearly all forms of government "interventionism," including Medicare, urban renewal, federal aid to education, "paying people to be non-productive," compulsory education, government mail service, social security, anti-trust legislation, foreign aid, child labor laws, and progressive income taxes.[37]

If Shuman and AFBF Secretary-Treasurer Fleming have not publicly lent their names to the groups we have been examining, they have frequently graced their platforms and their publications. Shuman and Fleming both granted long interviews to *Farm and Ranch* magazine when that journal was the leading publication of Birch council member Tom Anderson. Shuman has been a frequent guest on the Manion Forum, the weekly broadcast of Clarence Manion carried by more than 200 radio stations and about 50 TV outlets. Manion, former dean of Notre Dame Law School, is one of the top leaders of the Birch Society in the country. Shuman has also addressed Young Americans for Freedom and has been a frequent speaker at various Freedom Forums at Harding College. He has received Harding's highest award, "Distinguished American Citizen." Fleming has also been a familiar face at Harding. He told the *New York Times,* in response to stories about the Farm Bureau's right-wing activities, that "Dr. [George C.] Benson is a fine old gentleman. I've been on programs with Nyaradi and I'm happy to be identified with him."[38]

The major problem of the far right in this country has always been to achieve respectability. The Farm Bureau—by offering its publications and platforms to spokesmen of the extreme right—has contributed importantly to giving these individuals and causes respectability in rural America. The Farm Bureau carries the reactionary, accusatory, conspiratory message of the far right to the farm and rural population through one of the most extensive communications networks in the nation. It uses some of its great economic resources to promote often vicious, anti-government, anti-civil rights economic and political philosophy, with particular effect on the country's rural youth. And because of the Farm Bureau's tax exemption, the American taxpayers are picking up part of the bill.

*   *   *

Along with its support of the forces on the country's extreme right, the Farm Bureau has been an active participant in conventional party politics. The laws that regulate the political activities of organizations like the Farm Bureau are quite loose. The rules governing exempt organizations do not currently limit the political activities of groups like the Farm Bureau. The Federal Corrupt Practices Act—part of the United States criminal code since 1925—does prohibit corporations and labor unions from making contributions, including giving anything of value, in connection with any primary or election for President, Vice President, Senator, or Congressman. The American Farm Bureau Federation and many of the state Farm Bureaus are non-profit corporations, bringing them within the provisions of the Corrupt Practices Act. However, the Supreme Court has ruled that the law is not violated merely by the expression of opinion by a corporation, and some courts have refused to convict where the amount of an actual contribution has been insubstantial. In any case, very few prosecutions have been brought against corporations in the forty-five years of the statute.

Regardless of the state of the law, the Farm Bureau has steadfastly claimed to be strictly non-partisan.[39] But the Bureau has a strange view of what is involved in being "non-partisan." Non-partisanship usually means non-intervention in party politics, not support of the candidate of one party here and the other there. But supporting candidates in their campaigns, or as Fleming puts it more delicately, "help(ing) its members evaluate candidates . . ."[40] has been a pillar of the organization's political strength through the years. It is difficult to know how deep it goes. One interesting index, however, was the Farm Bureau claim some years ago that about one of every four members in Congress were members of the Farm Bureau and that more than 40 percent of the governors were members. (Most of the members of the House Committee on Agriculture that voted to disassociate itself from Resnick's investigation were members of the Farm Bureau.) On the local and state level the Farm Bureau claimed that 54 percent of the members of the county boards of supervisors (commissioners or county court members) reached in a survey were members of the organization.

Farm Bureau leaders assert that they have recently launched a renewed effort to recruit those sympathetic to their program, both farm and nonfarm, to become candidates "in both parties." The plan is for county and state Farm Bureaus to organize committees of "Farmers for so and so." AFBF officials admit they are also encouraging their members, as individuals, to give money to these candidates. They claim, however, that the effort will stop at the primary stage. Perhaps, but it has not always been that way in the past. Farm Bureaus around the country have been active in the election campaigns of a number of past and current Congressmen, as well as hundreds of state and local officials.

One of the organization's most effective techniques in past elections has been to publish and circulate among its members the voting records of incumbent candidates for office. The 1966 Congressional elections in Iowa offer a good example of what can be done with this device when the votes are judiciously selected. The Johnson landslide in 1964 had helped to carry a handful of liberal Democrats from Iowa into Congress. By 1966, the leadership of the Iowa Farm Bureau was determined to restore the Iowa delegation to more conservative and friendly hands. Ten votes were selected from the scores cast in the tumultuous 89th Congress. By coincidence of course, of the seven member House delegation from Iowa, of which the Democrats had a 6–1 advantage, the Republicans voted 100 percent *with* the Farm Bureau on the 10 particular issues selected and the six Democrats voted nearly 100 percent *against* the Farm Bureau on the issues selected.

The issues were selected with special care. Of the 10 issues used to inform the members of the largest farm organization in the country of their Congressmen's responsiveness, seven were non-farm issues, including rent supplements, Section 14b of the Taft-Hartley Act, the vote to create the Department of Housing and Urban Development, and Medicare. Of the numerous agricultural votes taken by the 89th Congress, only three were chosen and one of these was the vote on a cotton bill, not of particular importance to the grain farmers of Iowa. Obviously the Iowa Farm Bureau was shopping around for the right votes.

The report on these ten votes appeared in the Iowa Farm Bureau newspaper on the day before the election.[41] With even more impact than the newspaper article was the mass mailing of a piece of literature on the incumbents sent to every Farm Bureau member in the state shortly before the election. The first page was a letter signed by the president and "national policy committee" chairman of the respective county. Its most prominent feature was the capsulized summary of the candidates' voting records as selected by the Farm Bureau.

It did not take much deciphering to get the message. The Farm Bureau's active support was generally credited with being an important factor in the Republican near-sweep of Iowa in the 1966 election. As AFBF Secretary-Treasurer Fleming proudly announced to the national convention that year, "The effort on the part of the Farm Bureau members and other like-minded citizens throughout the country, sparked the civic renaissance culminating in the changes of the United States House of Representatives subsequent to the 1966 Congressional elections."[42]

In addition to purging its enemies, the Farm Bureau often manages to reward its friends in Congress. One good example of such friendship is the long and cordial relationship between the Illinois Agricultural Association and Congressman Paul Findley. The IAA has backed Findley in his Congressional races and Findley has been generally in line with the Farm Bureau in Congress. In 1962, redistricting in Illinois plunged Findley into one of the most difficult political challenges of his career. He was pitted against another incumbent Congressman, popular Democrat Peter Mack. In August, as the campaign heated up, Mack accused the supposedly non-partisan Farm Bureau organization of providing Findley with the use of its mailing list and addressograph machines—in fact of actually doing a mass mailing of Findley campaign literature to Bureau members. At first the IAA emphatically denied the charge, but upon reconsideration the next day, it issued a statement acknowledging it had addressed Findley's mailing because "his votes in Congress this year have consistently agreed with Farm Bureau policies." In a public letter to Mack, IAA (and now AFBF) President William Kuhfuss explained the thinking of the non-partisan organization: "We feel . . . that we need to support those Congressmen who pay heed to the letters and telegrams from Farm Bureau members and voted in support of the Farm Bureau position. We feel, also that we need to replace those Congressmen who turned a deaf ear to the concerns of farmers . . . Congressman Findley's actions in the Congress this year have consistently agreed with Farm Bureau policy positions." "You express surprise," continued Kuhfuss' letter to Mack, "that Farm Bureau addressed envelopes for Congressman Findley. Is it surprising that we help a Congressman who supported Farm Bureau positions as avidly as has Congressman Findley?" Not only did the American Farm Bureau Federation not disclaim the action or reprimand the Illinois organization for so openly flaunting the Farm Bureau's repeated claims of non-partisanship, it reprinted Kuhfuss's letter in the AFBF Newsletter.[43]

Paul Findley has not forgotten who his friends are. He has supported nearly all the strong Farm Bureau positions and introduced many of them into Congress in the form of bills. He introduced: the Farm Bureau-backed Agricultural Adjustment Act of 1969; a bill which would effectively have outlawed the NFO by making some of its activities a crime; the Farm Bureau-backed bill to turn the Rural Electrification Administration coops into stock companies; and a host of others. In fact, Findley's performance in Congress gives the Farm Bureau so much pleasure that he is featured in their weekly national newsletter more often than any other member of Congress.

The Farm Bureau's presence has also been felt in Presidential elections. Although the parent AFBF does not openly endorse candidates, the leadership makes its preference clearly known to the membership. *Nations Agriculture,* the American Farm Bureau Federation magazine with circulation of nearly 2 million, published an article in its November, 1964 issue about the Presidential candidates. After reiterating that "Farm Bureau does not endorse candidates," an assertion that as we have seen is less than candid, the magazine went on to assert: "Senator Goldwater has voted in accordance with Farm Bureau's policy recommendations most of the time. Representative Miller has followed many of the Farm Bureau's recommendations, but he has been somewhat less consistent than Mr. Goldwater. As a member of the Senate, President Johnson voted contrary to Farm Bureau's recommendations more often than he voted for them. And Senator Humphrey has been almost as consistent in his opposition as Mr. Goldwater has been in his support."[44]

After the election, Shuman bitterly attacked businessmen for their support of Johnson. "Apparently corporations are concerned only with prospects for immediate profits and care little about what is happening in agriculture," said Shuman. "They forget that once agriculture is socialized, other industries will be conquered quickly." It is interesting to note that in that interview, Shuman added that he did not mean to include all of business in his criticism. The Farm Bureau still had many friends in business, he explained, particularly in the insurance and investment industries.[45]

In 1968, the sympathy of the Farm Bureau was clear. Never having been happy with Hubert Humphrey, Richard Nixon was much more to the Bureau's liking. On October 23, 1968, during the homestretch of the tightening Presidential race, Charles Shuman and Roger Fleming met with Richard Nixon and his close advisor Bryce Harlow at Mr. Nixon's apartment. At that time Nixon pledged to the Farm Bureau leaders that, if elected, his administration would be more sympathetic to the Farm Bureau's outlook on farm policies.[46] What support was asked or offered in return is not known. However, in a letter to the President in early 1970, asking for Nixon's support for the Farm Bureau's general agriculture bill before Congress, Shuman pointedly referred to that meeting and to the fact that "farmers and small town residents were decisive in determining the election outcome." At the 1969 national convention of the Farm Bureau held in Washington, the Administration paid an unusual tribute to such an organization with surprise visits not only by the President, but the Vice President as well.

Despite the fact that it is a tax-exempt organization, politics has been a potent weapon in the Farm Bureau arsenal. The Farm Bureau has managed to combine both the economic resources of a $4 billion business operation and the political resources of an effective partisan organization. This awesome concentration of power is unchecked, resting in the hands of those who are not even accountable to their own members, let alone to the public at large.

11

Profiteering with Poverty

MOST URBAN AND SUBURBAN AMERICANS still believe in the rural America of the post cards—prosperous farms with freshly painted barns and well-scrubbed children; but there is also another rural America, and millions of the country's poor live there. About 10 million rural Americans live in poverty. Millions more—farmers and non-farmers alike—struggle to survive on desperately meager incomes, with little consolation that—by official standards—they are above the mystical poverty line. While national unemployment hovers between 4 and 6 percent, in rural America it soars to as high as 18 percent. More than 3 million rural Americans are illiterate. One in every 13 houses in rural America is unfit to live in. There are millions of chronically hungry children and even more who are undernourished. Millions of rural Americans, particularly low income farm families, have fled to the cities over the past few decades. Many of them now live in crowded urban slums and face a bleak, hard existence. Regardless of how bleak their lives, however, few return to the regions they left behind.

Because of its size, resources, and influence among rural Americans, the Farm Bureau has had more opportunity to alleviate rural poverty than any other organization outside the federal government. But not only has the Farm Bureau not been part of the solution, it has actually been part of the problem. While the Farm Bureau certainly did not create poverty in America, it can justifiably take partial credit for its continuing existence. It has erected roadblocks to decisive government action to help the poor—both rural and urban. It has fought efforts to improve the life of the country's farm workers; and it has led the advocates of a farm policy that would further widen the gap between rich and poor on America's farms.

It is interesting to note that in the nation's largest farm organization, with enough room for bankers, barbers, bowling alleys and body shops, a farm worker—as distinct from a farm owner—who spends his entire life working in agriculture, can only obtain a non-voting "associate" membership.[1] Not only has the Farm Bureau thus made farm workers second class citizens within the Bureau, it has also suppressed their attempts to form their own organizations. It is terrified of the movement to organize farm laborers and willing to commit the entire force of its resources to stop it.

There is no other issue on the Congressional front, except perhaps dismantling the government farm program, to which the Farm Bureau devotes more time, energy and money than farm labor legislation. The AFBF has vigorously opposed the extension of the National Labor Relations Act—the Bill of Rights of organized labor—to agriculture. Instead it has supported a watered-down farm labor bill, originally introduced by former Senator George Murphy of California, which would set up a separate Farm Labor Relations Board not bound by the years of labor relations precedent of the NLRB. The bill includes a sweeping prohibition on strikes that "might result in the loss of a crop" and excludes from its coverage seasonal workers who spend less than 100 work days in agriculture (which excludes about 2 million of the 3 million farm wage workers). The Farm Bureau has conceded that this is "somewhat more restrictive than necessary," and suggests that coverage only be denied to workers who spend less than 50 work days in agriculture, a provision that would still exclude about 1.5 million farm wage workers. The Farm Bureau also supports a provision that would exempt from coverage all farms that use less than 1,500 man-days of agricultural labor during 12 months, another broad limitation on the effect of the bill. Another crippling departure from general labor law advocated as part of the Farm Bureau's farm labor package would play on the high turnover rate in farm labor from year to year to introduce a degree of instability to farm worker unions avoided in all other unions.[2]

The Farm Bureau's Washington lobby has also worked against extending the coverage of social security unemployment insurance to farm workers. Although it claims it would support an unemployment insurance plan, if it could find one that is "workable," it has opposed even the modest proposal submitted by the Nixon administration that would cover only one third of the hired farm labor force. And the giant farm organization is opposing the coverage of farm workers by minimum wage and hours laws, since that would "involve great complexities of application and administration."[3]

In recent years the Farm Bureau has emerged as a leading opponent of the efforts to unionize farm workers. It has steadily increased the intensity of its assaults on Cesar Chavez and his United Farm Workers Organizing Committee and has committed its vast resources to frustrating the national boycotts, first of non-union grapes and, more recently, of lettuce.

In the fall of 1968, Farm Bureau leaders threatened to move their national convention from Kansas City when that city's council endorsed the grape boycott. At that convention, AFBF president Shuman, in a lapse from the organization's policy that the market place should not be used as a bargaining weapon, suggested a counter-boycott against stores which stopped selling California grapes. Early in 1969, Shuman engaged in an exchange with Chicago's Mayor Richard Daley, inviting him to tour the Delano, California, site of the strike after Daley endorsed the boycott. In late June of that year, the AFBF's board of directors called upon Attorney General Mitchell to investigate the boycott as a possible "conspiracy in restraint of trade," and if so, to "prosecute all parties involved."[4]

During the summer of 1969, the Farm Bureau joined forces with other conservative anti-labor groups such as the National Right to Work Committee and the National Association of Food Chains (a strange bedfellow for a farm organization). In a July, 1969, letter to local Farm Bureau leaders, an official of the organization revealed that, "several very reliable sources in the retail food trade have contacted the Farm Bureau asking for a campaign to offset the boycott."[5] Like a true friend the Farm Bureau began exerting counter-pressure on food stores which had stopped selling non-union grapes, while alleging that the strike activity is primarily the work of outside agitators—"New Left anarchists and rent-a-pickets."

After joining forces with such allies as the National Association of Food Chains, the Farm Bureau embarked on what it called a "crash program" to fight the grape boycott. The AFBF put its staff to work on anti-boycott activities, helping to launch local "Freedom to Market Committees" around the country. These committees, organized through the county Farm Bureaus, put pressure on local grocers to continue to sell grapes. They also attempted to bolster declining grape sales resulting from the boycott by distributing "buy more grapes" bumper stickers and posters. In June 1970, the Cook County (Illinois) Farm Bureau's board of directors blasted the Jewel Food Stores for refusing to sell grapes and called for a counter-boycott of the stores. The move was proclaimed to the entire organization in a front page story in the AFBF Newsletter.

Among the techniques sponsored by the Farm Bureau to promote grape sales during the national boycott was a national "grapestakes" contest. Forty-one state Farm Bureaus participated in the contest to promote non-union table grapes. The first prize, a 1971 pick-up truck, was announced at the American Farm Bureau Federation national convention in Houston, Texas, in December, 1970.[6]

Meanwhile the Farm Bureau was promoting Jose Mendoza, the grape growers answer to Chavez. Mendoza, spokesman for the self-styled California Farm Workers Freedom to Work Movement, travelled around the country carrying the growers' message that things are just fine among the workers down in the San Joaquin Valley.[7]

The Farm Bureau also distributed tens of thousands of pamphlets deriding the unionization effort. The more scurrilous of these, put out under the name of the "Consumer's Rights Committee" of Washington, portray the strike sympathizers as dirty, bare-footed and bearded "anarchists" and "activist ministers" who are promoting their goal by "threats, assaults, fire-bombing and vandalism."

The California Farm Bureau and its president, Allan Grant, have led the attack. The state organization committed substantial resources to coordinating the growers' resistance. A special program to provide assistance to the growers was established, including a newsletter on farm labor problems, a 24-hour clearing-house for growers with "labor difficulties," an educational program "to aid farm employers and their supervisors in learning to cope with labor problems and with unions." "Phase two" of this expanded labor program, announced Grant in the fall of 1970, "envisions on-the-farm labor relations assistance," including legal counsel, advice in "labor harassment situations, help in union negotiations if necessary, [and] assistance to growers who already have signed union contracts, and other aids." Grant was officially recognized by the California growers in 1969 as the man who contributed the most to the state's grape industry, "because of [his] contributions on [their] behalf against the grape boycott."[8]

Farm Bureau leaders also shadow Chavez as he travels around the country to promote his efforts. No forum, big or small, seems to evade the Bureau. When Chavez was interviewed on the "Today" show, Grant followed some days later for the rebuttal. Even when Chavez addressed a small church in New York City and urged the parishioners to support the unionization campaign, Floyd Hawkins, president of the Arizona Farm Bureau, flew in two weeks later to address the congregation of about 100 people.

Despite the Farm Bureau's strenuous efforts, however, the United Farm Workers Organization Committee achieved a stunning victory in the fall of 1970 when the California table-grape growers recognized the union as the bargaining agent for the farm workers. With that victory under its belt, the farm workers' union set out to unionize the lettuce workers of California and Arizona and called for a national boycott of lettuce raised on farms that do not recognize the UFWOC.

But if the union is in for the long-haul, so is the Farm Bureau. President Shuman, in his farewell address to the 1970 national convention, indicated continued Farm Bureau resistance to the union, as well as bitterness over its previous victory. "This was the year," said Shuman, "when the ruthless tactics of organized labor, combined with the prejudice-laden propaganda of misguided clergymen, forced the capitulation of certain chain stores to the demands of the grape boycotters. Farmers saw the fine principles of 'freedom to market' and 'freedom for consumers to choose' tossed in the ash can by the Chicago-based Jewel Food Stores which decided to cooperate with the boycott rather than risk the mugging of employees and the fire bombings of their stores. After the Jewel caved in, it was only a matter of a few days until California grapes were shut out of most markets unless the grapes were identified by the 'black bug' of the union."[9]

The ultimate success or failure of the farm worker unionization movement will be decided in part by the outcome of this head-on clash between the UFWOC and the Farm Bureau. Whether the outcome will be, as Grant describes it, "the establishment of law and order in the fields of this state,"[10] or, as Chavez describes it, the lifting of farm workers from their status as

second-class citizens through collective action, depends, in no small measure, upon the relative staying power of the union and the Farm Bureau.

*   *   *

The plight of the 3 million agricultural workers in this country is generally a bleak one. One significant group of farm workers is the migrant
laborers. According to the United States Department of Agriculture, there
were about 330,000 migrant farm workers in the United States in 1968, of
which about 280,000 were United States citizens. Counting families there
are about a million migrants in the United States. The life of many of them
makes existence in the worst urban slum seem cheerful by comparison. The
role of the Farm Bureau in relation to migrant farm workers has been, once
again, that of obstructionist to meaningful change and apologist for the
status quo. In the Middle Atlantic states, for example, the owners of large
fruit and vegetable farms bring in thousands of seasonal workers each year
to harvest their crops. One of the leading agents for supplying these migrants is the New Jersey Farm Bureau. The Glassboro Service Association,
an affiliate controlled by the New Jersey Farm Bureau, annually makes
about 10,000 migrant laborers available to its members. Each year it nego-
tiates a contract with the Puerto Rican government for most of these
workers.

The Association also runs a migrant camp—a waystation for the incom-
ing Puerto Ricans before they are parcelled out to their prospective employers. The Glassboro-run camp is not a bad one by migrant camp standards—nothing most of us would want to live in, of course—but at least
a source of the minimum necessities for decent human existence. The New
Jersey Farm Bureau, however, has been a leading opponent of action by
the state to censure and correct camps which do not satisfy even these
minimum conditions. It has continually fought social action agencies such
as the Volunteers in Service to America (Vista) and the National Association for the Advancement of Colored People which are seeking to improve
the life of the migrant.

During the New Jersey picking seasons of 1965 and 1966, there was a great deal of activity on the part of union leaders to organize the migrants; on the part of Vista volunteers and other anti-poverty workers to teach them; and on the part of newspapermen to report on conditions in some of the southern New Jersey camps, described as "squalid" by the *New York Times*. This activity produced repercussions throughout the state. Many of the farmer-operators reacted angrily to the outside intrusions. Some of them ordered Vista volunteers off their farms, accusing them of stirring up blacks and helping the labor unions to organize them.

Governor Richard Hughes named a task force on migrant farm labor to investigate the camps and make recommendations. The task force heard stories of deplorable conditions at some of the camps and of discrimination against the migrants by county welfare and other public officials. Vista volunteers and college students who had led a union organizing drive in the camps the previous summer described large numbers of blacks as "virtual prisoners, living in isolated hovels deep inside farms, miles from any neighbors." One county welfare director conceded: "Let's be realistic. The community justs wants the migrants to come in and pick the crops and then get out." This accounted, he acknowledged, for much of the hostility to the migrants from farmers and welfare officials.[11]

New Jersey Farm Bureau President Arthur West testified before the task force on behalf of the migrant employers in the Farm Bureau. "Over the years," he told the Governor's committee, "I have been more than an employer to these people [the migrants]. Dozens of them have become my friends. They turn to me when they need help, and I turn to them. They are not down-trodden slaves. They travel as family groups, closely associated together, for the most part happy in their work. They rank low in terms of education, but they are skilled in the planting, cultivating and harvesting of crops. They can do the kind of work that not too many others can do or will do. . . ." West claimed that the migrant workers in New Jersey were the best paid, best housed, best educated, and healthiest of those in any state in the country.[12]

Meanwhile, the Farm Bureau was taking steps to block future inter-ference by anti-poverty workers and other outsiders at the migrant camps. On March 22, 1967, the New Jersey Farm Bureau sent its members order blanks for *No Trespassing* signs to help "tighten up security on farms." The executive-director of the tri-county anti-poverty agency in southern New Jersey, upon learning of the new move, accused the Farm Bureau of "encouraging erection of barriers between the farm workers and the press, the clergy and the anti-poverty workers." He also charged that the Farm Bureau had called upon its members to clear all public statements on farm labor with the state organization. The Farm Bureau conceded that it had urged its members to "post signs on their property against trespassers or those who have no legal right to enter upon such private property without permission" and that it had also offered the service of the organization to members "in the field of press relations."[13]

The Bureau, at the same time, circulated to its members a "Guide to Farm Labor and the Protection of Property Rights." Included in this handbook was a remarkable document, an agreement to be signed between the farmer and the worker. The "sample agreement" read:

I, [employee's name], understand that the land owned by my employer [farmer's name] is private property, and I agree not to invite or receive any guests or visitors on [farmer's name]'s property unless I obtain written permission at least one (1) day in advance. If I should receive an unexpected visitor, I will notify my employer immediately, and will ask my visitor to leave if my employer does not grant permission for him to stay. I understand that the issuance of visitors' permits is in the sole discretion of my employer, and I agree to accept his decision.

[Signature][14]

How many farmers carried out this outrageous proposal is not known. The indenture would effectively imprison the migrants by giving the employer veto power on whom they could or could not see. The Farm Bureau did report a brisk business in *No Trespassing* signs, selling over 3,000 at $1.00 each. The signs prompted the NAACP Legal Defense Fund to go into court to knock them down as violations of First Amendment freedoms of speech and assembly. Defense Fund lawyers contended that the farmer forfeited his absolute right to privacy when he agreed to provide housing for his workers.[15]

The right of free access to migrant labor camps has been a hotly contested issue between migrant employers and officials of government and private social action agencies. During the summer of 1970, two anti-poverty workers were arrested on trespassing charges by the New Jersey state police when they refused to leave a migrant camp. At the same time in Oregon, the Valley Migrant League, a federally funded agency which helps 30,000 migrants in Oregon, had two of their workers arrested on the same charges.

Late in 1970, New Jersey Governor William T. Cahill proposed legislation to knock down the trespass signs and guarantee free access to the camps. "Refusals to permit federal and state anti-poverty, health, and education officials to visit migrant labor camps," Mr. Cahill said, "have too often frustrated attempts to improve the lives of seasonal workers."[16]

About the same time, the Department of Justice issued guidelines in the Oregon controversy which purported to insure for the first time the right of an agency aiding migrants to visit the workers in privately owned camps. Some anti-poverty workers, however, saw the guidelines as a capitulation by the Federal government to the growers, represented by the Oregon Farm Bureau in the negotiations leading to the guidelines. The federal guidelines permit anti-poverty workers to enter the camps only after working hours or on non-working days. They must leave in time "to allow a full night's sleep for the workers." Visits may be made during working hours only to provide services for migrant children and for non-working members of migrant families. The guidelines also require the anti-poverty agency to furnish the employers with advance copies of any materials being distributed to the workers, although the Justice Department has contended that "this shall not be construed to mean that the employer has a right of censorship."[17]

Despite the attempt to keep the world away from the camps, conditions of migrants in New Jersey drew national attention on November 28, 1967, when a fire in a migrant shack at a labor camp in Salem County, New Jersey, killed five children. They were five of the seven children of Mrs. Louise Taylor, a seasonal worker who was earning about $20 a week and who was working in the fields at the time. The chairman of the governor's task force on migrant farm labor, blaming "living conditions" at the wooden shack for the fiery deaths, called for immediate passage of a bill then pending in the state legislature to give the state the right to license migrant camps and keep them from opening if they failed to meet certain prescribed standards. The New Jersey Farm Bureau opposed this bill. "There is no dire emergency here," the New Jersey Farm Bureau president contended, and urged postponement of action for another year. This prompted the task force chairman to remark: "I wonder just how many more kids have to die before we have a dire emergency."[18]

The Farm Bureau campaigned loudly and strongly against the proposed inspection bill, arguing that the bill gave "broad and dangerous" powers to the state Labor Commissioner. It sent a memo to each member of the legislature warning that "some people" were attempting to use the fire deaths to cause enactment of the bill. But the outcry over the deaths of the children was too powerful to be smothered; the bill passed by a narrow vote, over the Farm Bureau protests.[19]

The following year another tragedy provoked another drive for legislation, and once again the Farm Bureau worked vigorously against it. A busload of migrants crashed, killing 18 of them. Legislation was proposed to insure safer transportation of migrants. The New Jersey Farm Bureau opposed it. Apparently there was still no "dire emergency."

In his testimony at Resnick's Washington hearings, the director of the anti-poverty agency for southwest New Jersey said he felt the officials of the New Jersey Farm Bureau place a higher value on the tomatoes than on the people who pick them. "That distorted sense of priorities leads them to find any given channel that permits them to slow down change. They have opposed almost every piece of social legislation that has come down the pike."[20]

The New Jersey Farm Bureau's current policies do little to dispel this charge. The Bureau claims that public opinion on the migrant situation has been distorted by "a deliberate campaign by certain groups and individuals to bring about certain changes" in the farm labor situation. In a most magnanimous gesture, the New Jersey organization has favored legislation to restrict 12-year-olds from working more than 40 hours a week. But the ultimate in fatherly concern is the New Jersey Farm Bureau's policy supporting "efforts to protect the privacy of farm workers who have moved into migrant houses."[21] All the time we thought that those *No Trespassing* signs were to keep lawyers and poverty workers and clergy and newspaper snoopers off the migrant farms, we were wrong. The Farm Bureau simply was trying to guard the privacy of the farm worker living in his wooden shack with a broken window and a hole in the wall.

The New Jersey Farm Bureau contends that it has shown enlightened leadership on the migrant problem, particularly with the Puerto Ricans who are handled by their Glassboro Service Association. Conditions are good, they contend. But others do not agree. In the fall of 1970, anti-poverty lawyers charged that hundreds of migratory farm workers had been jailed in southern New Jersey during the summer without ever seeing a judge, or without benefit of legal counsel. Max Rothman, the director of the farm worker division of a federally funded legal services agency that deals with migrants, charged that "a number of farmers are intimidating their migrant workers by threatening them with arrest and jailing on the slightest pretext, such as in cases where migrants dispute their wages or criticize the conditions in the camps where they live." The problems of the Puerto Ricans are compounded, according to Rothman, because they rarely speak English and thus never actually know why they are arrested. Upon hearing of these charges, the Puerto Rican Lawyers Association, headquartered in New York City, conducted its own investigation of the farms. Their findings prompted them to petition the Governor of Puerto Rico, with whom the Glassboro Service Association contracts for its Puerto Rican migrants, to stop sending migrant workers to the farms in New Jersey. And a Puerto Rican group in the United States, affiliated with the Roman Catholic and Episcopal churches and the United Church of Christ, launched a campaign to "alert farm workers in Puerto Rico to the problems they will be facing in the United States and where to go to voice their grievances."[22]

New Jersey does not have the only state Farm Bureau to show such enlightenment about the care and keeping of farm workers. The Oregon Farm Bureau's magazine recently reported on a meeting of farmers and the Farm Bureau director of farm labor with representatives of the state Board of Health. Although both sides agreed that there really ought to be showers at the camps, the farmers employing migrant workers wanted the number of showers to be determined solely by the number of workers and not by the total population of the camps—workers and their families. There was also "some objection" to requiring plumbed-in hand washing facilities as opposed to wash basins. But the greatest outcry was over the requirement for screen doors on the migrants' housing, obviously a dispensable luxury.[23]

In 1968, a committee of New York State legislators visited the migrant labor camps on Long Island. As they toured the long barracks-like buildings, lined with rows of cots, one of them remarked that it was worse than the Army; another described it as a "firetrap." The president of the Long Island Farm Bureau disagreed. Most of the camps, he said, were "superior to vacation camps in living space, fireproofing, sanitation and other accommodations."[24]

During his investigation of the Farm Bureau, Resnick also looked into the organization's relationship to migrant labor camps. The week before his Washington hearings began, a front page article in *The Washington Post* alerted him to the conditions in a Farm Bureau migrant labor camp in Cherion, Virginia. According to this article, "If you approach the Farm Bureau labor camp for migrant workers here from downwind, you may smell it a half a mile away." The disturbing report revealed that the Farm Bureau owned several camps on Virginia's eastern shore and operated them in an unsanitary and inhumane fashion, while collecting about $1,000 a week from the people who lived in them.[25]

Resnick invited the responsible Virginia state officials to testify before his hearings. Despite the obvious futility of the gesture, he also invited the Farm Bureau officials involved. The Virginia state officials charged with supervising the living conditions of migrant workers in their state told Resnick that the camps portrayed in the *Post* article continued in operation despite having been condemned by the state. (The camps were not far from Richmond, the state capital.)

It quickly became apparent during the hearings that the state officials were far more sympathetic to the growers than to the migrants whom they were charged with protecting. Even when confronted with pictures Resnick had obtained from the *Post,* showing open sewage ditches used as playgrounds, and broken-down wooden shacks serving as homes, they insisted that things were not so bad. (One must remember that there are considerably more farmers voting in Virginia than migrant laborers.)

Fortunately, the attention brought to bear on these camps by the day's hearings led to their inspection by federal officials. This resulted less than two weeks later in an announcement by the Virginia Employment Commission that it was immediately stopping its recruitment of migrant workers for the four Farm Bureau labor camps in Virginia,[26] because they failed to meet new federal standards. Rather than feeling any pleasure at this outcome, however, one can only be outraged that it required a Congressional hearing before anything was done.

The American Farm Bureau Federation has long opposed federal government intervention, including Department of Labor standards, to correct the migrant situation. It has blasted the National Council of Churches and the National Catholic Rural Life Conferences, both active in bringing public attention to problems of migrants, for lobbying on "purely secular issues and participation in farm labor disputes." As Shuman has put it: "Nowhere in the Bible is there any basis for the church participation in the political arena." (Shuman is a strict constructionist—of both the Constitution and the Bible.)[27]

In 1960, TV news commentator Edward R. Murrow poignantly brought the migrant problem to the attention of the American people with a moving documentary on the migrant condition entitled "Harvest of Shame." "We used to own our slaves," concluded Murrow, "now we just rent them." One of the people interviewed on the show was Charles Shuman. "I think that most social workers will agree," he remarked, "that it's better for a man to be employed, even if his capacity is such as to limit his income. And we take the position that it's far better to have thousands of these folks who are practically unemployable earning some money, doing some productive work, for at least a few days in the year."[28]

The broadcast, which pictured the pitiful state in which thousands of migrants live, provoked a storm of controversy and demands for Congressional reforms. The attack on the program was led by the American Farm Bureau Federation. The AFBF's board of directors passed a widely circulated resolution blasting the broadcast as "highly colored propaganda." The AFBF issued a critique of the program, the commentator, the producer and the network and supplied it to several Congressmen and Senators for use on Capitol Hill. The essence of the critique was that the show had been a total distortion of the "real" migrant, who, the Bureau claimed, was actually doing quite well.[29]

Ten years later, in 1970, NBC newsman Chet Huntley, moved by official inaction since the "Harvest of Shame" broadcast and by the continuing distress of the American migrant laborer, presented an updated documentary on the problem. His conclusion: there had been little improvement since 1960. He found that the average annual income for migrants was $891, and that they had an average life expectancy of 39 years.[30]

Once again the Farm Bureau felt compelled to act as an apologist for the giant corporate farms that sustain the migrant labor system. Even before Huntley's show went on the air, the Farm Bureau denounced it as "unreasonable" and "false."[31] Clearly then, if the country wishes to avoid another heart-rending documentary on the condition of migrant workers in 1980, it will have to overcome the vigorous opposition of the Farm Bureau first.

*   *   *

The stain of poverty on the hands of the Farm Bureau goes far beyond its role in the fight against migrant laborers and other farm workers. In his book, *The Other America,* which first brought the country's poor to national attention, Michael Harrington accused the Farm Bureau of having a "stake in poverty's survival." An examination of the Farm Bureau's recent statements and actions confirms this accusation.

The attitude of Farm Bureau ex-president Charles Shuman toward poverty in America is revealing, for it epitomizes the self-satisfied unconcern that has been so difficult for the nation to overcome. In an interview with the *St. Louis Dispatch,* Shuman defined poverty as "a combination of lack of education, training, and lack of ambition . . . . I don't think the Federal Government can do anything about it except spend a lot of money." At another point he explained, ". . . the very things which have made our Nation relatively free of poverty—freedom to work or play, freedom to spend or save, freedom to own a TV set and a Cadillac but live in a shack in order to do so. We are already too far down the road that leads to socialism —a morally decrepit philosophy which destroys the initiative to do better." Writing in *Nation's Agriculture,* he conceded that there are "poverty-stricken families" in the United States today but then asked, "What kind of poverty is this? With abundant educational and job opportunities on every hand, it must be primarily a poverty of the mind and soul—a lack of desire."[32]

These remarks by Shuman typify the policies of the Farm Bureau. Despite the fact that one in every four persons in rural America is poor, and that almost one of every three poor people are in rural America, the nation's largest rural organization fought against the anti-poverty program. The first witness to testify against the Economic Opportunity Act of 1964 at the Congressional hearings was the American Farm Bureau Federation. Instead of pleading for more attention to rural areas, an area sadly under-emphasized in that bill, the Farm Bureau representative declared that "this is no time to embark on massive increases in spending of the size proposed in this bill." He argued that "extraordinary progress" towards eliminating poverty in rural areas was being made and that Congress should give existing programs, such as the Vocational Education Act of 1963, a chance to work. Interestingly enough, the Farm Bureau opposed the VEA that year.[33]

When the anti-poverty program was enacted, the Farm Bureau quickly joined its most vocal critics, accosting the program even before it had had a chance to dig in. "One of the most costly, wasteful, and graft-ridden political patronage schemes ever imposed on the American people," charged Shuman in urging the voters to "register protest" in the 1966 Congressional elections.[34] The victory against the poverty program that they missed in 1964, they registered with the changes in Congress in 1966.

The President's Commission on Rural Poverty has reported to the nation: "Nowhere in the United States is the need for health service so acute, and nowhere is it so inadequate [as in rural America]. The statistical evidence is overwhelming, yet the statistics barely suggest the inequity and the discrimination against the rural poor in medical and dental care and in modern health services." Each rural birth presents a greater chance of an infant or maternal death than one in the city or in the suburbs. There is one non-federal doctor for every 500 people in metropolitan areas; one for every 2,000 people in isolated rural areas. At every income level, far fewer residents of rural areas are covered by hospital insurance than are their city cousins.

In the face of these disturbing realities the Farm Bureau was one of the chief allies of the American Medical Association in the AMA's relentless, and for many years successful battle against Medicare. In 1960, Roger Fleming called "all Government moves to supply medical benefits to the aged steps toward socialized medicine."[35] The Farm Bureau fought in Congress against the principle of a social security medical care program for the aged each year until its ultimate passage in 1965. It currently opposes any national health care plan.

Rural schools are generally smaller and less well-equipped than urban schools. The youngster going to school in a rural area is less likely to have modern facilities such as language and science laboratories. He is twice as likely to have an uncertified teacher, and his teacher will probably be paid less. Rural youth, consequently, drop out of school sooner and faster than urban youth. Less than half as many, proportionately, go on to college as city youth. Yet the Farm Bureau, in combination with groups like the

AMA, the National Association of Manufacturers and the United States Chamber of Commerce, defeated President Kennedy's federal aid to education program in 1961, and have fought it consistently since. Despite the program's enactment, opposition to federal aid to education remains Farm Bureau policy today.

One of the most fundamental problems in many scattered rural regions is the economic depression that has followed sharp declines in manpower needs resulting from the agricultural revolution. The difficulties in attracting new industry are compounded in many rural areas by inadequate transportation facilities, lack of coordinated planning, and depleted local leadership. Yet despite a certain amount of lip-service to rural redevelopment (the women's chairman of the AFBF recently served as chairman of President Nixon's Commission on Rural Affairs), the Farm Bureau opposed one of the most ambitious rural development programs the nation has ever undertaken.

The Public Works and Economic Development Act, ultimately passed by Congress in 1965, authorized $6 billion in grants and loans to assist America's economically distressed areas. The Act provided planning grants and loans for badly needed public facilities—like water systems and sewage plants—and for promoting industrial development in these regions. The program focused on distressed "redevelopment areas," a large portion of which would be rural, and provided for the creation of multi-county economic development districts to assist in regional planning. An important part of the program—about $4.5 billion over a ten year period—provided low interest loans for public facilities in target "redevelopment areas" and encouraged the development of private enterprises in such areas through interest subsidies.

The Farm Bureau opposed the Public Works and Economic Development Act, just as it had its precursor, the Area Redevelopment Act a few years before. The Bureau contended that it represented a serious erosion of state powers as well as an encroachment by the executive branch on the powers of Congress. Interest subsidies to encourage private business to locate in distressed areas represented, from the Farm Bureau's view, a mistake. "It would appear that to the extent this program is effective in 'bringing more stable and promising business enterprises . . . into depressed areas'," explained the Farm Bureau representative who testified to the Senate committee considering the bill, "investments induced thereby will inevitably be investments which would otherwise be made elsewhere. Investments which are relocated by interest subsidies represent an inefficient allocation of resources." As for the section of the bill authorizing regional planning commissions, the Farm Bureau saw "no real purpose" for them and expressed "continuing concern that regionalization of public programs has a tendency to impair state and local authority and responsibility."[36]

The Farm Bureau's share of responsibility for rural poverty is really twofold. It has been a relentless force against change in this country, especially when that change has involved government intervention into the areas of our greatest social need. Even more reprehensible, however, has been its failure as the country's largest rural organization to dramatize the dimensions of rural poverty, to demand corrective action, to cry out for equal opportunity for rural Americans, to commit the kind of energy and resources to the development of rural areas and the alleviation of rural poverty that it has marshalled for the elimination of the government farm program. The national policies of the American Farm Bureau Federation cover everything from ROTC to the National Council of Churches, from pornography to pay TV, from financing political campaigns to the international balance of payments. But the Bureau never mentions rural poverty.

12

Farming the Farmer

THE FARM POLICY pursued unrelentingly by the Farm Bureau for more than two decades now is one that would further widen the gap between rich and poor in farming and signify economic disaster for thousands of smaller operators.

The forces at work in the agricultural sector of the economy are turbulent and complex. Agriculture has undergone a quiet but dramatic revolution in this country, developing into the most efficient and productive in the world. But ironically the farmer has not generally shared the rewards of this revolution; in fact he has been the victim, not the beneficiary of his own productivity. The chronic farm problem faced by the United States has been the excess capacity of our farm system. Our commercial farms have been able to produce 5 to 10 percent more each year than the farm market, both domestic and export, has been able to absorb at reasonable farm prices. This surplus capability, of course, is translated for the farmer into lower prices for what he sells.

In 1950, 25 million Americans lived on the country's more than 5½ million farms. By 1970, nearly 15 million of those people had been squeezed off the farm. Because many of the farmers who survived bought the land of their departing neighbors, the less than 3 million farms remaining in 1970 averaged 80 percent larger than the farms of 1950 and produced a total output 35 percent larger than that year.

What remained by 1970 was really two worlds of commercial agriculture in the United States. Agriculture Department statistics say that the farmer is headed for trouble if he is not grossing at least $10,000 a year from his farm. But of the approximately 2 million full-time, commercial farms in the country, more than 1 million fall below that line. They average in size only slightly more than 200 acres, and are heavily in debt. The other world of farming consists of the approximately 400,000 farms grossing more than $20,000 from selling their products, with the top 150,000 farms averaging nearly 2,000 acres and grossing over $40,000. About 500,000 farms hover in the twilight zone in between.

If so many farmers are suffering, then for whom does the supermarket cash register bell toll? Despite ever rising retail costs for farm products, it has not tolled for the farmer. America's farmer has been victim, not beneficiary of inflation. In 1949, when Americans spent $45 billion a year for food, the farmer got about $20 billion of that and the middleman, $25 billion. In 1969, our yearly food bill was up to $90 billion. But the farmer received only $30 billion, only about 20 percent of the increase. The middlemen received $60 billion, getting about 80 percent of the increase. Let us take an example. In 1949, a one-pound loaf of white bread cost, on the average, 13.5¢. In 1969, its supermarket cost had risen to an average of 22.9¢. The baker and the wholesaler got 6.3¢ of that retail price in 1949; in 1969, they got 12.2¢. In 1949, 1.7¢ of the retail price went for milling, grain handling, and transportation; in 1969, 2.4¢ went for these. In 1949, 2¢ went to the other middlemen, including the grocer; in 1949, 5¢. In 1949, the farmer received 3.3¢ for the wheat and other ingredients that made up the loaf of bread. But in 1969, despite the nearly doubling of the retail price, the farmer still only received 3.3¢. "The problem with farming these days," explained an Idaho farmer recently, "is that somebody is making a killing and it isn't the farmer or the housewife. The trouble lies somewhere between the 2¢ a pound I get for potatoes and the 15¢ she has to pay. It's enough to drive a man to the point of desperation."[1]

Another farmer, who raises grain and cattle in Iowa, explained his situation this way: "Most of us are starting to lose a lot of our perennial optimism. We don't see any end to this economic bind. You decide you're not making a decent living, so you borrow money, increase the size of your operation, boost the efficiency, up the yield. It doesn't help, though, because while you're doing that, interest rates and seed and machinery costs spurt but crop prices don't change. In the past year or so, I've seen the cost of tractors go up almost a thousand dollars but I'm still getting only a buck a bushel for corn. So here I am—bigger and bigger, but I don't have any more to spend. Worst of all, I'm deeper in debt than ever."[2] The cost-price squeeze is more than economic jargon for the bulk of America's farmers.

Faced with this situation, the major farm organizations in the country have reacted quite differently. The National Farmers Union, the National Grange, and the National Farmers Organization look out and see agriculture in serious trouble. The head of the National Grange points out that the net income of farmers is 5 percent less than 20 years ago—while hourly earnings of manufacturing workers rose by 127 percent and corporate dividends by 251 percent. The president of the National Farmers Organization proclaims that "the core of family agriculture is struggling for survival because of low farm prices." And the president of the National Farmers Union speaks of the economic hardships of large segments of American agriculture. But the American Farm Bureau sees a strangely different world. Its 50th anniversary publication in 1969 proclaimed, "Despite a difficult cost-price squeeze, the farmers of our nation have earned a higher standard of living for their families than have any other agricultural people. All of this indicates progress."[3]

This differing perspective has contributed to a fundamental split among the farm organizations over basic farm policy. The basic question that has faced the government's agricultural policy-makers has been whether the federal government should step in and administer programs to raise farm prices above the level set by supply and demand, by making direct payments to farmers for reducing their production, thereby reducing the surplus that drives down prices. The other farm organizations answer yes; the Farm Bureau says no.

The basic thrust of our farm policy during the 60's has been for the government to subsidize farm income by direct payments to farmers who agree to limit their production in order to keep down surpluses. At the same time, the government has supported the price of basic commodities by means of loans to producers from the government Commodity Credit Corporation, with their produce as collateral. The CCC disposes of the stocks it acquires through this loan mechanism, partly on the open market and partly through non-commercial channels such as the Food for Peace program abroad and the school lunch program at home. This basic strategy has been supplemented by other programs such as Extension and the Farmers Home Administration, which helps farmers acquire land, equipment, and capital through low-cost loans.

In 1970, the price support programs, which would have expired if not extended, came up for reconsideration in Congress. Eighteen farm, commodity, and cooperative organizations, with the Farm Bureau conspicuously absent, surmounted traditional rivalries to join together in a National Farm Coalition to support the extension of the 1965 Act. Testified National Farmers Union President Tony Dechant to the House Agriculture Committee:

We believe it is a good law. Its most important aspect is that, while putting major responsibility on the shoulders of the Secretary of Agriculture to maintain a stable farm economy, it provides him with the machinery to do it. This machinery has never been used as effectively as it could be. But if used effectively, it can regulate production to prevent prices from falling to disastrous lows, and it can keep the farm program from being prohibitively expensive to the Nation's taxpayers. . . . Extension of the 1965 [Act] will not solve all the problems of agriculture. On the other hand, failure to extend the . . . programs would result in a loss in net farm income of over $5 billion a year.[4]

The Farm Bureau had different ideas. "The time has come to junk the whole sorry mess," said Charles Shuman.[5] Instead of ditching the support programs all at once, as it had advocated in the past, it urged a five-year phase-out. A former chairman of the House Agriculture Committee once described such a policy as "cutting off a dog's tail at the rate of an inch at a time."

One thing the last three national Administrations have agreed on is this: dumping our government farm program would have a devastating impact on the farm economy. Agriculture Secretary Freeman repeatedly warned that a return to a so-called free market agriculture "would mean instant disaster for much of agriculture." He cited studies by non-government economists at Iowa State, Oklahoma State, Cornell, and Pennsylvania State Universities which indicated that net farm income would plunge 40 to 50 percent. "This situation," he contended, "would bankrupt most farmers . . . and [bring about a] serious economic setback for the whole nation." President Nixon's Secretary of Agriculture Clifford M. Hardin, hardly tied by political vested interest to the old programs, more recently told the Senate

Agriculture Committee that elimination of the cropland adjustment program (which provides direct payments to farmers for diverting their land from production) would result in a drop in farm income ranging from $800 million to $1.3 billion.[6]

Professor Willard W. Cochrane, Dean of International Programs at the University of Minnesota and chief agricultural economist during the Kennedy and Johnson Administrations has argued: "The consensus among agricultural economists is that over-all net farm income would fall by 50 percent within a few years if all present commodity price and income support programs were eliminated. . . . And the price variability and . . . uncertainty that accompanied a free market for farm products would probably be more damaging to rational economic action than the initial price drop. . . . Few [farm economists] would advocate a return to the free market."[7]

The indirect consequences of such a change of direction should also be noted. The economically fatal blow to a large number of farmers would of course accelerate the concentration of food production into fewer and fewer hands at little gain in efficiency. "In sheer production efficiency," explains Cochrane, "an adequate-sized family farm is as efficient as any large-scale unit yet devised in the United States."[8] The displacement of farm families would further feed the flow to the cities, further depleting the essential human resources of rural America, while simply adding to the "municipal overburden" of our urban areas. Seventy percent of our population already crowds onto 1 percent of the country's land; it is a process we should be seeking to reverse, not intensify.

To meet these drastic consequences, the Farm Bureau's phase-out program would have provided little assistance. The Farm Bureau called for a modest program to take land out of production permanently, a land retirement program.[9] Under the plan, the Secretary of Agriculture would have been directed to buy not more than 50 million acres over 5 years (out of a total of nearly 300 million harvested). The purchases would be by competitive bidding, assuring that only that land which the farmer most wanted to get rid of was retired. It would have little effect on total production. To ease the human costs of virtually uncontrolled production, the Farm Bureau offered a meager plan for retraining and relocation grants. Under the Farm Bureau proposal, grants of not more than $1,000 would be offered to retrain farmers and adjustment assistance grants of not more than $5,000 would be offered to relocate them and their families. But the Farm

Bureau proposal would have limited these grants to farmers grossing less than $5,000. The 750,000 farmers who would therefore qualify produce only about 6 percent of the total agricultural output, so their displacement would have little effect in reducing production generally.

The approximately 1 million remaining commercial farms in the country produce over 90 percent of the country's food. Under the Farm Bureau scheme, these farms would be thrown into the "free market" battle for survival with virtually no controls on production. The sweat of the Farm Bureau plan would flow from the brow of the farms which now gross between $5,000 and $20,000 a year. These operations would be hard-pressed in an unlimited production situation to compete with the 400,000 largest farms (already producing more than 60 percent of our food). These middle-sized farms would be trapped under the Farm Bureau plan between the $5,000 ceiling for getting relocation or retraining moneys and the competitive resources of the very largest farming operations released from production controls. Moreover, the plan had no provision for the impact of all this on farm workers, or on rural communities. Late in 1970, the Farm Bureau plan was rejected by Congress and the 1965 Act, with certain modifications, was extended.

*   *   *

How does one explain what is behind the Farm Bureau's farm policy and why it differs so drastically from the philosophies of the other farm organizations? It is presented with much fanfare about saving the farmer from the imposing jaws of the federal government. It is heralded as farmer liberation. But that appears to be only part of the answer.

To the extent that the Farm Bureau plan primarily would benefit the larger farmers, the organization opens itself to the familiar charge that it is no more than the mouthpiece of the agricultural giants. This view is supported by the Farm Bureau's stance on the limitation on payments to individual farmers ultimately enacted as part of the new farm bill. While opposing farm subsidies to all farmers, the Farm Bureau opposed limiting payments to an individual farm to $55,000, a neat philosophical contortion.

But besides its large-farm bias and anti-government ideology, there are other pressures within the organization which produce a farm policy injurious to many farmers. We should not forget the business side of the Farm Bureau which has brought into the organization thousands of agri-business managers whose immediate responsibility is to run these operations on a businesslike basis. If the businesses succeed, the managers succeed; if the businesses fail, the managers fail. In the case of the large cooperatives, profits may not be the measure of success; nonetheless, the managers and executives want to be associated with ventures that are growing and expanding so that their interests may be not too different from those of the managers and operators of large private farm suppliers and processors.

There are, then, informal but powerful pressures on the organization to advance the success of the business operations. To this, add the fact that many state organizations rely upon the success of the business operations for sizeable portions of their own operating revenue, and the actual tensions that exist in such a two-headed operation begin to emerge.

Are the interests of those who supply the farmer, those who process farm products and those who market food antagonistic to the farmer? Once again Cochrane: "There is no question about the policy goal of firms in this group [non-farm suppliers, processors, and marketers]; they want volume, the maximum farm production possible. High-level farm production enables them to expand the market for farm producer goods and supplies and the volume of product processed and handled. This group persistently opposes all forms of supply management, or production control programs . . . processors and marketers favor low farm prices because they are purchasers of farm products. . . . All these agri-business groups want the farmers producing at full throttle; the question of a little or a big surplus, and who bears the cost of carrying it, does not disturb them."[10]

Uncontrolled production, then, means selling more Farm Bureau fertilizer, feed, and seed, more insurance and oil, and having more produce available to market through Farm Bureau marketing associations. But to thousands of already hard-pressed farmers it means lower prices and economic disaster. This fundamental difference presents a frightening conflict for the organization that claims to speak for these farmers in the halls of government.

The Farm Bureau has only fanned the flames of charges that it really speaks for interests other than strictly those of the farmer. Such policy positions as support for the oil depletion allowance and for turning over the business of the Federal Crop Insurance Program—which competes with Farm Bureau companies—to certain unnamed "private companies," most clearly appear to be for the benefit of their businesses at the expense of the farmers. And their frequent alliances and affiliations over the years with the large private firms who process farm products and supply the farmer with his fertilizer, machinery, feed and seed have done little to dispel fears about where the Farm Bureau's heart really lies. For example, the American Farm Bureau Federation has been a major participant in closed "summit conferences" with the leaders of the Chamber of Commerce, the National Association of Manufacturers and other sympathetic groups held each year at the Greenbrier Hotel in the West Virginia mountains. These sessions plan joint strategy on major issues facing Congress.[11] For many years, one of the most controversial affiliations of the Farm Bureau was the National Food Conference. Organized by the Farm Bureau and headed by Charles Shuman, the NFC was made up of about 65 of the nation's largest food processors and marketers including Armour, Campbell Soup, General Foods, the A&P, Kraft Foods, Quaker Oats, Ralston-Purina, Safeway Stores, and the American Can Company. Although the Farm Bureau claimed that the only purpose of the association was to promote food and improve the diets of teenagers, some of the other farm groups did not see it that way, charging that the Farm Bureau was "selling out" the American family farmer. In any case, the heat increased to the point where the NFC was dissolved in 1969.[12]

As long as the Farm Bureau has several billion dollars of business interests up its sleeve, its support—in the name of the farmer—of an agricultural policy in agreement with most of the country's largest agri-businesses and in opposition to most of the country's other farm organizations will be suspect. The organization will be open to charges like that expressed by an Illinois farmer who angrily remarked: "The fact is they are a big business themselves and here lies their greatest interest in the farmer."

Regardless of the organization's motivation, the resulting split among the nation's farm organizations has been costly for the farmer. As the farm population has dwindled the political power of the farmer has waned. Only about 35 of the 435 Congressmen now represent districts with a farm population of more than 25 percent. At the same time, the urban liberals in Congress, long the backbone of support for the government farm program, are growing restless as pressing needs in their own back-yard compete with all other items in the budget for a greater share of the tax dollar. Along with this diminishing political strength, the discordant voice of the largest farm organization has prevented the farmer from pre-senting a united front of their own forces. Many feel that if the farm groups could have come together, the farm problem would have been solved long ago. What has resulted instead is a political stalemate that saps the remain-ing political strength of the farmer.

The chasm between the small farmer and the large farmer, between the rural well-to-do and the rural poor, between the farm worker and his city counterpart is in no slight degree the product of the emergence and as-cendancy of the Farm Bureau. And the saddest part is that it has all been done in the name of the American farmer.

Notes

THE GREATEST SOURCES OF INFORMATION about the Farm Bureau are its own publications, brochures, newspapers, reports and broadcasts, and the speeches, writings, and newspaper interviews with its leaders. Wherever possible, these sources have been footnoted. Personal interviews by the author, including interviews with Farm Bureau officials, have generally not been footnoted, nor have letters to Congressman Resnick or to the author, unless the name of the speaker or writer or his position is of particular interest. Many of the quotes used in the book are taken from the transcript of Congressman Resnick's one-man hearings in Chicago, 4 August 1967; Omaha, 5 August 1967; Washington, D.C., 28, 29, 30, 31 August 1967; and Cleveland, 17 November 1967. Since the official transcript of the hearings is in the possession of the author and has not been published, these quotes have not been footnoted, unless the witness' name or position is of particular interest.

Where to do so eliminates more confusion than it creates, multiple references in a single paragraph have been combined into one note, indicated at the end of the paragraph.

Chapter 1
Introduction

For the Farm Bureau's description of itself, see the brochure: *This is Farm Bureau* (Chicago: American Farm Bureau Federation, 1969).

Chapter 2
"The Resnick Affair"

During his investigation, Congressman Resnick submitted periodic reports into the *Congressional Record*. These reports furnish a thorough history of the Resnick investigation. They can be found in the *Congressional Record* for the following dates: 18 July 1967; 17 August 1967; 18 September 1967; 19 September 1967; 20 September 1967; 21 September 1967; 25 September 1967; 26 September 1967; 2 October 1967; 3 October 1967; 17 October 1967; 18 October 1967; 20 October 1967; 23 October 1967; 24 October 1967; 7 November 1967; 8 November 1967; 14 November 1967; 5 December 1967; 15 December 1967; 6 February 1968; 26 February 1968; 20 March 1968.

1. Lynn's testimony from: U.S., Congress House, Committee on Agriculture, Subcommittee on Rural Development, *Effect of Federal Programs on Rural America: Hearings,* 90th Cong., 1st sess., 21 June 1967, p. 468 et seq.

2. Roger Fleming, *Annual Report of the Secretary-Treasurer* (Chicago: American Farm Bureau Federation, 1967).

3. Resnick press release, 28 June 1967.

4. Fleming's testimony from: *Effect of Federal Programs on Rural America: Hearings,* pp. 647 et seq.

5. Cohen to Resnick, 10 July 1967.

6. *Des Moines Register,* 9 July 1967.

7. *Effect of Federal Programs on Rural America: Hearings,* p. 659.

8. Fleming to Poage, 7 July 1967.

9. *Congressional Directory: 90th Congress.*

10. "Statement by Members of [House] Subcommittee on Rural Development, Committee on Agriculture," 12 July 1967.

11. Ibid.

12. *Kingston* (New York) *Daily Freeman,* 15 July 1967.

13. *New York Times,* 13 July 1967.

14. *Washington Star,* 12 July 1967.

15. Joseph McCaffrey, "Big Brotherism on Capitol Hill" (Broadcast editorial on WMAL-TV, Washington, D.C., 12 July 1967).

16.   Shuman to Resnick, 6 September 1967; *Effect of Federal Programs on Rural America: Hearings,* p. 648; see, for example: Charles Shuman, "This We Believe," *Nation's Agriculture,* December 1967.

17.   "Resnick Farm Organization Hearings: Washington," 30 August 1967, transcript p. 206.

18.   *New York Times,* 3 September 1967; *St. Louis Post-Dispatch* (AP dispatch), 1 September 1967.

19.   *Poughkeepsie* (New York) *Journal,* 6 September 1967.

20.   Rowland Evans and Robert Novak, "Farm Bureau Purge," *Washington Post,* 10 September 1967.

21.   *New York Times,* 19 October 1967.

22.   Roger Fleming, *Annual Report of Secretary-Treasurer* (1967).

23.   *Farm Bureau Policies for 1968* (Chicago: American Farm Bureau Federation, 1968), p. 29.

Chapter 3
Membership for Merchandising

Statistics on number and kind of farms, farm population, and characteristics of farm operators are from: U.S., Department of Commerce, *Statistical Abstract of the United States: 1970,* pp. 582–589; U.S., Department of Commerce, *Statistical Abstract of the United States: 1968,* pp. 594–595; and *American Farm Bureau Federation Official Newsletter,* 19 January 1970. For information on number and nature of Illinois farms, see: Illinois Department of Agriculture, Cooperative Crop Reporting Service, *Illinois Agricultural Statistics: Assessors' Annual Farm Census,* 1970, S.F.C.–33, December 1970.

1.   U.S., Congress, House, Committee on Agriculture, Subcommittee on Rural Development, *Effect of Federal Programs on Rural America: Hearings,* 90th Cong., 1st sess., 28 June 1967, p. 653.

2.   Kuhfuss to Resnick, 31 July 1967.

3.   *Hoard's Dairyman,* 10 March 1964.

4.   *The Louisville Courier-Journal,* 15 November 1967.

5. Willard W. Cochrane, *The City Man's Guide to the Farm Problem* (Minneapolis: University of Minnesota Press, 1965), p. 14.

6. "The Farm Bureau Safemark Tires Are Here," Wyoming Farm Bureau Federation, Laramie, Wyoming (brochure).

7. *Wall Street Journal,* 14 December 1967.

8. *Both Rural and Urban Families,* Missouri Farm Bureau Federation, Jefferson City, Missouri (brochure).

9. "Report of Investigation by Robert C. Londerholm, Attorney General [Kansas] Re: Kansas Farm Bureau Insurance Companies and the Kansas Department of Insurance," 7 November 1967, exhibit nos. 1 & 2.

10. *Buckeye Farm News,* July 1969.

11. Ibid., January 1969.

12. "Official Board Proceedings of Boone County Supervisors," Boone County, Iowa, 2 January 1964.

13. *Colorado Farm Bureau News,* June 1969.

14. Walter Randolph (Statement to Democratic Platform Committee Hearings, 19 August 1964); *Florida Farm Bureau: The Voice of Agriculture,* Florida Farm Bureau Federation, Gainesville, Florida (brochure); *Join Your County Farm Bureau,* Virginia Farm Bureau Federation, Richmond, Virginia (brochure); *Partners for Progress,* Ohio Farm Bureau Federation, Columbus, Ohio (pamphlet).

Chapter 4
Insuring the Farm Bureau's Future

Information on the Farm Bureau insurance companies, including operating figures, control relationships, directors and officers, and corporate restrictions is primarily from: *Best's Insurance Reports: Life-Health (1969)*; 64th annual edition (Morristown, N.J.: A.M. Best Company, 1969); and *Best's Key Rating Guide: Property-Liability;* 63rd annual edition: (Morristown, N.J.: A.M. Best Company, 1969); and *Farm Bureau Insurance,* American Farm Bureau Federation, Chicago, Illinois (brochure). For material on the Illinois Agricultural Association and the Country Insurance Companies, see: *Annual Report: 1968,* Illinois Agricultural Association,

Bloomington, Illinois. For information on Nationwide Insurance and its relationship to Farm Bureau, see: *Best's* (above) and *Partners for Progress,* a pamphlet issued jointly by the Ohio Farm Bureau Federation, Landmark Coops, and Nationwide Insurance.

1. Murray Lincoln, *Vice President in Charge of Revolution* (New York, McGraw-Hill Book Co., 1960), p. 69.

2. Loudoun County Farm Bureau to Singer, 5 July 1967.

3. The *Madras* (Oregon) *Pioneer,* 20 August 1967; *Illinois Consolidated Telephone Directory,* classified section, p. 53; *Economic Services,* Virginia Farm Bureau Federation, Richmond, Virginia (brochure).

4. Lincoln, *Vice President in Charge of Revolution,* p. 102.

5. Robert F. Mark (manager, Farm Bureau Insurance Company of Nebraska) to policyholders, 28 December 1951.

6. *Annual Report: 1968,* Illinois Agricultural Association, Bloomington, Illinois, p. 57.

7. *Birmingham News,* 8 October 1967.

8. Ibid.

9. This explanation, and the following material about the IAA, is based upon interviews by the author with IAA officials, July 1969, as well as the IAA *Annual Report: 1968.*

10. See, for example: "Report of Investigation by Robert C. Londerholm, Attorney General [Kansas] Re: Kansas Farm Bureau Insurance Companies and Kansas Department of Insurance," 7 November 1967; *Partners for Progress,* Ohio Farm Bureau Federation, Columbus, Ohio (pamphlet).

11. "Report of Attorney General [Kansas]," pp. 7–8.

12. *The State and the Columbia* (South Carolina) *Record,* 12 February 1967.

13. *Charlotte* (North Carolina) *Observer,* 22 February 1967; *Charleston* (South Carolina) *News and Courier,* 22 February 1967.

14. As of September 1967, Farm Bureau insurance companies had 2 percent interest in: KGFF, Shawnee, Oklahoma; KGNC, Amarillo, Texas; KSOK, Arkansas, Kansas; WIBW, Topeka, Kansas; KSEK, Pittsburg, Kansas.

15. *Origin and Growth of North Dakota's Farm Bureau,* North Dakota Farm Bureau, Fargo, North Dakota, 1965, pp. 31–32.

16. Ibid.

17. *Best's Insurance Reports: Life-Health (1969);* 64th annual edition (Morristown, N.J.: A.M. Best Company, 1969), pp. 223–224.

18. See, for example: "The Resnick Affair," *IAA Record,* September 1967, p. 11.

19. Lincoln, *Vice President in Charge of Revolution,* p. 124.

20. Orville Merton Kile, *The Farm Bureau Through Three Decades* (Baltimore: Waverly Press, 1948), p. 348.

21. Ibid., p. 354.

22. Lincoln, *Vice President in Charge of Revolution,* p. 220.

23. *Partners for Progress* (pamphlet published jointly by Ohio Farm Bureau Federation, Landmark Cooperatives, and Nationwide Insurance), pp. 1, 14.

24. *Buckeye Farm News,* June 1968.

25. "Farmer-Businessman Heads Nationwide," *Buckeye Farm News,* July 1969.

26. *Buckeye Farm News,* May 1969, p. 25; Ibid., February 1969.

27. *AFBF Official Newsletter,* 25 April 1966.

28. U.S., Congress, House, Committee on Agriculture, Subcommittee on Rural Development, *Effect of Federal Programs on Rural America: Hearings,* 28 June 1967, pp. 653–654.

29. *AFBF Official Newsletter,* 24 March 1969.

30. Ibid., 26 October 1970.

31. Aaron Trupin (Director, Insurance Research and Statistics, State of New York Insurance Department) to Modesto Aregenio (*Buffalo Courier-Express,* Buffalo, New York), 1 August 1967.

Chapter 5
The Farm Bureau Supermarket

The information on the Farm Bureau business operations has been taken largely from annual reports and other publications of the businesses themselves. For information on the Farm Bureau cooperatives, see: *FS Services, Inc.: Annual Report* (31 August 1968), Bloomington, Illinois; *Building for Better Farming: 42nd Annual Report* (1968), Indiana Farm Bureau Cooperative Association, Indianapolis, Indiana; *Landmark: 1968 Annual Report,* Ohio Farm Bureau Cooperative Association, Inc., Columbus, Ohio; *Farm Bureau Services, Inc.: 39th Annual Report* (30 June 1968), Michigan Farm Bureau Federation, Lansing, Michigan; and U.S., Department of Agriculture, Farmer Cooperatives Service, *Statistics of Farmer Cooperatives (1965–1966),* FCS Research Report No. 1. For information on cooperatives generally, see: U.S., Department of Agriculture, Farmer Cooperative Service, *Did You Know?,* Information 49 (revised, June 1969); U.S., Department of Agriculture, Farmer Cooperative Service, *Cooperative Criteria* (February 1965). Other useful material for this chapter was found in: "Fact Sheet: Central Farmers Fertilizer Company," Chicago, Illinois, March 1969 (mimeo.); "Central Farmers Fertilizer Company: Member Companies," Central Farmers News Service, Chicago, Illinois; "Michigan Farm Bureau History in a Nutshell," Department of Education and Research, Michigan Farm Bureau; Harvey Hull, *Twentieth Century Pioneer* (Indianapolis: Indiana Farm Bureau Cooperative Association, 1968); *A Look at FS,* FS Services, Inc., Bloomington, Illinois (pamphlet); *Indiana Farmers' Off-the-Farm Business,* Indiana Farm Bureau Cooperative Association, Indianapolis, Indiana; *Illinois Agricultural Association, the Country Companies, FS Services, Inc., and Other Affiliated Companies,* Illinois Agricultural Association, Bloomington, Illinois (brochure).

1. From interviews by the author with Illinois Agricultural Association officials, July 1969.

2. *Partners for Progress* (pamphlet published jointly by Ohio Farm Bureau Federation, Landmark Cooperative, and Nationwide Insurance), p. 17.

3. U.S., Congress, House, Committee on Ways and Means, *Hearings on Tax Reform,* 91st Cong., 1st sess., pt. 3: 1025 et seq.; *AFBF Official Newsletter,* 4 August 1969; Ibid., 8 September 1969.

4. Ibid., 20 October 1969.

5. Ibid., 27 October 1969.

6. Williams testimony from: "Resnick Farm Organization Hearings: Washington," 30 August 1967, transcript pp. 249 et seq.

7. *Cleveland Plain Dealer,* "Editorial," 19 October 1967.

8. Ibid., 15 September 1967; Ibid., 16 September 1967.

9. Ibid., 12 October 1967.

10. Ibid., 19 October 1967; Ibid., 12 October 1967.

11. *Kent* (Ohio) *Record Courier,* 17 October 1967.

12. Hoiles testimony from: "Resnick Farm Organization Hearings: Cleveland," 17 November 1967, transcript pp. 2 et seq.

13. *Landmark: 1968 Annual Report,* The Farm Bureau Cooperative Association, Columbus, Ohio, p. 12.

14. *Hearings on Tax Reform,* pt. 13: 4744.

15. *Buckeye Farm News,* December 1968.

16. *Birmingham News,* 9 October 1967; Ibid., 6 July 1967.

17. *California Service Agency,* California Farm Bureau Federation, Berkeley, California (brochure).

18. *California Farm Bureau Federation: Its Services to Members,* California Farm Bureau Federation, Berkeley, California (brochure).

19. *Macon* (Georgia) *Telegraph and News,* 13 October 1967.

20. *Birmingham News,* 8 October 1967.

21. *Opportunity at Illinois Agricultural Association and Affiliated Companies,* Illinois Agricultural Association, Bloomington, Illinois (brochure).

22. *Farm Bureau Mutual Fund: Annual Report (31 March 1969),* American Farm Bureau Federation, Chicago, Illinois.

23. Advertisements for Farmer-to-Farmer tours are found in nearly any issue of *Nation's Agriculture.*

24. "American Farm Bureau Service Company," American Farm Bureau Federation, Chicago, Illinois (mimeo.).

25. Kenneth Hood, "A Year of Challenge" (speech delivered to 1968 annual meeting of the American Agricultural Marketing Association, Kansas City, Missouri, 12 December 1968); Idem., "Marketing Activities in Farm Bureau (speech delivered to Southern Regional Staff Conference, New Orleans, La., 30 April 1969).

26. *American Farm Bureau Research Association,* American Farm Bureau Federation, Chicago, Illinois (brochure).

27. *AFBF Official Newsletter,* 19 October 1970.

28. Associated Press, 13 June 1965.

Chapter 6
Representation Without Taxation

For the basic tax provisions that govern exempt agricultural organizations, see: *Internal Revenue Code of 1954* (hereafter, IRC), § 501(c)5; *Department of the Treasury Regulations* (hereafter, Treas. Reg.) § 1.501 (c)(5); and U.S., Department of the Treasury, Internal Revenue Service, *Exempt Organizations Handbook,* MT(11)671-27 §§ 931–942. For the basic tax provisions regarding unrelated business income, see: IRC §§ 521–522; Treas. Regs., §§ 1.512-1–1.522-4. For provisions on advertising revenue of exempt organizations and taxation of income from controlled businesses, see: *Tax Reform Act of 1969* (PL 91-172), §§ 121(c); 121(b)(2).

1. Treas. Reg. § 1.501(a)-1(2).

2. Trinidad v. Sagrade Orden de Predicadores, 263 US 578; T.D. 3548, C.B. III-1, 270 (1924).

3. U.S., Department of the Treasury, Internal Revenue Service, *Exempt Organization's Handbook,* MT(11) 671-15, 13 December 1966, § (26)-12(2).

4. *Best's Insurance Reports: Life-Health (1969);* 64th Annual edition (Morristown, N.J.: A.M. Best Co., 1969), pp. 223–224.

5. "The Resnick Affair," *IAA Record,* September 1967, p. 11.

6. Treas. Reg. § 1.501(c)(5)-1(a)(2).

7. Treas. Reg. § 1.513-1(d)(4); Rev. Rul. 55-676, C.B. 1955-2, 266; Rev. Rul. 60-86, C.B. 1960-1, 198.

8. *Exempt Organizations Handbook,* § (26)-33.

9. *Annual Report: 1968,* Illinois Agricultural Association, Bloomington, Illinois, p. 24.

10. Ibid.

11. Rev. Rul. 70-95, 1970, IRB No. 8, 16.

12. Rev. Rul. 60-228, C.B. 1960-2, 200.

13. *Oklahoma Cattlemen's Association v. U.S.,* 1970-1 USTC ¶ 9165 (W.D., Okla., 1970).

14. U.S., Department of the Treasury, Internal Revenue Service, TIR-899, 14 April 1967; *Congressional Quarterly,* 12 July 1967.

15. *Glenwood* (Iowa) *Opinion Tribune,* 19 August 1967.

16. Information on effective tax rates supplied by office of U.S. Rep. Henry S. Reuss (Dem.–Wisc.); *New York Times,* 24 November 1969.

17. *Best's Insurance Reports: Life-Health (1969).*

18. *Building for Better Farming: 42nd Annual Report,* Indiana Farm Bureau Cooperative Association, Indianapolis, Indiana, 1968.

19. *Annual Report: 1968,* Illinois Agricultural Association, Bloomington, Illinois. This includes 1967 figures for four insurance companies.

20. Treas. Reg. § 1.501(a)-1(a)2.

21. Rev. Rul. 66-105, C.B. 1966-1, 145.

22. Treas. Reg. § 1.501(c)6-1.

23. Rev. Rul. 60-86, C.B. 1960-1, 198.

Chapter 7
The Rock Against Radicalism

The history of American agriculture, agricultural policy, and the Farm Bureau, have been taken largely from the following sources:

Andrews, Stanley. *The Farmer's Dilemma.* Washington, D.C.: Public Affairs Press, 1961.

Block, William J. *The Separation of the Farm Bureau and the Extension Service.* Urbana: University of Illinois Press, 1960.

Cambell, Christiana McFadyen. *The Farm Bureau and the New Deal.* Urbana: University of Illinois Press, 1962.

Cochrane, Willard W. *The City Man's Guide to the Farm Problem.* Minneapolis: University of Minnesota Press, 1965.

Fite, Gilbert C. *American Agriculture and Farm Policy Since 1900.* American Historical Association, Service Center for Teachers of History Publication No. 59. New York: Macmillan Co., 1964.

Goldman, Eric F. *Rendezvous with Destiny.* New York: Alfred A. Knopf, Inc., Vintage Books, 1952.

Hofstadter, Richard. *The Age of Reform.* New York: Alfred A. Knopf, Inc., Vintage Books, 1955.

Kile, Orville Merton. *The Farm Bureau Through Three Decades.* Baltimore: Waverly Press, 1948.

Lincoln, Murray. *Vice President in Charge of Revolution.* New York: McGraw-Hill Book Co., 1960.

McCune, Wesley. *Who's Behind Our Farm Policy?* New York:Frederick A. Praeger, 1956.

McConnell, Grant. *The Decline of Agrarian Democracy.* Berkeley and Los Angeles: University of California Press, 1953.

1. Block, *Separation of Farm Bureau and Extension,* p. 4.

2. Kile, *Farm Bureau Through Three Decades,* p. 24.

3. Dale Kramer, *The Truth about the Farm Bureau* (Denver: Golden Bell Press, 1964), p. 3; See also: Benton J. Strong, "Rock-Ribbed Farmers," *New Republic,* 28 February 1949.

4. Cambell, *Farm Bureau and New Deal,* p. 5.

5. Kile, *Farm Bureau Through Three Decades,* p. 40.

6. McConnell, *Decline of Agrarian Democracy,* p. 48.

7. Goldman, *Rendezvous with Destiny,* p. 229.

8. Ibid.

9. Kile, *Farm Bureau Through Three Decades,* p. 58.

10. Ibid., p. 70.

11. Lincoln, *Vice President in Charge of Revolution,* p. 69.

12. Ibid., p. 72.

13. "The Farm Bureau," *Fortune* (June 1944), p. 156.

14. Kile, *Farm Bureau Through Three Decades,* p. 188.

15. Ibid., p. 205.

16. McConnell, *Decline of Agrarian Democracy.*

17. Ibid., p. 81.

18. Ibid., p. 118.

19. Ibid., p. 106.

20. Kile, *Farm Bureau Through Three Decades*, p. 296.

21. Block, *Separation of Farm Bureau and Extension Service*, p. 43.

22. McConnell, *Decline of Agrarian Democracy*, p. 23.

23. Kile, *Farm Bureau Through Three Decades*, p. 315.

24. Ibid., pp. 317–318; "The Farm Bureau," *Fortune* (June 1944), p. 156.

25. Kile, *Farm Bureau Through Three Decades*, p. 220.

26. Kile, *Farm Bureau Through Three Decades*, pp. 330–331.

27. Andrews, *The Farmer's Dilemma*, p. 84.

28. *Nebraska Farmer*, 6 April 1963.

29. *Time,* 3 September 1965.

30. *Des Moines Register,* 17 December 1961; Charles Shuman, in Foreword to Alan Kline's *Reflections on Freedom* (Chicago: Information Division, American Farm Bureau Federation, 1967); Charles Shuman, "This We Believe," *Nation's Agriculture* (June 1969), p. 4.

31. Roger Fleming, "Annual Report of Secretary-Treasurer" (before the 50th annual convention of the American Farm Bureau Federation), Kansas City, Missouri, 10 December 1968, p. 14.

32. *Boston Globe,* 8 December 1970.

Chapter 8
Divorce, Farm Bureau Style

The complete story of the separation movement up to 1960 is told in William J. Block's *The Separation of the Farm Bureau and the Extension Service* (Urbana: University of Illinois Press, 1960).

1. "The Farm Bureau," *Fortune,* June 1944.

2. Block, *Separation of Farm Bureau and Extension,* p. 14.

3. Ibid., p. 6.

4. Ibid., p. 25; Dale Kramer, *The Truth About the Farm Bureau* (Denver: Golden Bell Press, 1964), p. 16; Block, *Separation of Farm Bureau and Extension,* p. 58.

5. Ibid., p. 125.

6. Ibid., p. 108.

7. Ibid., p. 125.

8. Roy Battles (NFU press release), 2 December 1954.

9. National Farmers Union (press release), 26 December 1951.

10. Block, *Separation of Farm Bureau and Extension,* p. 207.

11. U.S., Department of Agriculture, "Activities of Department Employees with Relation to General and Specialized Organizations of Farmers," Memorandum No. 1368, 24 November 1954.

12. *St. Louis Post-Dispatch,* 27 November 1954.

13. Ibid., 2 December 1954.

14. Ibid., 3 January 1955.

15. "The Relationship of the Cooperative Extension Service of the University of Illinois and the United States Department of Agriculture and Farm Organizations in Illinois" (report of Study Group appointed by President, University of Illinois and Secretary, Department of Agriculture), Urbana, Illinois, March 1955, Appendix F.

16. Ibid., Appendix E.

17. Ibid., p. 23.

18. Claar to Resnick, 11 August 1967, p. 2.

19. W. D. Murphy (Acting Director, Cooperative Extension Service, University of Illinois) to Resnick, 24 August 1967.

20. "Resnick Farm Organization Hearings: Chicago," 4 August 1967, transcript pp. 143–144.

21. "Resnick Farm Organization Hearings: Chicago," testimony of Ray Watson, president of Illinois Farmers Union, transcript pp. 9 et seq.

22. *Buffalo Courier-Express,* 6 August 1967.

23. "Resnick Farm Organization Hearings: Washington," testimony of Dr. N. P. Ralston, Deputy Administrator, Federal Extension Service, 31 August 1967, transcript p. 282.

Chapter 9
"Do I Have to Agree to Belong?"

1. *New Republic,* 15 October 1951, p. 10; *Indianapolis Star,* 31 August 1951.

2. Wesley McCune, *Who's Behind Our Farm Policy?* (New York: Frederic A. Praeger, 1956), pp. 4–5.

3. Roland G. Nelson (president, Nebraska Farm Bureau Federation) to County Farm Bureau Presidents and National Affairs Chairmen, 4 May 1967.

4. Christiana McFadyen Cambell, *The Farm Bureau and the New Deal* (Urbana: University of Illinois Press, 1962), p. 16.

5. Donald Burkman (president, Minnehaha County Farm Bureau) to Holiway, 31 October 1962.

6. Roger Fleming, *Annual Report of Secretary-Treasurer (1967),* American Farm Bureau Federation, Chicago, Illinois.

7. Grant McConnell, *The Decline of Agrarian Democracy* (Berkeley and Los Angeles: University of California Press, 1953), p. 156.

8. Orville Merton Kile, *The Farm Bureau Through Three Decades* (Baltimore: Waverly Press, 1948), p. 392.

9. *St. Louis Post-Dispatch,* 4 November 1956.

10. *Ever Try to Smear a Dirt Farmer?* National Farmers Union, Denver, Colorado, 1951 (pamphlet).

11. Memo from: Donald E. Hirsch (Assistant Director, Commodity Division, American Farm Bureau Federation), 23 August 1963.

12. *Lincoln* (Nebraska) *Star,* 19 September 1962; *Lincoln* (Nebraska) *Sunday Journal,* 3 September 1961.

13. Charles Marshall (president, Nebraska Farm Bureau Federation) to County Farm Bureau Presidents, 8 September 1961.

14. *Nebraska Farmer,* 6 October 1962.

15. *Lincoln* (Nebraska) *Star,* 19 September 1962; "Resnick Farm Organization Hearings: Washington," 30 August 1967, transcript pp. 128 et seq.

16. *Nebraska Farmer,* 5 October 1963.

17. U.S., Senate, Committee on Agriculture and Forestry, *Hearings,* 11 February 1964; "Resolution of the Board of Directors of the Nebraska Farm Bureau Federation," April 1964.

18. "Resnick Farm Organization Hearings: Washington," 30 August 1967, transcript pp. 128 et seq.

Chapter 10
The Right Wing in Overalls

Much of the background material on the organizations and individuals associated with the far right was obtained with the cooperation of Group Research, Inc., Washington, D.C. *Group Research Report,* a bimonthly publication, reports the activities, speeches and writings of a wide range of right wing people and groups. In addition, Group Research issues periodic reports on a single individual or group, collecting its statements and giving the original source. For much of the information used in this chapter on the following individuals and groups, consult the respective Group Research Report: Tom Anderson, Dr. George Benson, Reed Benson, Kenneth Ingwalson, Dr. C. L. Kay, Robert LeFevre, Fulton Lewis, Jr., Clarence Manion, Lewis Munn, John Noble, Nicholas Nyaradi, Herbert Philbrick, W. Cleon Skousen, Willis Stone, Frank Wooley, Americans for Constitutional Action, American Security Council, Foundation for Economic Education, Harding College, and the John Birch Society.

1.   Daniel Bell, ed., *The Radical Right* (Garden City, N.Y.: Doubleday Anchor Books, 1964), p. 242.

2.   *New York Times,* 5 July 1970, p. 34.

3.   Peter Schrag, "America's Other Radicals," *Harpers,* August 1970, p. 39.

4.   *Farm Bureau Policies for 1970,* American Farm Bureau Federation, Chicago, Illinois; Charles Shuman, "This We Believe," *Nation's Agriculture,* 8 July 1969.

5.   *Missouri Farm Bureau News,* December 1967; Ibid., April 1968, p. 10; *Farm Bureau Policies for 1969,* Idaho Farm Bureau Federation, p. 2; *Farm Bureau Policies for 1969,* Texas Farm Bureau Federation, pp. 26–27.

6.   *Wall Street Journal,* 30 January 1958.

7.   *New York Times,* 18 May 1961; *Michigan Farm Bureau News,* 1 April 1961.

8.   *Nebraska Agriculture,* May 1961.

9.   Jack Nelson and Gene Roberts, Jr., *The Censors and the Schools* (Boston: Little, Brown & Co., 1963); *Farm Bureau Policies for 1969,*

Idaho Farm Bureau Federation, p. 18; *Farm Bureau Policies for 1969,* Wyoming Farm Bureau Federation, p. 4; *Farm Bureau Policies for 1969,* Texas Farm Bureau Federation, p. 35.

10. *Missouri Farm Bureau News,* September 1967; *Badger Farm Bureau News,* August 1962.

11. *Kansas City* (Missouri) *Star,* 27 June 1965; Ibid., 30 June 1968.

12. Missouri Freedom Forum (press release), 27 June 1967; *Minneapolis Tribune,* 30 October 1963.

13. Ibid.

14. *East Bay Labor Journal,* Oakland, California, 26 January 1962.

15. Missouri Freedom Forum (press release), 27 June 1967.

16. John Birch Society, *Bulletin,* April 1960.

17. *Missouri Farm Bureau News,* July 1967.

18. *Kansas City* (Missouri) *Star,* 30 June 1968; Missouri Freedom Forum (press release), 28 June 1968.

19. *Kansas City* (Missouri) *Star,* 30 June 1968.

20. Nicholas Nyaradi, "Free Enterprise or Disaster" (speech to Tri-State Credit Association, annual meeting, Albuquerque, New Mexico, 1960), broadcast by Public Service Co. of New Mexico.

21. *The American Liberal,* July 1962.

22. *Montana Agriculture,* July 1969.

23. *Washington Post,* 30 December 1954; See also: *Atlantic,* May 1955, p. 63.

24. *Kansas City* (Missouri) *Star,* 27 June 1965.

25. *Montana Agriculture,* July 1969; *Kansas City* (Missouri) *Star,* 30 June 1968.

26. *Missouri Farm Bureau News,* July 1967.

27. *New Republic,* 28 February 1949.

28. "Resnick Farm Organization Hearings: Omaha," 5 August 1967, transcript p. 101.

29. *Facts* (published by Anti-Defamation League of B'nai B'rith), November 1969; Schrag, "America's Other Radicals," *Harpers,* August 1970, p. 36.

30. Bell, ed., *Radical Right,* p. 264; Associated Press dispatch, 26 Au-

gust 1964; *Springfield* (Missouri) *Leader-Press,* 15 May 1964; *New York Times,* 15 October 1967; Ibid., 18 October 1967.

31. John Birch Society, *Bulletin,* 2 March 1964.

32. Ibid., May 1963, p. 13.

33. *New York Times,* 17 December 1961; *Newsweek,* 4 December 1961.

34. *Missouri Farm Bureau News,* October 1959.

35. Allan Kline, speech to National Institute of Animal Agriculture, 1955.

36. "1976 Committee" (brochure); *Milwaukee Sentinel,* 3 May 1966.

37. *Notes from the Foundation for Economic Education,* Irvington-on-Hudson, N.Y., January 1968.

38. *Farm and Ranch Magazine,* June 1963; for Shuman appearances on Manion Forum, see, for example: "The Vicious Cycle" (Weekly Broadcast No. 669), Manion Forum, South Bend, Indiana; *New York Times,* 15 October 1967.

39. *This is Farm Bureau* (Chicago: American Farm Bureau Federation 1969).

40. Roger Fleming, "We Must Work At Improving Government," *Nation's Agriculture,* January 1966, p. 4.

41. *Iowa Farm Bureau Spokesman,* 5 November 1966, p. 15.

42. Roger Fleming, *Annual Report of Secretary-Treasurer (1967),* American Farm Bureau Federation, Chicago, Illinois, p. 9.

43. *Illinois State Register,* 1 August 1962; Ibid., 2 August 1962; *AFBF Official Newsletter,* August 1962.

44. *Nation's Agriculture,* November 1964.

45. *Washington Post,* 8 December 1964.

46. *AFBF Newsletter,* 30 March 1970.

Chapter 11
Profiteering with Poverty

For statistical information about rural poverty generally, and the condition of farm workers specifically, see: *The People Left Behind,* Report by the

President's National Advisory Commission on Rural Poverty (Washington, 1967); U.S., Department of Commerce, *Statistical Abstract of the United States (1970)*, pp. 95, 236, 579–622; and *Poverty Amid Plenty, Report of the President's Commission on Income Maintenance Programs* (Washington, 1969).

1. Kuhfuss to Resnick, 31 July 1967.

2. *AFBF Official Newsletter,* 26 January 1970; Ibid., 23 February 1970.

3. *Farm Bureau Policies for 1969,* American Farm Bureau Federation, p. 42.

4. *AFBF Official Newsletter,* 23 June 1969.

5. Jeffrey W. Cain (Director, Marketing Programs, Illinois Agricultural Association) to presidents, marketing committee chairmen, executive secretaries, 18 July 1969.

6. *AFBF Official Newsletter,* 14 December 1970.

7. Ibid., 16 December 1968.

8. Ibid., 21 September 1970.

9. Ibid., 7 December 1970.

10. Ibid., 9 November 1970.

11. *New York Times,* 11 June 1967; Ibid., 14 June 1967.

12. *This Week in Farm Bureau,* New Jersey Farm Bureau, Trenton, New Jersey, 18 March 1967.

13. Ibid.; *Atlantic City* (New Jersey) *Press,* 9 June 1967; Ibid., 8 June 1967.

14. *Guide to Farm Labor and the Protection of Property Rights,* New Jersey Farm Bureau, Trenton, New Jersey, May 1967, Appendix G.

15. *Philadelphia Inquirer,* 1 June 1967; *New York Times,* 14 June 1967.

16. *New York Times,* 8 November 1970.

17. Ibid.

18. *Atlantic City* (N.J.) *Press,* 28 November 1967; Ibid., 1 December 1967.

19. Ibid.

20. "Resnick Farm Organization Hearings: Washington," testimony

of Joe Wilkins, Executive Director, Southwest Citizens Organization for Poverty Elimination, 28 August 1967, transcript pp. 19 et seq.

21. *1969 Resolutions and Policies,* New Jersey Farm Bureau, Trenton, New Jersey, pp. 1–2.

22. *New York Times,* 17 August 1970; Ibid., 20 September 1970.

23. *Oregon Agriculture,* 25 July 1969.

24. *New York Times,* 17 February 1968.

25. *Washington Post,* 20 August 1967.

26. Ibid., 10 September 1967.

27. Farm Bureau Policies for 1969, p. 43; Charles Shuman, "This We Believe," *Nation's Agriculture,* April 1966.

28. "Harvest of Shame" (broadcast over the CBS Television Network, 25 November 1960).

29. *Congressional Record,* 2 February 1960, House: 1686, et seq.

30. "Migrant: An NBC White Paper" (broadcast by NBC Television Network, 16 July 1970).

31. *AFBF Official Newsletter,* 13 July 1970.

32. *St. Louis Post-Dispatch,* 28 January 1966; Charles Shuman, "This We Believe," *Nation's Agriculture,* May 1964; Charles Shuman, "What Kind of Poverty?" *Nation's Agriculture,* 1966.

33. *Washington Evening Star,* 13 April 1964.

34. Charles Shuman, "What Kind of Poverty?"

35. *New York Times,* 15 May 1960.

36. U.S., Congress, House, Committee on Public Works, *Hearings on HR 6991: Public Works and Economic Development Act,* pp. 184 et seq.

Chapter 12
Farming the Farmer

1. *New York Times,* 23 April 1970; *Boston Globe* (AP dispatch) 27 August 1969.

2. *New York Times,* 23 April 1970.

3. John W. Scott (letter to Editor) *New York Times,* 24 November 1969; U.S., Congress, House, Committee on Agriculture, *Hearings on*

General Farm Program, 91st Cong., 1st sess., pp. 293, 252; *This is Farm Bureau* (Chicago: American Farm Bureau Federation, 1969).

4. U.S., Congress, House, Committee on Agriculture, *Hearings on General Farm Program,* p. 251 et seq.

5. *Nation's Agriculture,* January 1967.

6. *Time,* 3 September 1965; *AFBF Official Newsletter,* 30 March 1970.

7. Willard W. Cochrane, *The City Man's Guide to the Farm Problem* (Minneapolis: University of Minnesota Press, 1965), p. 134.

8. Ibid., p. 22.

9. *Nation's Agriculture,* June 1969.

10. Cochrane, *City Man's Guide,* p. 142.

11. Donald Hall, *Cooperative Lobbying: The Power of Pressure* (Tucson: University of Arizona Press, 1969), p. 192.

12. Charles Marshall (president, Nebraska Farm Bureau) to county Farm Bureau presidents, 16 April 1963; National Farmers Organization (press release), 24 April 1964.

Index